Hal Swiggett

on North American DEER

A Jolex PUBLICATION

Published by JOLEX INC., Oakland, New Jersey

Published simultaneously in Canada by Plainsman Ltd., Vancouver, B.C.

Distributed by:
John Olson Company, 294 West Oakland Avenue, Oakland, New Jersey 07436

Library of Congress Catalog Card No. # 79-65959

ISBN: 0-89149-047-7 paperback
ISBN: 0-89149-048-5 cloth

COVER painting and illustrated chapter headings by
Don Keller of San Antonio, Texas

Printed in the U.S.A.

Dedication

This book is dedicated to the memory of Louis
Hawthorne Spray who died more than a quarter
of a century ago . . .
a man who insisted a six year old lad
was of sufficient age to learn to shoot and hunt . . .
then proceeded to teach him both plus
to love and respect the out-of-doors . . .
my grandfather.

Hal Swiggett

Swiggett has hunted over most of the Western and Northwestern United States, a good deal of the Midwest, a little of the North, about that same amount of the Southeast and absolutely none of the Northeast. His heart is definitely west of the Mississippi. Hunting in several provinces of Canada, a bit in Mexico, Central and South America and a little in Europe, Hal feels these United States offer more hunting and fishing than any man or woman can get to in one lifetime so why waste any of it going off someplace else.

Serving in the United States Air Force in World War II Hal was discharged in San Antonio, Texas, and remained there to call that city home.

He was a photographer for the San Antonio Express-News for twenty one years, leaving in 1967 to devote full time to writing about shooting and hunting. His freelancing career started in 1947 with his first sale a story on trapping and the use of a .22 revolver on the trap line.

With many hundreds of articles published in all the major outdoor magazines over the past 33 years Hal settled on guns and hunting some fifteen years ago and seldom writes on any other subject anymore. His talents run towards helping manufacturers test guns, bullets and loads because of his constant, on a year-round basis, hunting. One load, the Remington .44 Magnum Medium Velocity cartridge, now so popular among handgunners, was his doing in total — started by taking handloads to the factory, if you can believe such a thing.

He has been active in outdoor club work serving as a vice president in the Texas Wildlife Federation, the forerunner of the Sportsmens Clubs of Texas now active in the Lone Star State. As a member of the Outdoor Writers Association of America Swiggett served three years on its Board of Directors and three terms as secretary – treasurer of the Texas Outdoor Writers Association. This was followed by two terms as president of that organization, which kept him active on the state level.

On the Advisory Committee of the International Handgun Metallic Silhouette Association Hal was at the founding meeting in El Paso and holds membership card number one with a Life Membership. He's also a Life Member of the National Rifle Association and the Texas State Rifle Association.

His name is included in the International Authors and Writer's Who's Who 1976, Who's Who in the South and Southwest (16th and 17th editions), Men and Women of Distinction, Personalities of America and the 10th edition Book of Honor.

The Outstanding American Handgunner Awards, started in 1973, recognized Swiggett as one of the "Top Ten" in 1973, 1975, 1978 and 1979.

Currently he is Associate Editor of GUN WORLD Magazine, Handgun Editor of Guns, Game & Shooting and a Contributing Editor to GUN DIGEST.

Married to the former Wilma Turner on March 1, 1942, Hal and Wilma have two sons, Gerald and Vernon, two daughters-in-law, Ida and Linda, and five grandchildren, Donna, Leah, Darryl, Katherine and Stuart. He is a Deacon, church treasurer, Sunday school director and music director.

About our contributing authors

✦ BOB ZWIRZ (Chapter 3) is Editorial Director of Gun World Annual, Gun World Hunting Guide, puts out his own Fishing Annual and Fishing Guide, is Editorial Director of Gun World Magazine, author of some DBI books, is active in industry P/R and as a consultant to several gun and tackle companies. Bob lives near Ridgefield, Connecticut.

✦ CHARLEY DICKEY (Chapter 4) is a full-time freelance writer/photographer on hunting, fishing, travel and related subjects specializing in the Southeast. He has authored books on quail hunting, dove shooting, trout fishing and is Outdoor Columnist for the Tallahassee Democrat. He is well known for his humor and has a page in many publications displaying that talent. Charley lives in Tallahassee, Florida.

✦ ED PARK (Chapter 6) is a full-time freelance writer/photographer with talents in hunting, fishing, camping, backpacking, travel, RV's, conservation, wildlife and scenic photos. He has a degree in wildlife management, is a book author and has served as President of the Northwest Outdoor Writers Association. Ed lives in Bend, Oregon.

✦ JEROME KNAP (Chapter 9) is a full-time freelance writer/photographer with positions as Canadian Editor, Field & Stream; Gun Dog Editor, Peterson's Hunting; Gun Editor, Ontario Out of Doors; and Outdoor Writer, The Hamilton Spectator. He has authored 10 books and has a degree in wildlife management. Jerome lives in Stoney Creek, Ontario.

✦ JUDD COONEY (Chapter 13) is a freelance writer/photographer covering all outdoor subjects. He is a big game specialist and was a Colorado game warden for 13 years. Besides his writing he guides elk, deer and bear hunters. He is an authority on bow hunting having killed many varied head of big game with a "sharp stick." He is Colorado Editor for Western Outdoors and writes a monthly column on bow-hunting for Archery World. Judd lives near Pagosa Springs, Colorado.

✦ B.R. HUGHES (Chapter 18) is an authority on knives. He authored "American Handmade Knives of Today" and co-authored the "Gun Digest Book of Knives." Bill is Editor of the Muzzleloader Magazine, Associate Editor of Gun Week and has appeared in most gun-oriented publications. In his spare time Hughes holds down a position as Dean at Texarkana College. Bill lives in Texarkana, Texas.

✦ SYLVIA BASHLINE (Chapter 20) is a freelance writer/photographer who specializes in gastronomic delights from game, fish and fowl. She is a regular contributor to the food pages of Field & Stream Magazine and is Supplement Editor of Pennsylvania Forest. L. James Bashline is also a well-known outdoor writer/photographer but his real claim to fame is in being Sylvia's husband. The Bashlines live near Honey Creek, Pennsylvania.

All of these writers, and the author of this book, are active members of the Outdoor Writers Association of America. Ed Park, Jerome Knap, Judd Cooney and Hal Swiggett have each served terms on the Board of Directors of this august 1300 plus member organization.

Table of Contents

Chapter 1

WHAT THIS BOOK IS ABOUT

For the first time, under one cover, we are attempting to present the North American deer hunting picture. The intent is to offer hunters throughout the North American continent something on their immediate locality and at the same time aid hunters from other states, those hunters interested in hunting a different animal, whitetail versus mule deer for instance, or perhaps simply looking for a new area.

Along with this we will offer suggestions on the proper rifle, handgun, muzzleloader or shotgun, knives and other steel and how these items should be used and cared for. What to do with the deer after it is down. And finally how to cook it.

Several of these chapters are written by authorities in the areas under discussion, authorities on the scene to give first-hand information. If I, as the author, felt someone else could present any given segment better, I assigned that chapter to him, or her, in one case. My publisher allowed me this privilege because our only concern is to offer the most thorough book on deer hunting that has been done to date.

Illustrations the same: photographs can't always show exactly what is needed. Don Keller, cowboy turned lawman turned artist, is well-known through the southwest for his wildlife work. Particularly is he famous for depicting South Texas whitetail bucks in the rut. All of Don's deer paintings show the animal with the neck swollen which is an obvious feature during mating season. Many hunters, the majority in fact, never see a big buck in this condition. It becomes so extreme the animals often appear pin-headed. This is when South Texas bucks "come to horns" as rattling is called. Keller did all the sketches in this book along with the cover.

Truly a fine painter of deer in their most impressive raiment Don is also well-known for his excellent paintings of Texas Longhorns.

Some of the photographs are by Perry Shankle, Jr., and in each instance his work is given credit by the picture. Perry is one of the better-known wildlife photographers in our country.

Though books of authority list many subspecies of deer, and we will cover most of them, it's still essentially a whitetail and mule deer situation insofar as hunting is concerned.

The whitetail is hunted in many states far removed from his original habitat. Primarily an eastern deer, Virginia whitetail no less, he has worked his way throughout the south, midwest, southwest and far west to the point he is now in all 48 of the original United States. Plus Canada and Mexico.

I was born in Kansas in 1921 and didn't leave there until 1935. During that period we hunted everything there was to hunt (I was blessed with a grandfather who was convinced six years of age was the proper time to start a young man hunting) which included rabbits, squirrels, doves, quail, ducks and geese. No Kansan in my part of the state ever saw hide nor hair of a deer. Now they are hunted there extensively. And some grow to mighty impressive sizes.

The same is true in many other states. A little of the saturation would be credited to migration except that we all know whitetail deer do not migrate.

11

Some of it stems from deer becoming so plentiful they are forced to move in search of food but more realistically it comes from game departments importing animals to stock an area.

All of this can be attributed to sportsmen. Hunters if you will. Without their interest in supporting wildlife through self-taxation, without their interest in supporting game departments with financial help as well as physical labor in many instances, none of this would have been possible.

Bird watchers, preservationists, environmentalists, ecologists, all have had their say of late, yet it is only the hunter who offers time and money for the work.

Witness Colorado. They offered a $5 stamp for the non-hunter to raise money for work with non-game species. They didn't sell a double-handful in several years of issue. These groups are far more affluent with their mouths than with their pocketbooks.

The true conservationists have proven to be the hunters. What they do for game animals, and no one will deny it is done to improve hunting, also benefits non-game animals every bit as much. Habitat improvement benefits every living thin thing in the area, not just hunted species, yet no mention is made of these efforts by those fighting us.

I think it can be safely said that regardless of where a hunter lives there is good deer hunting within a short drive of his home. If this isn't a tribute to game management and hunter/conservationists I'd like to know what is. And all other wildlife has gained because of it. End of editorial and back to deer hunting.

East of the Rocky Mountains whitetail deer are the primary big game animal. Basically, from these mountains on west it becomes mule deer country. With a few exceptions, of course: Eastern New Mexico (and south along the Mexican border), Eastern Colorado, Eastern Wyoming and likewise Montana, harbors both mule deer and whitetail. Same goes for South and North Dakota and Nebraska. In much of this country a hunter can see deer of both species on any given hunt.

On a hunt in Montana some years back, a mule deer hunt, the only really shootable buck I saw was a whitetail. Since I live with whitetails I left him for someone else. The same thing happened in New Mexico. Often hunters shoot one thinking they are getting the other in these overlapping areas. A friend hunting in West Texas watched two mule deer bucks go over a mountain. He topped out as fast as a seashore dweller could at that elevation. Two bucks were running across on the next mountain. He shot one and got a fine whitetail. Obviously not one of the pair he had seen earlier because he really does know the difference. Two deer went over. He saw two deer and shot without further checking. A wasted trip for him since he, too, lives with whitetails every day.

More deer are killed on this continent than all other big game combined, by seven or eight times, so prolific is our favorite game animal.

Whitetails seem to thrive even better when forced to associate with humans, up to a point. If said humans wipe out their habitat then it's all over. But just moving close doesn't seem to bother that waver of the white flag at all. Homeowners on the edges of every town and city in deer country have a problem with the animals eating their flowers at night.

Mule deer don't seem to be so willing to share an area. They require more distance between them and "folks." As a result they are being forced out of many parts of their terrain. And in a few cases whitetails are moving in.

Back in pioneering days mule deer not only inhabited their current range, but extended on eastward into the great plains. This was as little as a century and a half ago. They have been put back into some of this somewhat marginal country and are hunted in the Dakotas and Nebraska to some extent.

These big-eared animals simply do not like people. They are not prone to come into town edges and eat flowers. Quite the contrary. Lumbering, mining and even heavy grazing of livestock will cause him to move farther back and higher. Whatever it takes to get away from people.

Because of this the mule deer, as we know him, will one day become a rarity. Human beings are expanding. Bodies need someplace to survive. Whitetails will make it so long as there is a little cover and he is granted a bit of watchcare and protection. All that care and protection is for naught with old big ears. He wants to be alone.

Only bucks wear antlers in the deer family. Whitetails and mule deer differ in the design of those antlers. Whitetail bucks are decked out with a single main beam on each side with tines growing up off the master, or main portion. Much in the way roses sprout and grow off a single cane when it is tied into a horizontal position. Mule deer antlers are

Whitetail – photo by Perry Shankle, jr.

John Amber, long time editor of Gun Digest, killed this heavy-horned whitetail in the heart of mule deer country on the Mescalero Apache Reservation. One of the overlapping areas Swiggett tells about in this chapter.

a series of forks. A fork off the main beam then another fork off that offshoot.

In each case mature bucks usually have four points to the side. Easterners count brow tines which makes it five, then add the two together which turns into a 10-pointer. Westerners stick to only the main points on a single side for their count. Often mule deer are described as 4 × 4, meaning four points to the side. Brow tines do not count in this measurement.

Some count anything big enough to hang a ring on as a point. Others say it should be longer than it is wide at the base. Boone and Crockett, in their scoring system, require that a point must be at least 1 inch in length. As you can see, how many points a buck has is totally dependent upon who is doing the talking.

Mule deer and whitetails vary in looks as well as antler formation. The mountain deer is more of a blocky, heavier-bodied animal. He stands taller than a whitetail of the same weight. Coats vary as well. During hunting season, when most of us see them, mule deer are dark, almost steel gray in color and the older bucks become quite Roman-nosed with decidedly black, gray and white markings on the face. They are tawny colored during the warmer summer months.

Whitetails are brown to the point of almost red during hot summer months but take a turn towards gray as fall approaches, so that by the time hunting season rolls around they are definitely gray. Older animals are darker, normally, than the younger whitetails.

The period of gestation of a doe is about 210 days, which places the dropping of fawns from April to June, depending on the locality. Twins aren't at all uncommon in either whitetail or mule deer. Fawns are spotted at birth, but lose them in a few months.

Antlers drop off shortly after breeding season. Occasionally, during hunting season in Texas where the hunt runs through to the first weekend of the year in much of the state, new growth starts immediately and can be seen, usually in April or May. Covered with a sort of "fur" as they grow, antlers are described as being in velvet during that period. Once the antler has reached full growth, usually by August, blood circulation ceases, which allows the antler to harden and the velvet to dry up. As it begins to peel, bucks rub the substance off on small trees and brush.

Occasionally a buck will injure his genitals. Sometimes it's a birth defect or injured through fence jumping or spines off cactus or other thorny flora. When this occurs the antlers never harden but remain in velvet. Bucks in this category are often referred to as "stags".

Once in a great while a doe will grow antlers. I've seen only one in my life. It was an 8-pointer and she had a head of antlers of a quality to make any buck proud.

Besides a difference in appearance through body shape and antlers, whitetails and mule deer run differently. Whitetails take off in a smooth stride that appears almost effortless, often making leaps of 18–20 feet or more with ease. In Texas seven foot fences are called "deer proof" but any self-respecting whitetail can easily clear such a barrier when he or she really wants to.

Mule deer run with sort of a bouncing-ball gait. Remember those old movies where a bouncing ball

Two small muley bucks during late season – photo by Gudd Cooney.

directed viewers to words on the screen? That's the way mule deer usually run. And they cover a lot of ground in a hurry. The gait is very deceiving. With their four feet almost bunched together they sort of pogo-stick their way across the country.

Another difference in the two is the whitetail's ingrained nature to stay home. Whitetails stick mighty close to where they are born, unless forced out through habitat destruction. Drought often causes death from lack of food and water when they might have migrated to better living conditions a few miles away.

Mule deer, on the other hand, live in the high country in summer and come down into the valleys and lowlands for winter, primarily travelling with the winter snows. But should no snow come, most will eventually work their way down anyway. Regular migration routes are common. Trails are often walked into a deep rut the same as cattle make in a pasture. That's the reason why late-season mule

deer hunts are so popular, especially for the true trophy hunter. Big bucks will be forced down out of the high country through migration and be yarded up so that several, or many, can be looked over before the tag is used.

Whitetail hunters never have this aid to a bigger rack. Their only natural help comes when seasons run with the rut (mating season) because at this time bucks get downright careless. Mule deer seasons seldom hit when this rut is in progress.

There really isn't all that much difference in weight of the two animals either. Whitetails can run both bigger or smaller than mulies.

Mule deer, the desert variety, probably average 125–140 pounds with an occasional 90-plus pounder thrown alongside that 170–180 pound exception. The bigger mountain deer will average close to 200 pounds or at least 185–190. There too, some will be smaller and a few will approach the 300 pound mark. Very few at this top weight, I guarantee. I've never seen one that big in more than

30 years of mule-deer hunting and while watching check stations for story material. But it does happen on occasion. Most of those biggies are guessed weights not put to the test of scales.

Whitetails run from a low of 70 pounds to as high as 400 but again, this upper figure isn't reached by many. Some years back I saw a release from Saskatchewan quoting a 400-plus pound kill, but it hastily pointed out that it wasn't to be taken as an average happening. Another printed epistle from that Canadian Province lists their whitetails as from 85 to 250 pounds. Kansas has produced some real monsters in the weight department as has Iowa and Missouri.

Antler size does not have any bearing on body weight.

Mule deer hunters, normally, are blessed with sufficient time to judge a head, often to the point of comparing two or three top bucks in a bunch. This is something seldom offered a whitetail hunter. He sees, he judges, he shoots or passes in an instant. Only in a rare situation will he be allowed time for second guessing. The only exception here is during the rut when bucks come to horns in South and Central Texas. Bucks rattled up are coming to fight in most instances, sometimes out of curiosity, but normally with sex as their objective. When he comes in this attitude his eyes are red with fire, his neck swollen all out of proportion to his body size, the hair on the back of that huge neck bristled and standing straight up, and with no desire to leave suddenly unless the hunter is careless. Here, and only here, can a whitetail hunter get a long and sure look at his trophy.

There is always the exception, after all, that's what makes the rule, but whitetails don't get big by letting hunters look them over. There are not enough trophy hunters for that sort of thing.

In the most recent listing of hunting-license purchases Pennsylvania leads with 1,281,323 followed by Michigan at 945,735 and Texas with 855,729. Fourth showed New York with 768,686 while Wisconsin was fifth with 707,287. California garnered the sixth spot with 611,564 licenses.

Non-resident listings placed Montana first with 127,822 (this out of a total license sale of only 222,878) then Pennsylvania at 101,619; Wyoming 98,237; Colorado 85,862 and sixth was West Virginia with 49,189 non-resident hunters.

One thing became instantly apparent in this listing from the Department of the Interior's U.S. Fish and Wildlife Service. Many of the Western states that do their utmost to keep non-resident hunters out are blessed with game departments surviving on revenue from those non-residents.

In alphabetical order: Colorado listed 27% of their licenses to non-residents; Idaho 15%; Montana 57% (over half); New Mexico 12%; Utah 7%; and Wyoming 60% (well over half). With the heavily increased fees charged out-of-staters these ratios are quite revealing as to who really supports state game departments. In the case of both Montana and Wyoming more than half the licenses go to non-residents, yet those from out of state pay several times as much for a license. Even Colorado with 27% non-resident sales receives more from out-of-staters than locals, because their rates are definitely more than four to one pricewise.

Maybe I'm talking out of school here, but it appears, at least on the surface, that some states could be in serious trouble, financially, if only residents bought licenses. Yet that is the trend. Save it for our own residents is more and more the theme.

It is going to be interesting to find out if those residents are really willing to pay the freight in bearing the full financial responsibility of their game departments. (Only an editorial comment. Maybe I shouldn't have brought it up.)

It is hard, even after half a century in the woods, for me to realize deer are color blind. It is primarily motion that sets them in motion. Along with smell.

I have sat still on a log, and by still I mean motionless, and had whitetail does walk within fifteen feet. I'll never forget one young buck that became very curious. More so than any other I've had contact with. I was sitting on a stump watching a squirrel tree (this was in the fall — just before deer season) when I heard something coming. It was close so I couldn't turn to look. Didn't need to, really, because the step never faltered. Whatever it was, obviously, was going to pass right close. As he drew alongside, maybe ten steps at the most, he sensed all wasn't as it should be, but unlike a smart old whitetail buck he waited to check it out. He stopped. I blinked one eye winking at him. He reacted with a slight muscle quiver. I winked again, never allowing any other movement whatever. That time he stomped a foot. I winked a third time and he stomped the same foot again. Then I threw caution to the wind and tapped my foot lightly. That was too much and off he went.

Once I actually moved he knew he didn't belong there. I never will know why the wink didn't spook him because I've seen numerous other deer spooked by blinking eyes. Just a rarity I guess, a curious whitetail buck, a young buck, let me add. And the way he was behaving, chances are he never grew into an old buck.

I'm not at all certain deer hunters need camouflaged clothing, but dark clothing, I feel, is almost a necessity. Quietness, slow motion, moving into the wind, all are more important than what is worn. Many, or most, western states require the use of "blaze orange" in many hundreds of square inches. I feel like a Christmas tree when so decked out and can't help but feel a deer can see it, and if nothing else, hear it, since the color is so loud. But I do have to admit I have experienced no incident where the color has kept me from getting a deer.

One western state, New Mexico, doesn't require blaze orange on the grounds they don't want hunters thinking they can shoot anything they see moving that isn't so outfitted. Their reasoning makes good sense to me. Blaze orange states could inadvertently set up a killing through a hunter shooting at a moving object which could turn out to be a rancher or even a hiker who wandered into hunting country.

Maybe I'm not realistic, but if a person is capable of going hunting he should be capable of not shooting until he knows what the target is — beyond the shadow of a doubt. Could be that that in itself is the reason I've become a trophy hunter and like to associate with other trophy hunters. A fast shot is out of the question in our game. We first have to judge the size of the head. I've seen a lot of strange things in my life but never among them was another human with antlers.

The whitetail is a prettier, sleeker-looking animal. His rack is an impressive work of nature's art (that of a big buck) and he is so much smarter than a mule deer that there is no comparison. He has a bag full of tricks to keep from getting shot at, even if he's seen, for that matter, because whitetails can be awfully close yet remain totally out of sight. They are masters at sneaking away from danger.

But – – –.

I still like to hunt mule deer best. There is a majestic appearance that hovers around a truly great buck that can never be reached by a whitetail. I don't know what it is and I'm not clever enough to describe it, but every mule-deer hunter knows what I'm talking about and every whitetail hunter will learn it on sighting his first big mulie.

Chapter 2

TEXAS WHITETAILS

Second only to Alaska in size, the State of Texas takes a back seat to no one in deer population. "More deer than any other state" is the claim of the Lone Star state and they can back it up with facts and figures.

Not only does Texas have the most deer but they also offer the most varied types of hunting. Terrain runs from the piney woods of East Texas through lush southeastern Texas rice country to the arid Brush Country of South Texas (where everything either sticks, scratches or bites) back north through Central Texas and the Hill Country, then on to West Texas which again is arid and somewhat mountainous.

Much of West Texas is classified as the place where "jack rabbits carry lunch baskets" but in spite of the apparent lack of vegetation a few deer can be found.

Most of the hunting takes place in the Hill Country of Central Texas for this reason – that's where we find the best food, water and cover. There is a good deal of cedar and lots of live oak. Much of the country is rocky, "extremely rocky" I believe would be a safe term to use.

Hunting here is on small ranches. Some as little as 50–100 acres. Most, however, will run in the 1000 to 5000-acre bracket. There are a few larger, but not in any great number. The world famous Y.O. Ranch is the largest, by far, in this section. Hunting on more than 100 square miles they operate on a "No Kill – No Pay" basis which is day hunting at its best. The hunter books a hunt, is assigned a guide, and owes nothing unless he gets his buck.

Here we should probably explain that there is practically no public hunting in the state of Texas. The Texas Parks and Wildlife department owns a few small areas scattered around the state and holds public drawings for hunts, but because of the limited areas involved, the number of deer to be killed is naturally very small, so only a few hunters can be accommodated. It's a great idea and worthy of note, but with so little public land it is only a small drop in a mighty big bucket.

Other than these small areas handled by public drawings ALL hunting in Texas is on private land which means, in almost every case, it has to be paid for. Leases in other words, paying for the privilege of going on the property to hunt. As a result, Texas does have the largest deer population. Ranchers devote both time and money to maintaining deer herds far in excess of what state game departments could do by themselves.

On the other hand Texas has very few non-resident hunters because there is no place for them to hunt. Same as residents, they have to find a lease and pay for the privilege. Good leases are valued mighty highly. Many have been with the same group of men thirty years or longer. It is often the paying hunters who spend the extra money to help the landowner better his hunting. After getting the lease, it is the hunter who spends still more money putting up blinds or stands, builds feeders to keep deer in the area, clears "senderos" for shooting lanes and sometimes even helps with fence-mending and gate-repairing. A good lease is valuable, no

A hunter's first deer warrants the X on the forehead. With the animals blood. This doe was shot with a Savage bolt action .222 Rem.

When you find a tree rubbed bare like this you can be sure there is a buck in the area.

hunter will take a chance on anything happening to keep him from renewing it year after year.

Time has taken its toll and prices have skyrocketed. Leases that used to go for $50–100 per gun now bring $1,500–2,000 per gun and a few, even more. A sad but true fact – deer hunting in Texas has just about left the working man's bracket. He's a victim of the times. Landowners can't be criticized for getting all they can from the use of their ranches. Many big ranches have stayed in business through hunting lease money when cattle prices are down and when cattle couldn't be run in the pastures because of droughts.

Leasing, too, is the reason why more deer aren't killed in the Lone Star state. Let's take, for example, a ranch in South Texas. It's in this part, south from San Antonio to Laredo, hard on the Mexican border, then back northeast to Carrizo Springs and Crystal City, that the most money is paid for leases. Ranches here might be upwards of 100,000 acres and harbor good herds. If it is leased to 10 men, or let's say 20 for the sake of argument, chances are no more than 40 bucks will be taken in any one hunting season. Two per hunter is the state law and does are a no – no in that part of Texas.

As a result we have 40 deer coming out of an area that might well provide three, four or even five times that number without hurting the deer population at all. In fact, in many cases, it would improve the quality of the herd. A sad note – several hunters on a lease in this part of Texas will often qualify as true "trophy" hunters and might go several seasons without killing a single buck, which lessens even more the actual kill on each ranch.

Cap't Bob Snow (Texas Game Warden, retired) and Pat Flenniken demonstrate horn rattling. Cap't Snow is an authority on this type of hunting. The area they are watching is small clearing just across the draw.

There are a few "day leases" throughout the state. Most are in the Hill Country north of San Antonio, but occasionally one can be found in the Brush Country of South Texas. Usually "day leases" are on small ranches with few deer. The success ratio is mighty small, but folks still grab at the chance to go hunting. This writer knows of one such place that uses about 30 blinds on 1,000 acres. Spaced so as to be perfectly safe, no problem here, but since there is so little likelihood of a shot anyway, danger is no problem. As many as 20 hunters a day sat in these blinds one year, throughout the six week season. Eight deer were killed, at $25 per day, per man.

The man offering that hunting didn't get rich after he paid for the lease, built his blinds and delivered his hunters to and from those blinds. Feeling guilty on occasion, because so few deer were killed, he always got over it when one was brought in. There were deer in the country so he was doing nothing wrong. I'm just pointing out how willing hunters are to pay for the chance to try for a deer.

Since I've mentioned blind hunting maybe we'd best take a moment and go over all the types of hunting Texas has to offer. In deep East Texas, along the Louisiana border, dogs are used to drive deer. Only in these few counties is it legal and only in these few counties are shotguns used in the Lone Star state.

The rest of Texas, except in the far west, hunts mostly from blinds built on the ground or stands built like towers. Tower blinds might be a better description. These might be from 10 to 30 feet high, depending upon the area. Looking like outhouses

His first buck for a mighty young hunter.

with legs, they usually have a hole in the floor through which the hunter climbs or else a door in the side. Once inside there is a seat or two. Sliding panels are opened on each of the four sides for shooting purposes. These might be a foot or two long and maybe eight or ten inches high. These are usually left year-round so they become part of the landscape.

Sometimes stands are built in trees except that over most of Texas trees large enough for stands are somewhat conspicuous by their absence.

Sometimes feeders are built near blinds or stands. When kept filled with corn they aid in keeping deer in the area. Seldom ever is a buck killed around a feeder, especially one of any size. They are far smarter than that. If they feed in them at all it is in the dark of night. The greatest aid from feeders is

they keep does around and nature being what it is, bucks will hang around the does.

Hunters usually go into these blinds or stands before daylight and leave around 9:00 or so, then go back at mid-afternoon and stay till dark. And it is here they goof up more often than not. Hunters the world over have become brainwashed by "daylight and dark". Good, true, are those hours, but so is mid-day, especially in areas hard-hunted early and late. If hunting from blinds or stands I encourage you to make a day of it. Nap if you must during those warmer hours of day, but before you do, say a prayer and ask God to cause any deer that comes by to walk heavy.

In case that sounds silly to you — I have been awakened several times by deer staring at me. That is, staring at the blind I was in. And a few of them

Women get in the act too. A really fine trophy, heavy of horn, plenty of spread and lengthy tines.

A really fine Hill Country whitetail buck. Non-typical and very impressive.

were shot, all because I elected to stay in the blind all day.

Lots of hunting from vehicles takes place in Texas, and it is perfectly legal on private property. Sometimes, when a buck is sighted, the hunter makes a stalk on foot, but more often he shoots from the vehicle or at most the nearest tree.

Vehicle hunting might not sound sporting to some but if you haven't tried it, don't knock it. Like the old Indian said, "Don't criticize a man until you have walked a mile in his moccasins". Deer aren't dummies, at least whitetail deer aren't. It takes them only an instant to catch on when shots are fired from a vehicle. Often they stand and watch as pickups (most popular in Texas) or Jeeps go by, maybe only 50 or so yards away. Let that vehicle slow down and the deer becomes more alert. Slow

enough to stop and that deer suddenly becomes very full of life. Let it stop and that buck is gone. Instantly!

It takes a mighty fast man with a rifle to drop a buck from a pickup or Jeep.

There is very little walking done by deer hunters in this biggest of states; most have figured out better and easier ways, except in far West Texas. West of Del Rio the country goes from hill size clear up to mountains near New Mexico. A wide stretch of the eastern side of this country is inhabited by both whitetails and mule deer. It isn't at all uncommon for a hunter to walk through this area looking for mule deer and come home with a whitetail because he shot when the buck jumped without taking time to see what kind of buck he was drawing down on.

A typical Hill Country 8 point whitetail buck. A young deer, as can be seen by the small antlers which appear heavier than they really are because of being in velvet. He is probably 2½ years old.

The author with a better than average Texas whitetail sporting 16⅞ inches spread and fairly heavy antlers. His rifle is a Model 70 Winchester Featherweight .243.

This hunter has picked himself out a comfortable tree and shows how he safely gets his rifle up there. Note the bolt is open and he is using his sling as attached to the front swivel to lift the rifle.

A pair of happy hunters with better than average West Texas whitetails. Both of these bucks came to horns being rattled.

Long shots are a possibility any place there are deer, except maybe in deep forest country, but in West Texas the long shot is the rule rather than the exception.

One area I've neglected, and probably should leave it so because of the rarity of opportunity, is our coastline. The Intracoastal Canal running from Aransas Pass to the southern tip of Texas goes through some of the finest deer country in the state. Texas law doesn't allow any trespassing whatever, so hunting on the adjoining ranches is out of the question. Hunting on some of the islands is not. Some mighty good bucks hang out in this soggy, swampy country. Hard to get to, that's for sure, and they are even harder to hunt because of the mushy sogginess of the terrain. But a possibility for the few willing to make the effort.

What about the size of deer in Texas?

"Not very big" is the kindest I can be. Northern and eastern states top our sizes by so much it is no contest in body weight. Antler size, however, places them second to none as indicated by the Boone and Crockett record book. The point here is that it does not take a hand cannon to kill a whitetail. More is said in chapter 16 on guns for deer but let me mention only that there's no place in the state where a hunter will find a "magnum" necessary.

Old favorites like the .30-06 Springfield, .270 Winchester, 7 × 57 Mauser and .257 Roberts are all that is needed.

Hill country deer run to maybe 100 pounds field dressed, if they're big ones. Sure, on occasion a few 15 or 20 pounds heavier might be found. On the other hand the majority will weigh in the 70 to 80 pound bracket. I once saw a handsome little 8-pointer with a spread of some 15 or so inches that weighed 56 pounds, field dressed. South Texas bucks, Brush Country deer, occasionally go over 200 pounds, field dressed, but the majority will weigh between 125 and 140 pounds with a good many 100 to 110 pounders thrown in. The rest of the state falls sort of in between these figures.

How does one go about setting up a deer hunt in Texas? Resident and non-resident alike have the same problem. I'd suggest getting a map of the Lone Star state and picking the town in the center of the area you wish to hunt. Write to the Chamber of Commerce. Most of them maintain working lists of ranches available to the hunter. Do this in the spring or early summer at the latest. Even planning a year ahead won't hurt.

Once you have a rancher's name and address it becomes a matter of finding out if he has any openings left. You might contact a lot of ranchers before you hit pay dirt or you might luck out on the first try. But that's how it's done – and about the only way I know, short of driving into the area and spending a lot of time meeting people and asking questions. This is best, of course, if time is of no consequence. One more comment – Texans are like good people

John L. Turner killed this buck on opening day of the 1977 season. It took top honors on the Y.O. Ranch, where it was killed, and top Hill Country honors in the Texas Trophy Hunters Association annual awards. It placed second in the TTHA statewide awards. A South Texas buck was first. It scored 375.6 BTGRW points.

Vernon Swiggett with an "eatin'-size" whitetail dropped at 150 yards with his Remington Model 600 .308 Winchester. His ammo was handloaded by the author – 51 grains of 4895 under Speer's great 130 grain hollow point.

everywhere, if they like you they will try to help, if they don't, you could be standing in the center of an available lease and never know it.

As to the time of year for the best hunting, Texas offers one of the longest seasons. Most of the state opens on the Saturday nearest November 15th and runs through the first weekend in January, sometimes seven or eight weekends. The number of deer is equally generous: Four, if full advantage is taken. One of those has to be a mule deer, which are limited to far West Texas and only a few day's hunt. One of the remaining three has to be a doe. Two whitetail bucks are legal and both of those tags can be used for does if the landowner has sufficient doe permits. Often hunters, wanting the meat, spend the entire season seeking fat, dry does and, or, young bucks.

I must admit they sure do eat good – or as a friend of long standing phrases it, "They make mighty good grazin'."

Hill country bucks have been known to start the rut in early October – long before hunting season opens. When this happens hunting becomes a bit more difficult because there is less activity. It is when bucks are interested in does that one enjoys the best hunting conditions.

If hunting this part of the state I prefer the first two or three weeks of the season. Not for any particular reason, really, except that most of the ranches have a good deal of hunting pressure and the bigger bucks aren't quite so spooky. If the rut is late then I'd hunt later.

South Texas, the Brush Country, is a late season effort, in most instances. In know a good many hunters of long years experience who only consider that final week, between Christmas and New Year's, as

Dr. Gerald Swiggett walks up to a good 8 pointer dropped with his .270 Winchester.

For the hunter who has never killed a whitetail, or one who has hunted eastern deer most of his life and never seen more than one or two bucks a season (and maybe not killed more than one or two in his life) the Texas Hill Country is the place to go. Deer are extremely plentiful, though they won't be of heavy antler. In most cases, bucks only a year and a half old will sport 8-point headgear. Bucks a year older will usually have slightly heavier antlers and are sometimes 10-pointers. It takes age to make heavy antlers but these little deer are great trophies.

A well-known eastern outdoor writer and syndicated radio personality visited the Y.O. Ranch and got so excited her guide almost had to take her rifle away to keep her from shooting. Hunting in her part of the country, a fork-horn was considered exciting game. She told of many hunters spending several years in the woods trying for their first deer. On the Y.O. she saw deer everyplace. Six and 8-pointers were commonplace.

Her guide was able to calm her down and on the second day found a right nice 10-pointer of fairly heavy horn and impressive spread. She dropped it with a single shot from her .308 Winchester.

Having hunted all my life (well, almost, because I started when I was six) I have a full half-century of experience in the woods behind me as this is written. This has caused me to have some strong opinions about many things. Maybe not right – but strong. One of them is about youngsters or any beginning hunter and their first deer. Here I go, mentioning the Y.O. Ranch again, but they have a rule of "8-points or better" before a buck is legal game. Many fathers bring their sons to this famous ranch because of the guaranteed hunt. Not that the child will get a deer because that isn't always the case, but because they are put with guides who are experienced in handling young folks and first-time hunters. Then, of course, it probably doesn't hurt that there is no charge unless an animal is killed.

My complaint is that 8-point minimum. Youngsters or first-time hunters have no business killing a buck with eight or more points as their first deer, unless it happens to be the first buck they see. In that case I'm all for it. But to search out a trophy for the first kill – no way. Where do they go from there? Most of the country considers a buck such as this a top trophy. This leaves the first-time hunter with no chance, or at least very little chance, of improving his record on future hunts.

their deer season. They hunt earlier but not with enthusiasm. The rut usually starts about mid-December in this part of Texas. Because of the cover, mesquite and head-high cactus, bucks are near impossible to find if they aren't moving.

Some mighty impressive sets of antlers come out of this South Texas Brush Country. Boone and Crockett records reveal more trophy heads from here than any other single location other than Saskatchewan.

For the hunter bent on bagging a real trophy, South Texas probably has more to offer than any other place on the continent. It is also the hardest place on the continent to set up a hunt because of all the private land, so start early and work hard if you have such a thing in mind. It could be a bit expensive but then so is everything else these days.

Bottle-fed by this South Texas rancher this young buck lived to be 4½ years old and was a fair-to-middlin' 10 pointer when he wandered too far from the house and got shot.

A South Texas whitetail doe. Those hunting specifically for meat should never pass up an opportunity such as this — where does are legal, of course.

Linda Swiggett brings home her own venison dinners.

I feel it takes the edge off and may even keep that person from going on future hunts. I'd much rather see first-time hunters kill spikes or fork-horns on that first hunt. The thrill is still there, yet they have something to look forward to on future hunts.

One of my sons is a fine example; his was a mule deer, but the meaning is the same. I took him to Colorado for his first mule deer hunt of any consequence after he graduated from college with a PhD. He tried a few times in Oregon, where he attended graduate school, but didn't have time to take it seriously – and didn't get a buck. Knowing the country well, I told him we would do our best to get him a 24–25 inch head, but knew better than to promise such a thing. First off, a head such as this makes a mighty fine trophy yet leaves working room for improvement in later years. As luck would have it the first buck we saw, forty-five minutes into the hunt, measured 28½-inches after he dropped it with a single shot from his .270 Winchester. A high-antlered trophy in anyone's book. Spread, height, a perfect shot and accomplished in less than an hour. He's been after mulies several times since, and has killed maybe half a dozen deer, but nothing close to equaling his first buck. I can't help but feel it must

be harder for him to work up enthusiasm for a hunt knowing he has little chance for a bigger head than that already on his wall. Maybe I'm wrong; I hope I am.

There are some good trophy bucks in South Texas and there are some right handsome bucks in the Hill Country. One was killed this past season, again on the Y.O., that fell just a few points short of the Boone and Crockett minimum. There are more deer here than in any other state except, maybe, Pennsylvania. Hunting becomes a matter of selection. A bit nerve-wracking, true, but selection is the name of the game if size is the aim.

Maybe that first buck sighted is the biggest one you'll see, and he might just look that way because he's first. Trophy hunters will be able to pass him up. First-timers probably won't. Which one is right?

It is a bit hard to encourage a non-resident to hunt for meat because of the high cost of travel, hunting fees, licenses, etc. This is the reason I continually refer to trophies. A trophy can mean something different to each hunter, but basically I think it should be a good representative head from the area. Not necessarily a record-book head, just something at least average.

29

A fine whitetail buck – photo by Perry Shankle, jr.

A typical 8 point whitetail. Not very wide but heavy enough to be interesting.

A whitetail family, or rather the makings of one. A couple of months later and this buck will have his antlers rubbed out, polished and be chasing does – not posing with them.

Charles "Fibber" McGehee posing with a really fine Hill Country whitetail buck. Taken on the Y.O. Ranch, famous for its "No Kill-No Pay" policy. This buck was 5 1/2 years old.

With his antlers in velvet this 8 point buck appears to be much larger than he really is. Even so — most hunters would like to get their sights on him. Particularly in this position.

When the blood stops circulating in the antlers they harden und the velvet dries. To remove that dried velvet bucks take on trees, rubbing them completely free of bark sometimes. The bigger the buck the bigger the tree he uses.

Some Texas ranchers have "pet" bucks. "Bucky" was always around camp and enjoyed nothing better than getting in the tent and scattering contents to the four winds.

Which leads us to the advantage of hunting whitetails in Texas. During any given season any hunter will get to look at so many bucks he will have the opportunity to choose one to his liking. Sometimes he might end up with one a bit smaller than he wants, after passing up larger heads while sweating out just the right one. But then, that's what deer hunting is all about.

Hunting whitetails in the heaviest deer-populated state is not a handicap under any set of standards, or circumstances.

There is one more aspect to whitetail hunting in Texas that bears mention. It is here, in the Lone Star state, where "rattling" gained fame. "Rattling up a buck" is calling him in for the shot. What this amounts to is taking a set of antlers and hitting them together to simulate a buck fight. This only works during the rut when bucks are fighting over does. But it really works then. Though considered a Brush Country trick many Hill Country bucks are also taken each year by being lured to the gun through the rattling of antlers.

Buck fights get very noisy sometimes. Not only do their antlers clash, but struggling feet kick rocks loose, knock over brush, and in general tear up a bit of the countryside.

Every hunter has his own technique – some even carry a small container of "skunk oil" and set it on the downwind side to destroy the human odor.

Bucks come best to horns, as it is called, on cold, clear, still mornings. Foggy mornings sometimes are good. Windy weather is out. Same as with any other calling.

Often a buck will charge the "rattler" with his head lowered, ready to fight, and with the hair standing up on the back of his swollen neck. A downright spooky situation when it happens. Others will sneak in to see what is happening. In either case the result is the same: a shot at a buck of usually larger proportions than can normally be found; A real trophy buck and sometimes an honest-to-goodness record book buck.

Hunkered down under a mesquite or alongside a pear (cactus) it isn't uncommon to lure a rutting buck to within 50 feet, sometimes closer. Yes, feet, fifteen or less yards. Close. Real close. So close they are much easier to miss than hit.

If a hunter doesn't get buck fever when this happens you might as well go ahead and bury him. He's already dead.

Chapter 3

PROVEN TECHNIQUES FOR...
...EASTERN AND NORTHEASTERN WHITETAILS
by Bob Zwirz

You might not be reading this book if it were not for the indisputable fact that year after year the most hunted game animal in the United States and Canada continues to be – deer.

In this chapter I'm devoting most all of my coverage to the whitetail deer and the various methods employed for hunting him. I'll also discuss deer herd populations, average sizes of the deer you may encounter and a broad outlook as to future expectations in this extensive area.

Though I've already stated that this will deal exclusively with the only species that inhabit this geographical area of the country – whitetails, I will also draw comparisons from time to time, so as to relate it to mule deer and what has become known as the Columbia River blacktail. The blacktail being a much contested species, since a number of noted biologists continue to believe it is not in truth a separate species at all, but a close cousin of the muley.

The reason for my comparing hunting methods, terrain, calibers and even weather, as they apply to a whitetail versus mule deer is simple. Once the marked differences are obvious, it is no longer a mystery to a less-experienced hunter to realize what makes them perform in their natural habitat as they do, and why specific calibers, even different types of rifles, are often a factor worthy of careful consideration. Once clearly identified by habit and terrain, the whitetail will become far easier to out-guess, even in its own chosen surroundings.

The hunter who will concentrate on the proven techniques for taking whitetail, particularly in the type of cover found throughout most of the east-northeast U.S., will not find it overly difficult to connect with a mule deer if and when an opportunity to hunt them presents itself. As for that disputed blacktail, we can dismiss him here and now by stating that you will find your game inhabiting exactly the same type of dense cover and terrain as the whitetail in, as a prime example, New England. Again, and briefly stated, due to the heavy foliage in blacktail country, the rifles and calibers I'll recommend for most of your east-northest whitetail hunting will serve you well. In addition, their foraging habits are not all that dissimilar, as you will soon learn as we zero in on the whitetail.

For the sake of the record I've hunted both whitetail and mule deer since I was a lad of 11. I've put down for keeps eighty-one whitetail and twenty-three mule deer. Not a single blacktail. However, I continue to demonstrate adequate humility where smart deer are concerned. Almost every year I find myself badly out-classed by the savvy and almost human reasoning power of some buck – often a whitetail in one of my favorite haunts in New England, southern Canada or New York. That particular buck I rarely collect.

I truly believe I'm lucky when it comes to hunting deer. I feel this way simply because I always seem to see, hear and sense deer when a number of my companions are still far from being alert or truly interested in what they are supposed to be doing. On more than one occasion I've shot my buck, or, at times, a doe for the camp larder, long before less interested hunters have disciplined themselves enough to throw away that first lighted cigarette of the morning. I am patient and exceptionally observant of my surroundings and I am continually disciplining some inner drive that pushes me into thinking I must rush and cover ground as fas as the hunters around me. Experience, once reviewed, tells me such haste simply isn't necessary, nor wise.

Only three times in my life have I ever had to take a shot at 250 yards for a whitetail. One was across a small, high-country lake in New York's Adirondacks; in the other two instances, the shots were down inclines as I mooched along deserted logging roads. Most other shots were well under two hundred feet and a vast majority were from sixteen to ninety feet. It is the very nature of our thick second growth in the east and northeast that makes short range shots so common.

For a big guy, I'm not all that obvious in the woods. I utilize cover and try in every way possible to mask both the cadence and noise of my feet and hunting clothes. The ofttimes close proximity of whitetail in our geographical areas and the type of cover make this more important than when working terrain for the average-situation mule deer. When I actually stalk my deer, it is around swamps and fresh game trails, as well as along ridges that provide sufficient cover for wise old bucks. Areas of heavy blow-downs are favorite areas of mine – and the wary deer.

I particularly like to stalk hot spots during windy periods, when it is raining or snowing, or when a previous night's rain or snow has covered or softened the leaves underfoot. Under these circumstances, with the air or wind currents not against me, I love nothing better than to move in short, slow treks through the second growth and deadfalls, constantly alert for that telltale twitch of an ear or tail, or some other movement of feeding or anxiety that will tell me I'm not as alone in that area as it would seem.

I spend as much time peering around from the protection of a tree, as I do walking along slowly. Never do I hasten my steps or push too fast. Usually it's while the careful hunter is standing motionless, with all senses alert, that he spots or hears nearby game; there is a reason for this. Your body is working as close to perfection as it ever will, short of a combat situation. Your basic hunting sense has been sharpened by those old juices that lie within us all, unless, of course, we've allowed ourselves to become too completely dulled by living overly close to the civilized mode of things.

A typical average-size buck, representative of the northeast. They come significantly larger and with finer racks than this would be run-of-the-mill adult. (Taken with camouflaged camera and remote shutter release, plus tele-lens.)

If and when you have an opportunity for a clean shot, it usually will have to be a quick one. Dense woods and tangled second growth allow many a whitetail in these areas to put enough real estate between you so that a second or third shot often is no more than a branch-cutter. Whatever you are carrying, whether a rifle or slug gun, it should be on its way to your shoulder in an instant and your first shot should be quickly but carefully aimed. If you doubt whether you can hit your target, don't shoot. Oftentimes you can stealthily walk up game again, but rarely ever if you actually fire your rifle and put the woods into panic.

Whitetail hunters in my part of the country have learned a good deal from Texas hunters and others in similar terrain where deer can move through fairly high and dense growth. More and more of my hunting friends are beginning to place greater faith in such excellent hunting accessories as the Baker

Nothing much handier than a lever-action in .35 Rem. or even the supposedly outdated .30-30 to bring down a New England buck. This one lived in a pulp forest loaded with young second growth foliage. An abundance of food. (This buck weighed over two hundred pounds.)

Tree Stand and Seat – this not only gives you far greater ability to spot a deer that cannot be spotted from the ground, but it serves admirably when wind or air currents are not in your favor.

Remember, during the fall air currents tend to move up or down a slope or mountain, as well as laterally. Height often gives you a chance of going unscented, at least at a distance; often the view from your high perch gives you an opportunity for a longer, unobstructed shot before you are spotted or scented. Probably the only art you will not see performed here to any degree, and one favored by many Texas deer hunters, is "rattling". Few have tried it and fewer know how. It's different in moose country – it is widely practiced, as is calling; quite a few hunters, and numerous guides do both well.

Another favorite gambit of whitetail hunters calls for long sessions of ridge running. With my wife, or a few friends hunting together, one pushes whitetails off the tops of ridges while "Glad" or others work along about a quarter of the way down the ridge and about two hundred yards ahead of the top party, which can be heard moving noisily along, on purpose. Usually, if I'm the ridge walker I can pace myself exactly to my wife's or friends' movements simply by stopping and catching the occasional sound of the lower party's journey. In her case, when she's alone, it's close to an art – she long ago learned to be that silent a walker. If it is noisy underfoot, she reverses her procedure and holds back one or two hundred yards behind me. Such changes in tactics are discussed prior to our splitting up.

When moving through the woods in this manner, "Glad" and I both tend to choose light, fast-handling sporting arms; "Glad" leans strongly towards a Winchester, Mossberg or Marlin lever-action carbine. For the past twelve years she has placed most of her faith in two favorites – a nicely stocked Marlin in .35 Remington or a Winchester Model 94 in caliber .30-30. She had me install rear aperture peep sights in place of the open factory hardware, and both are equipped with carrying slings. They're handy coming down mountains, or when she is forced by circumstances to drag a dressed deer to a spot where I can locate her. She dresses her own deer, antelope, bear and small game. On moose and elk she waits out big-daddy's return!

As for my preference, I normally carry either an old Winchester, Marlin or Ruger .44 Mag. carbine. The Marlin is in .35 Rem., the Winchester, chambered for the old but still adequate .30-30; my favorite load for this one incorporates 34.0 grains of IMR 4895 behind a Sierra 150-grain FN bullet; a combo that allows for a velocity of close to 2300 fps. Occasionally I may tote a test rifle such as a Mannlicher-stocked 7 × 57 or a Mauser Model 660 in a variety of calibers, thanks to its versatile, interchangeable, barrel system. If the weather is fair-to-middlin', I just may use any one of these rifles with a 1.5–4X Bushnell scope. The scope, however, is practically always set at the 1.5-power mark. When the days are rainy, snowy or foggy, I carry nothing longer or heavier than my Ruger carbine in .44 magnum. It is by far the fastest, deadliest close-range tool I could use on a whitetail in my section of the country. It is even great medicine for close-in black bear.

When it comes to calibers for whitetail in typical brush or second-growth timber, you don't need lightning-fast lightweight bullets (or calibers in

"Glad" Zwirz drops a buck from atop author's Cedar Mountain private hunting grounds in New England. In minutes it was in husband's 4-wheeler and back at house for hanging and dressing. (She handles her own field dressing – sans Eskimo fur coat.)

general). This is the country for the .30-30, .35 Remington, .308 Winchester, .300 Savage, or even the .30/06. Other cartridges falling within this general size and power range can be substituted. However, stay away from the easily upset, fast-moving bullets or calibers that are simply too much for the distances involved during better than 95% of your hunting. I don't care how up-to-date anyone tells you they are, many of the newer fast-traveling lightweights don't belong in the average habitat of eastern or – northeastern whitetail terrain.

Whitetail deer seem to have a sight problem when moving in snow or on a bright, sunny day, particularly where the glare or rays are in front of them, and this to a greater degree than that experienced by mule deer inhabiting more open country. On six recent occasions, my wife and I had bucks and does walk practically over us as we sat motionless with our backs against fallen logs, our rumps deep down on a waterproof cover placed on the ground. Almost invariably it was near midday, as we were drinking tea and eating sandwiches.

On one occasion a buck accidently kicked over a light backpack I had leaning against a tree not more

than six feet from our booted toes. I couldn't reach my rifle without getting up, so I carefully drew my service .357 Ruger Security-Six for a fast snap-shot. My spouse, however, beat me to the punch and fired her carbine from the knee. She missed at six short paces, shooting right over his neck! I never did get to shoot. Later, she alibied that she had mustard on her fingers and the carbine slipped just at the inopportune second. A rare occurrence for this modern-day Annie Oakley.

When just two hunters push whitetail around, as "Glad" and I are often prone to do, it cannot be described as driving in the usual sense of the term. Driving in our kind of terrain usually requires a minimum of from three to four hunters to a dozen or more. I personally don't like driving at all. It simply isn't my idea of old-fashioned hunting, though it does account for hundreds of downed deer each season in whitetail country. Sometimes it's the only way to move them out of a swampy alder area or a heavy concentration of pulp forest. This is a technique requiring a percentage of hunters to be posted around points that are in line with the termination of the drive. Occasionally a driver will have

A small whitetail buck – photo by Judd Cooney.

an opportunity for a snap-shot, but it still tends to be more dangerous and less of a challenge to the individual's skill.

Still-hunting, interspersed with periods of short moves, is still the most successful method I know. It is not, however, for everyone. Each season a number of hunters tell me it's their last resort. Ants in their pants! Most cannot or will not discipline themselves to stay absolutely quiet and immovable for one or two hours in a concealed spot. That, ol' buddy, is why so many never get to see that whitetail, much less collect one. Most hunters, I'm sorry to say, do little more than frighten and push deer to and fro through the woods and swamps. It's rare when the inexperienced hunter, who blunders along like this, gets his deer. Instead, another nearby hunter luckily spots the fleeing deer and manages to get off a carefully aimed shot or two. Nothing more to worry about but tagging it, dressing it and dragging it out –.

Experienced hunters agree that, done with stealth, still-hunting is deadly. Those willing to climb high along the ridges, close by a well-used game trail, are the ones who will take the trophy-

size bucks during early season, if they are willing to be in a concealed position offering good visibility at least a half hour before dawn. This is so the area you have chosen can calm down in time for that magic moment of first shooting light. Deer and other game are returning to their resting areas after a night of feeding and drinking in the lowlands and fields, or returning from a night of bliss spent with a doe or two.

Most of my larger bucks have been killed early in the season. They also have been shot from a sitting position as I fired downhill at relatively close range. The worst shots are not all that bad, with, say, sixty degrees of angle and a maximum range of about 150 to 190 feet. Past that range it probably wouldn't have been possible to pick up a clear enough path for the bullet. Worse, the whitetail could have slipped through with not much more than a snap and a crackle, unseen in the dimmer light and shadowy cover of foliage.

Second to dawn is the late afternoon. Rarely do I hit a well-known area or outroad until about twenty minutes before dark. We pick our pre-dusk hunting sites so we will have the least amount of trouble reaching a known return route when the time comes to get out of the woods safely. This is the time when you make certain you are looking over the areas leading from the high country, not to it. Many bucks, and particularly does, have built-in alarm clocks that tend to go off between 3:30 and 4:00 p.m.. From that point on they become eager to return to the previous night's goings on; usually it will take them anywhere from one hour to two or three hours to mooch down from their daylight haunts.

Early in the hours of first light and again when light is fast fading, there is a definite advantage to having your rifle equipped with a top-quality scope. But as I've stated before, a scope of low magnification. It should have all the light-gathering potential possible, so keep that power *low*.

If you are alone and kill a big buck just at dark, you must dress it out, dark or not. Always carry a flashlight when you intend to hunt late and when you are far from a road or camp. For reasons of safety don't try to carry or drag a buck at night, especially if alone. Instead, clean it as well as you can, then cover it with brush and leaves – always leave some article of clothing on it to help keep other predators from working it over during the night, but there's no guarantee that if you leave your drawers animals will stay away! I know from experience that a long rope, a high limb and a wire cage make a better guarantee. And then, it's a visual invitation to a game thief. By the way, attach your game tag or you could be inviting game warden trouble.

Not that it is an unbreakable rule, but when a dyed-in-the-wool whitetail hunter goes into prime mule deer terrain, he finds himself working country that, to him, is veritable open country. Yet even the rules here can fool you; I've shot muleys at five hundred and forty yards off a ridge as they watched me far below. I've also bushwhacked a fine buck in a grown-up wash at forty paces. Be ready for anything, and flexible, is the key to deer-hunting success.

As something of a guide-line I'm going to list here some fairly recent statistics as they relate to a number of states that make up our east coast and what is considered to be the northeast. I'll only give you reported kills by firearm and bow hunters, combined. I'll also give you the *average* field dressed weight. We all know there are bucks that weigh well over two-hundred pounds and have racks that are spectacular. We all want to collect a few in a lifetime. However, I'd rather be realistic and give you honest weights, dressed, as checked by Fish & Game Departments. Just add the guts weight and you have a better braggin' figure if you are prone to this.

Note: Though this chart is slightly over two years old, it is the latest data compilation available.

STATE	* DEER HARVEST	AVERAGE DRESSED WEIGHT	FORECAST
Alabama	120,727	80 lbs.	Good
Connecticut	834	94 lbs.	Good
Delaware	1,272	110 lbs.	Excellent
Florida	55,000	85 lbs.	Good
Georgia	57,893	80 lbs.	Good to Excel.
Kentucky	10,000	100 lbs.	Fair
Louisiana	76,769	82 lbs.	Good
Maine	34,765	107 lbs.	Good
Maryland	9,727	100 lbs.	Excellent
Massachusetts	5,525	95 lbs.	Good
Mississippi	37,000	100 lbs.	Excellent
New Hampshire	8,351	108 lbs.	Fair
New Jersey	12,688	90 lbs.	Excellent
New York	103,225	120 lbs.	Good (northern zone – Fair)
North Carolina	53,000	80 lbs.	Excellent
Pennsylvania	138,200	95 lbs.	Good (except S.E.)
Rhode Island	111	85 lbs.	Good (based on state size)
South Carolina	46,000	85 lbs.	Excellent
Tennessee	14,890	115 lbs.	Good (West zone) Fair (remaining areas)
Vermont	11,545	100 lbs.	Excellent (asking for more hunters)
Virginia	63,443	82 lbs.	Excellent
West Virginia	35,336	114 lbs.	Excellent

* For one season.

North-country whitetail buck, still in velvet.

Zwirz likes lever-actions and fast-handling carbines such as the Ruger .44 Mag., but also uses auto-loaders, pumps, and bolt-action rifles in slower calibers than those used in Western areas. In whitetail country range is usually limited. He calls for scopes to be set a lowest magnification in heavy cover – if too dense – no scope!

41

Chapter 4

SOUTHEASTERN WHITETAILS
by Charley Dickey

There's good news for deer hunters in the southeast ... and a rosy future. The state herds have expanded beyond most hunters' expectations and the seasons are long with liberal limits.

The whitetailed deer was first scientifically described in Virginia but at least 30 subspecies from Canada to Panama are now recognized by wildlife biologists. The Virginia whitetail, *Odocoileus virginianus virginianus,* is the dominant strain from Virginia to Kentucky to Louisiana to Georgia and most points in between.

The Osceola subspecies occurs along the Gulf Coast from Louisiana to Florida. The Seminolus subspecies is in southeast Georgia and much of Florida. There are four subspecies on islands off the coast of South Carolina and Georgia. The little Key deer, about the size of a collie dog, is found only in the Florida keys, most of the remaining 500 being strictly protected and concentrated in the National Key Deer Wildlife Refuge in Monroe Country.

Classifying deer means a lot to wildlife biologists but little to hunters. It really takes an expert to tell the difference and there are many gradations where even the scientists argue. The whole situation is confused even more because sportsmen's clubs and state game departments have imported deer from Wisconsin, Texas, Missouri and other states and stocked these different subspecies with the native subspecies. They've readily crossed. A buck in rut, or a doe in heat, doesn't worry about technicalities such as subspecies.

Hunters don't care much for the formal Latin names of the subspecies. Can you imagine a hunter missing a buck on Blackbeard Island off the Georgia Coast and yelling, "I just missed an eightpoint *Odocoileus virginianus nigribarbis!*" He's more likely to scream, "There goes that *# *$ & #* with his heart shot out!"

The key point about the various subspecies of whitetail is that a whitetail is a whitetail is a whitetail. That is, while they may vary a bit in color, size and bone structure, they are basically the same deer no matter where you hunt them. Their reactions to hunting pressures are the same. They instinctively know how to use cover and avoid danger. They have the same keen senses which enable them to outwit hunters most of the time. For instance, a recent Florida survey showed that it takes, on the average, about 34 man-days of hunting to bag one whitetail buck.

Until 20 or 30 years ago, the whitetail deer was all but extinct in most of the southeast and had been in that condition since the turn of the century. Most of the deer still hanging on were in remote mountains or impenetrable swamps. Since 1950, there's been a deer explosion in the southeast and hunters are bagging big bucks in central Georgia where they were unknown only 10 years ago.

The deer came back to the southeast for several reasons: there has been a change in land pattern use, much of it favoring deer. They have better habitat, with much of it due to the cutting of timber and pulp to let a new succession of plants start.

Charley Dickey, the author of this chapter, looks over some prime venison. Note his gun. Even in the dense woods of the South he prefers a rifle.

Thanks to sportsmen, the public has a better understanding of deer. The public wants them around, whether for the pleasure of watching or the fun of hunting. Also, because of sportsmen concern, there's better law enforcement. Wildlife biologists now know more about managing county or statewide herds. With sportsmen money and cooperation, deer have been trapped from well-populated areas and moved to other areas where there were few or no deer.

Give the whitetail reasonable protection during the non-hunting season, ideal habitat and plenty of territory and the bucks and does take care of the multiplication. On a healthy range, a doe drops twins, or sometimes triplets, every year. It doesn't take long for a local herd to bounce back.

That's exactly what the whitetailed deer has done in the southeast. Other than Alaska, South Carolina has the longest season of any state in the union with no danger of the herd being overshot. Their season opens Aug. 15 in the eastern part of the state and continues until January 1 in some parts of the state. That's four and one-half months of deer hunting!

Alabama is bursting at the seams with a deer herd of one million. For the 1977–78 hunting season, Alabama allowed hunters to take one buck a day. With a 65-day season, that meant a hunter could legally take 65 bucks – assuming any hunter is good enough to bag one a day. In Florida, where the herd is close to 600,000, a hunter could legally take *two* bucks a day.

In fact, the biggest deer problem on the horizon in much of the southeast is too many deer. When there are too many deer for the range, the animals are subject to malnutrition and when that sets in it's usually followed by an outbreak of disease. A given amount of territory, with only so much deer food such as browse and mast, will only support so many deer. When the carrying capacity is passed, most of the deer are affected. If the situation continues, the inevitable result is an undernourished herd and finally a variety of fatal diseases.

Farmers in many sections are complaining that deer are robbing their gardens and crops. They don't want to see the deer totally removed, but the numbers reduced to some reasonable figure. The best way to reduce deer herds is to let the hunters handle it. Hunters work free.

After more than 75 years of intensive study of deer management, wildlife biologists know that a deer herd cannot be managed wisely without cropping some of the does. And that's where the headaches start! The public, many legislators and some poorly informed hunters are opposed to taking any does, much less just a reasonable number to keep the herd roughly in balance with available food. State game departments are subject to political pressures and sometimes they are reluctant to make decisions based solely on biological fact.

Anyway, Alabama, Georgia, South Carolina and Florida, plus other states in the southeast, now have short statewide doe seasons or do it on a county or regional basis. The way the deer keep multiplying, they may have to have longer doe seasons. One thing is sure, if hunters are not allowed to keep the herd in line with available food, nature will step in and do the job with malnutrition and disease.

The southeastern deer, regardless of subspecies, on the average doesn't grow as large as the northern woodland or some other subspecies of whitetails. However, with improvement in the range in the southeast, most of the states are producing some relatively spectacular bucks. A rebuilding of de-

The "work" part of hunting. Note the heavy cover, yet this hunter is using a rifle.

The moment of truth.

High in a tree this hunter is above the line of sight — and smell — of his quarry.

What it's all about!

*Why don't they ever
pose like this during hunting season?*

pleted soils in the southeast with fertilization and nutritious crops, is giving deer a balanced diet and their weights and antlers are showing it. Central Georgia is producing an encouraging number of bucks with antlers scoring from 120 to 160 under the Boone and Crockett system of measuring. So is Alabama.

In 1972, Boyd Jones, a Tallahassee contractor, killed a buck in south Georgia that weighed 255 pounds field dressed and examined by two biologists. That's the same weight as a buck taken in Maine which many considered the largest whitetail ever bagged.

Big ones are around, and indications are that there will be more of them, but the average deer in the southeast still does not compare with those taken in Wisconsin, Michigan, Pennsylvania and other northern states. However, the challenge of taking *any* buck in the southeast is the same as for whitetails anywhere. What the southeastern hunter has going for him are long seasons and liberal bag limits and plenty of open land upon which to hunt. And he doesn't have as much competition from other hunters as, say, in New York or Wisconsin.

The southeast has abundant rainfall and long growing seasons and this means lush cover. No matter where you find whitetails, they are seldom far from dense escape cover. Most of the bucks taken are shot at distances of less than 50 yards. The southeast is traditionally a shotgun region but that's rapidly changing. Hunters have found that a rifle with telescopic sights pays off for short shots and, of course, there are opportunities at 100 to 200 yards which can only be handled with a rifle.

Shotguns, loaded with either buckshot or rifled slugs, are on the way out, although they will be a long time dying. The hunter with the proper scope and rifle has the odds with him. The word is getting around and more hunters are converting.

For the hunter who deliberately wishes to handicap himself by hunting with bow and arrow, muzzleloader or even a handgun, the southeast offers unlimited opportunities. The low dense cover, so prevalent, often works to his advantage. It helps him get within range for the capabilities of the weapon he is using.

In many parts of the southeast, especially the wild mountain areas and the desolate swamps, hunters use dogs to drive deer to standers. In fact, in some of the rugged country there's hardly any way to get within range of deer without drives. Hunting with dogs is greatly misunderstood. The dogs simply

Mighty Mite tree stand and Hand Climber.

A moment of rest during the long drag out.

Charley Dickey, the author, checks to see if his buck is really down for the count.

Not very big but he sure will taste good.

Lever guns are popular throughout the Southeast.

A mighty fine buck for the Southeast or any place else.

Charley Dickey, the author of this chapter, looks as if he is wondering about the success of his shot – since it brought about having to use a knife and all the work that goes with it.

An archer dressed to blend in with his surroundings. A necessity for bow and arrow hunters.

flush and push the deer. They don't catch the deer or leap at their flanks and chew them to pieces.

In more open country, or where it's easier to get within range of deer, hunting with dogs is not necessarily the most efficient way of putting venison on the table. A great deal of time is spent chasing does, rounding up lost dogs, moving from one drive area to another and holding long tactical sessions (arguments). Hunters mostly use hounds because they enjoy hunting with dogs. The performance of their dogs is more important than someone shooting a buck.

Of course, with wild packs of dogs that belong to no one and who roam free all year, there is damage done, especially to pregnant does in the spring and fawns in summer. Sportsmen and state game departments try to keep these hungry and vicious packs under control. But this has no relationship whatsoever to good sportsmen in the fall using hounds to drive deer to standers.

The two main ways for hunting deer in the southeast are the same as for anyplace else. The hunter sits and waits at a likely spot or he sneaks carefully through the woods "still" hunting, moving cautiously a few feet and then looking intently. It's more of a "stop and go" method or "pause and look." Of course, the two methods can be used together.

Whitetails do most of their moving, as far as hunting is concerned, around dawn and dusk. That's when it's best to have earlier scouted an area, chosen a place to sit and to be there early and patiently wait. You let the deer come to you. During the middle of the day, when the deer are mostly bedded down, you "stop and go" hunt. You go to the deer, perhaps flushing one from a bed for a quick running shot.

It takes an excellent woodsman to move towards a buck without spooking him. Whitetails have a keen sense of smell. No one knows just how sharp it is, but it's many thousand times more efficient than our own. Although deer do not distinguish color, they have sharp eyes for detecting movement. Their large cupped ears are magnets for sound and any unusual noise, especially one which means danger, causes the deer to ease into dense cover or flee.

Because of these heightened senses, compared to a human's, the best bet for most hunters is to choose a spot and let the deer come to him. Sitting and waiting is a patient art difficult for most of us to learn. We'd rather be moving.

Leaving in a hurry!

A .30-30 Winchester was all the gun needed for this whitetail buck.

This 21 point buck killed in Beaufort County is perhaps the largest recorded killed in the Southeast. While hunting near Gardens Corner, John W. Wood took this trophy rack which tallied 208⅝ points on the Boone and Crockett scale. This puts it in a class with the largest deer ever killed in the United States. (S. C. Wildlife Resources Department photo by Ted Borg.)

Selecting a stand or a place to sit at dawn, or an hour or so before dusk, is more than finding a comfortable place for your rear end. It means scouting and choosing an area where deer are abundant. The hunter ideally scouts before the season opens and locates the general movements of the deer. The best way to scout deer is to actually see them. They're pretty much creatures of habit. A buck has a regular range, perhaps no more than 200 or 300 acres.

The hunter checks droppings, rubs, scrapes, browse and runways. If he is planning to watch a runway, he sets up back from the trail perhaps 25 to 50 yards so that he will get a broadside choice of shots. He picks a spot with the prevailing wind in mind. Then he picks a spot as an alternate on the other side of the runway in case the wind changes. He rakes out the dry leaves and limbs so that when he moves he does not make noise. He sits down in the spot and checks visibility. Does he need to cut a few weeds or limbs that would be in his way while swinging his rifle?

On the scouting trips, he plans everything he can. Then when he walks to his chosen spots in the dark an hour before sunrise he's all set. He has planned everything he can. His task is to sit quietly and patiently wait: the buck may come, or not come, but at least he's done all he can to control the tactics.

Because of the dense understory or low cover in much of the southeast, the hunter is forever fighting visibility. He can't shoot a deer if he can't see him. In most cover situations, the hunter would prefer a few added feet of height for his observation post. If he could sit five feet higher, his visibility would be doubled. With 10 feet, he could see nearly everywhere.

That's why tree stands are becoming more and more popular. There are two general types – permanent and portable. For a permanent tree stand, the hunter, after obtaining permission from the landowner, builds a large and comfortable stand in a tree. It takes considerable effort to make a permanent stand so the hunter scouts thoroughly before selecting a tree. It overlooks main runways of travel, perhaps a favorite feeding field or a milling area.

The trouble with a permanent tree blind is that the deer may change their patterns a bit because of hunting pressure, weather or other conditions. The hunter is stuck, unless he wants to build another blind in another scouted area.

Thousands of deer hunters, especially the bow hunters, are now using light portable tree stands and self climbers. If one tree doesn't pay off, the hunter folds his stand, puts it on his back and moves to another area which looks better.

There are a number of excellent portable stands on the market designed especially for deer hunters. For free literature on a variety of models, you may wish to write Jim Baker, Baker Manufacturing Company, P. O. Box 1003, Valdosta, Georgia 31601.

Of course, whenever you use a climber and tree stand, you must be careful in going up or down the tree. Your rifle should be unloaded and you'll find a sling or rope handy so that both hands are free for holding onto the tree.

The best time to hunt bucks in the southeast is during the rut when the bucks have their minds on sexy does. The bucks lose much of their normal caution and do a lot of rambling within their home range. Bucks are usually in rut for three to five weeks and the peak of the rut comes about the same time every year, in a given region. The farther

Deep South hunting is sometimes almost a social event shared by a good many friends.

north, the earlier the rut, since decreasing hours of daylight are what set off the hormones. For instance, in Pennsylvania the rut comes in middle November. In north Florida it peaks about Christmas or New Year's.

New studies have shown that deer rub saplings with their antlers as the rutting season approaches, similar to earlier rubbing in autumn to remove velvet. The rubs are advertising markers, often near the boundaries of a buck's territory, to warn other bucks to stay away and to let does know the buck is ready. The rubs are usually from one to three or four feet off the ground and sometimes a tree is almost debarked.

Scrapes are a sexual advertisement. The buck paws out the ground about the size of a bucket or washtub. He may scrape his antlers through the dirt. The scrapes are usually made in a small clearing beneath overhanging branches. The buck urinates in the scrape, deliberately spilling some on his hocks which he rubs together, and has a stationary marker as well as being a walking advertisement for does.

The buck may make several scrapes. He checks them often. If a doe in heat, or about to become proud, finds a scrape and the buck is not there, she urinates in the scrape and dribbles some on her hocks. When the buck returns, he has no trouble sniffing her down.

If you find fresh rubs and scrapes during the rutting season you know there's a buck around. The scrape is the best sign you can find. Many hunters grab a handful of dirt from the scrape and sniff it, the strong urine giving an indication of current usage by the buck. The hunter sets up 25 to 50 yards from the scrape and patiently waits for the buck to return. The chances are that he'll be back, may be unwary and offer you a great shot.

The future of deer hunting in the southeast is bright, although some areas are over-populated and does need to be thinned. Many areas have yet to hit carrying capacity, or ideally just a little below. All of the state game departments have progressive programs of keeping land open for public hunting. The southeastern hunter never had it so good.

53

Chapter 5

MIDWESTERN AND NORTHERN WHITETAILS

Some of the largest deer on our continent call this area, "home." They're grain fed almost to the point of prime beef.

It is here, too, that we find some of the smartest whitetails since, until we move into the northern evergreen forests, they are in close proximity to man all year long. Meaning they not only learn to live with man but learn how to avoid him as well.

Hunting in this segment of these United States differs little from those methods used elsewhere in most instances, in spite of what one might hear from time to time. Corn field hunting is corn field hunting regardless of the state. Likewise for forests.

As with other parts of the country, most hunters are out the first few days of the season and that's when most of the deer are taken. I think it would be safe to say the average deer hunter spends three to four days at his sport and these make up the first three to four days of the season. This would be true coast to coast, except, perhaps, in Texas, where it is not only private land hunting but where the ritual includes the entire season from mid-November through January 1, in most counties.

Because of this it becomes mandatory for the successful hunter to devote more than that number of days to bagging venison, but not during the season! It's the number of days spent in the woods BEFORE the season opens that determines the success of opening weekend. Properly done, in fact, the hunting season could be a mighty short one. The secret, if there is one, comes in that pre-season scouting. A week spent in the woods prior to opening day could easily reduce a hunter's actual hunt to a single day, even half a day in some instances.

Knowing which tree to lean against, which trail to watch, which grain field (and what portion of it) to watch makes the difference between deer hunters and deer baggers on opening day. This is when hunters are stationed at opportune locations, using to advantage those other hunters who waited until opening day to hit the woods. It is this preponderance of manpower, clumsily stumbling through the brush, that causes deer to keep moving and that makes the odds go up in favor of that prepared hunter.

Hunting public land is an art, though one easily learned. It coincides with learning the land. Deer have a decided preference for food and cover and the trails between the two. Only under duress will they change. Learn where they feed, where they bed down, the trails they use to go back and forth. With this knowledge your deer season chances of success are greatly improved. Even in heavily hunted areas.

Why?

Because you know where to plant yourself, long before the light of day on opening morning, to take advantage of the animal's natural daily habits before those scurrying about spoil the area. Even with the extra activity in their habitat deer will move around a good deal before leaving. Should a buck fail to use the trail you selected during those first few minutes of the hunt, he may well come along later while

A small whitetail in typical habitat.

being driven by those hunters who were not willing to work at their sport ahead of time.

Remember, more than 90% of the deer killed are dropped by hunters at stands; by hunters like yourself who took time to learn where to go BEFORE the season opened.

How does one go about scouting an area?

My preference is to simply get out and walk over the country I'm going to hunt. From side to side and front to back. Then, from the other direction, back over that same country again if there is time. Deer will be seen while doing this, or at least some waving white flags will be seen. Fortunately, there is an animal attached to each one.

The reason I advise going backwards over the same country will become obvious once you've done it. Ridges look different from the other side, fields, too, and forests. From one direction a spot might be casually dropped from consideration for one reason or another, yet, from the other side it might look good because of what you had been standing in while looking it over the first time. This same reasoning applies to hunting strange country. Look back over your shoulder every so often. It sure helps when finding your way back to camp.

In some midwestern and northern states scouting can be effectively accomplished by water routes. A canoe trip along a few miles of stream, or lakeshore, can prove mighty revealing.

Another good method, where it can be done without tangling with a game warden, is to drive around at night with a spotlight. This is a prime way to locate bucks of a stature that places them in the trophy, or record, category.

A mighty good whitetail for this lucky hunter. More probably it wasn't luck for a buck of this size.

Much of the country allows spotlighting so long as there is no gun aboard. Be careful here because finding the biggest buck in the state wouldn't be worth losing the right to hunt him through conviction on a game law violation. Often all that is necessary is to notify your game warden where you will be to protect him from making an unnecessary run should he receive a call about a "spotlighter."

Just because a big buck is located at night, with a light, doesn't mean he will be seen in daylight. But it does add encouragement to the hunt to know a big one lurks in the vicinity.

On scouting forays watch for tracks, droppings, rubs, scrapes, anything that indicates deer are using the area. Rubs and scrapes are particularly sought out by buck hunters because these are obvious signs of male deer. Scrapes are pawed places on the ground and urinated on by the buck to mark his boundaries. A doe in season comes along and urinates in the same spot. Bucks check out their scrapes by making rounds. That calling card left by the urinating doe means she is ready. The buck tracks her down and another fawn is conceived.

Rubs are found on small trees. Bark will have been rubbed off as the buck rubs the velvet off his hardened antlers just prior to the rut. Since whitetails are homebodies, seldom wandering more than a mile, at most, from where they were born, a rub means a buck is in the vicinity. If fresh, it is possible he will return periodically and "fight" that same tree a few more times as he prepares for breeding season. A worthy spot to keep under surveillance. Also watch for trails that show regular use. Beds. Water holes. Even when there is a good

57

An excellent northern whitetail.

deal of water or food in an area, animals often have a preferred spot for their daily repast.

Once these selected spots, be they food, water, bed, scrape or rub have been located, set about finding a good stand from which to hunt. If legal in your state (this varies a bit from state to state so check local regulations carefully) a tree stand is best for several reasons. It gets you above the animal's line of sight as few ever look up. Next it tends to let your scent float over the immediate area, above your quarry. Don't ever short-change a deer in this department. He trusts his eyes, that's for sure, but he trusts his nose even more. I would rate their sensitivities as scent, sound and sight, in that order. A deer that smells or hears a hunter isn't about to wait around and see how he is dressed or what kind of gun he is carrying.

Being color blind a deer's vision depends on movement. A motionless hunter is home free. Unless he makes some slight sound, such as when stifling a cough or sneeze, crackling paper as he ever so slowly removes the wrapper from a candy bar, or any other sound he might think didn't travel beyond the length of his rifle barrel. Rest assured it does and it will often get a buck's attention, making his eyes and nose even more sensitive.

Let a whiff of air carry the hunter's scent to that oversensitive nose and brother whitetail is long gone. Instantly. No questions asked. From distances you wouldn't believe.

If hunting from the ground pick a spot against a tree or stump, if you are the motionless type. If fidgety, like me, you'd better pick a spot behind some light cover. It doesn't take much to break up the outline of the human body. Sometimes I slip inside such cover. The main thing to watch here is that you don't become so concealed a shot is impossible when the time comes. Figure out where shots may be offered and then make sure there is an opening to them.

Regardless of how carefully this is done, sooner or later a buck will get away without a shot being fired because he did the unexpected. And he'll usually be the "bull of the woods." Which is precisely how he got that way, outsmarting old homo sapiens.

Murphy's Law will usually win out. If anything can go wrong, it will. Just try to see ahead and avoid all possible pitfalls. You'll never thwart them all, and even if you did, it would destroy the intriguing part of hunting. It's the unexpected that makes it the great sport it is.

The new World Record Whitetail (typical) killed in 1914 by James Jordan and owned by Dr. Charles T. Arnold. The Boone and Crockett score a whopping 206 5/8.

Sometimes it is possible to put up a permanent tower or stand, especially if privileged to hunt private property. When this is done leave it up the year round. Animals soon come to accept these installations as part of the terrain and pay no attention whatever to them.

Moving on into evergreen forests, what has already been said still holds true except distances here can be handshaking at times. The closer the deer, the easier he is to miss! That's for sure. Also, the closer he is the more careful a hunter has to be about scent, sound and motion.

Though possible for a really fine woodsman, a neophyte hunter will stand little chance against a whitetail buck by trying to hunt afoot. At best he'll see an occasional white flag as it disappears through the trees. It is here, for sure, that the inexperienced hunter is well-advised to find a likely spot and wait out his quarry.

It is this type of cover that generates strong feelings about guns. Shotguns, where legal, can prove ideal. Especially when used with buckshot for those 15 to 25 yard shots. Most prefer large-bored rifles with big, heavy bullets, the kind often referred to as "brush busters." See chapters 15 and 16 for more details on this. I go along with those preferring .30-30's, .35 Remington's, .44 Magnums and .444 Marlin's for this type of hunting, particularly when a low-powered scope is added. The man has not been born that can convince me iron sights are best; except, and I will accept this single instance, where shots never exceed 35 to 40 yards. Providing, of course, that the hunter has near-perfect eyesight. (Sort of limits my acceptance, doesn't it?) Even here scopes will show the way through brush, should a standing shot be offered that would never be seen by the naked eye.

Low-powered scopes allow hunters far greater precision in directing bullets through brush and even more importantly, permit precisely-placed shots when early morning and late evening iron sights cannot be defined. In forests and woods this occurs every day of the season during legal hunting hours. Such conditions, more often than not, account for missed and crippled deer.

Semi-automatic rifles are sometimes preferred by those with little experience, because of fast repeat shots. Having hunted for more than a half a century I've never been able to buy such thinking. Spraying forests and woods with bullets might, for some, be what deer hunting is all about. Not yours truly. A careful first shot that misses is not very good justification for fast repeats. If the carefully placed first shot misses, how in the world can anyone expect faster, less-carefully-aimed repeat shots to do better. Maybe that's where fortune cookies and tea leaves take over, I don't know.

All of this, of course, applies to all forms of deer hunting, not just in the midwest or northern states.

Deer are hunted in similar fashion wherever they are. Slight variables occur due to local conditions but a woods hunter from the deep south will kill deer in Minnesota just like a hunter from Iowa will kill deer in Texas. He will use the same gun, the same knife, the same rope, but he might sight in for a longer or shorter distance. Other than that, whitetails are whitetails. All of them, are smarter than the hunter on an eyeball to eyeball basis. The best you can do is think ahead and be there before he is – waiting.

Which means, I guess, man is smarter than deer when he applies himself. Fortunately for the deer population, most hunters fail to do this.

This chapter had been put to bed and was to have been mailed the next morning when a news release arrived from the North American Big Game A-wards Program, Hunting Activities Dep't., 1600 Rhode Island Ave., N.W., Washington, D.C. 20036. This is the National Rifle Association address as they have taken over the awards program of the Boone and Crockett Club (whose address is listed at the end of chapter 11).

Often someone sincerely interested in a subject will go to great lengths to search out details on a subject to make sure the proper person receives credit. Dr. Charles T. Arnold performed that feat in the case of a set of enormous whitetail antlers he had acquired in his hobby of collecting big deer heads. Because the deer had been killed in Wisconsin it has been included here.

I can do no better than give you that entire release:

"WORLD RECORD WHITETAILED DEER TROPHY FROM WISCONSIN"

"Some 65 years have now passed since James Jordan shot a whitetail buck with an exceptionally large rack near Danbury, Wisconsin, along the Yellow River, in 1914. Although no one viewing this rack could remember a larger one, no one suspected this trophy of being a world record. The date was long before the formal records-keeping for native, North American big game was begun by the Boone and Crockett Club in 1932. Through a peculiar series of events, Jordan would not again see his trophy for more than a half-century.

Shortly after killing his deer, Jordan accepted the offer of a part-time taxidermist, George Van Castle of Webster, Wisconsin, to mount his trophy for 5 dollars. Van Castle took the rack and hide to his home to work on it, but soon moved to Hinckley, Minnesota, after the death of his wife. Jordan later heard that Van Castle had moved to Florida, making a trip to Hinckley to recover his trophy useless, although Jordan himself moved to Hinckley in his later life.

When Van Castle moved to Florida, he left Jordan's mounted deer head behind in the home he had occupied. Apparently, it then gathered dust in an attic corner until it was purchased in 1964 at a rummage sale for 3 dollars by Robert Ludwig.

Passing through Sandstone, Minnesota, Ludwig decided that the exceptional antlers were worth the price although the cracked and peeling mount

would have to be thrown away. Ludwig retained the antlers in his home in Sandstone until he sold them to Dr. Charles T. Arnold of New Hampshire, whose hobby is collecting exceptional deer antler racks.

In 1964, Bernard A. Fashingbauer of St. Paul, Minnesota, measured this rack in his capacity as an Official Measurer for the Boone and Crockett Club big game records and found it to surpass the score of the then world record. Later, a select panel of judges, chosen from the ranks of the Official Measurers, certified this trophy as the world record at 206-5/8 points. At that time, the trophy was still the property of Robert Ludwig. By the time it was first published in the records book (1971 edition: *North American Big Game)* it was the property of Dr. Arnold so that it was shown with hunter "unknown".

In 1964, when James Jordan first viewed the huge deer rack owned by Robert Ludwig (a distant relative) he knew it was the same deer he had shot so many years ago. For more than a decade, Jordan would be frustrated in his quest to be recognized as the hunter for this deer in the records book.

Jordan's claim to this trophy was convincing to many of those who talked to him about the matter. Ron Schara, Outdoor Writer for the Minneapolis Tribune, featured Jordan's story on several occasions. The current trophy owner (Dr. Arnold) wrote to the North American Big Game Awards Program (NABGAP) in late 1977, suggesting that Jordan's story be fully explored and that he be des-

ignated as the hunter, if the records office were convinced.

The NABGAP office asked Bernard Fashingbauer to gather all evidence that he could find on this trophy, in order that Jordan's claim could be fully considered by the Boone and Crockett Club's Records of North American Big Game Committee. Under the terms of the 1973 records keeping agreement, the club renders the final decision in cases such as this, while NRA staff perform the everyday program administration.

Information gathered by Fashingbauer, and from other sources, was considered by the Records Committee at their December 1978 meeting. After review, the committee decided to list James Jordan as the hunter for the world record whitetail deer (typical antlers), with a kill date and location of 1914 on the Yellow River, near Danbury, Wisconsin.

The next edition of the records book, *North American Big Game,* will be corrected with this information; expected publication is in 1983. (The current edition was published in 1977; usual publication cycle is six years.)

Unfortunately, James Jordan died in October 1978, at age 86, before he could be informed of the decision. His heirs have been informed of the decision, and they are pleased that his hunting achievement of more than a half-century ago has finally been properly recognized."

Chapter 6

BLACKTAIL & SITKA

PHANTOM OF THE RAIN FORESTS
by Ed Park

Those who have lived along that waterlogged strip of muddy land and dripping vegetation of the Pacific coast from northern California, through Oregon, Washington and British Columbia, and into southeastern Alaska, will appreciate the comment of a native Portlander, when asked if it rained often there.

"Naw," he replied, peeking out from under his soggy hat brim, "it's only rained once in the 63 years I've lived here. Once, continuously!"

But all this rain does have some advantages. It grows the country's finest crops of giant trees for timber, and produces dozens of great rivers and streams for salmon, trout and steelhead.

In between these towering trees and mighty rivers is a seemingly unpenetrable mass of ferns, brush, vines and other assorted plants that make up the well-known Pacific coast rain forests.

Finally, someplace in that dark and dank tangle lives one of this country's most elusive big game animals – the blacktail deer.

Those who have hunted both will tell you the blacktail is a more crafty, harder-to-hunt animal than the highly-reputed whitetail of the east. The blacktail lives in rougher country, more densely covered with brush, and in an area where adverse weather is a certainty.

Anyone doubting the secretiveness of the blacktail need only review the details of a controlled hunt carried out in Oregon in the early 1960s.

This hunt took place within an area of just 340 acres of typical blacktail habitat, surrounded by a deer-proof fence. At the time of the hunt, it was a known fact that at least 47 deer were inside the enclosure. A total of 50 hunters, a maximum of 8 at one time, would hunt this small area for 22 days. The first 13 days would be for bucks only while the last 9 would be either sex.

Many of the hunters were recognized experts at hunting blacktails so some persons expected a 100% kill, a total of 47 or more deer.

The hunting began at daybreak, and within the first few hours the initial eight hunters took three blacktail bucks. The slaughter had begun.

When sunset of the 22nd day arrived, 47 of those 50 hunters came away with nothing but a classic case of frustration, for not one more deer was killed after those three taken in the opening hours.

Comments recorded from the participating hunters indicate how well the native blacktail deer can adapt to heavy hunting pressure. Many were completely convinced that there wasn't a single deer in the whole enclosure. Others thought a few might be present, but based this opinion entirely on tracks they'd seen. Only a few even saw deer, but most of those failed to get a shot off.

The same scenario, expanded to cover the entire blacktail deer's range, is repeated each fall. Many blacktails are taken – but many more completely outwit the hunter in the rain-drenched jungles of this area.

The blacktail deer was once considered to be a separate species, but taxonomists now consider it merely a subspecies of mule deer, just as the Coues

Blacktail doe.

deer of Mexico and our own southwest, and the tiny Key deer of southern Florida are considered subspecies of the whitetail.

The scientific name of the mule deer is *Odocoileus hemionus hemionus* while the two subspecies that interest us here are the Columbian blacktail, *Odocoileus hemionus columbianus,* and the Sitka blacktail, *O. h. sitkensis.*

The Columbian blacktail is found along the coast and on most coastal islands, from about central California north to central British Columbia and inland roughly to the summit of the Cascades and Sierra Nevada mountains.

The Sitka blacktail, a smaller subspecies, is found immediately north of this, on the coastal islands and mainland of southeastern Alaska, and in British Columbia from about Prince Rupert north into the southern Yukon territory.

The differences between the Sitka and Columbian blacktail deer are so slight as to not be appar-

ent in the field, so differentiation must be based on range. This difference is even further confused by the many hybrids which occur where the two ranges overlap.

There are, however, very real differences between the blacktail subspecies and the mule deer.

Both have antlers that fork, then fork again, as opposed to the main beam and individual tines of the whitetail, but blacktail antlers are much smaller than those of the mule deer. This is clearly shown when we note that the top ranking blacktail rack in the Boone & Crockett records falls many points short of even making the minimum for inclusion in the mule deer listings.

The tail is the most obvious difference, with the blacktail's tail appearing to be somewhere between the long, broad flag of the whitetail and the thin, ropy tail of the mule deer. While not as large as the whitetail's, the blacktail's tail is longer and broader than the mule deer's and is dark on top and white

Blacktail doe.

underneath like the whitetail's. The mule deer's tail is thin and white, with a black tip.

The metatarsal gland on the outside of the lower hind leg is about 2½ to 3 inches long in the blacktail while about 5 to 5½ inches long in mule deer.

The habits and habitats of the Sitka and Columbian blacktails are similar. They are both highly secretive, completely capable of withstanding tremendous hunting pressure, and both live in the wettest, most heavily vegetated areas of this continent.

How then do successful hunters bag blacktails?

Basically most big game is taken by one of four general methods: Spotting and stalking, still hunting, driving, or sitting on a stand. Blacktails are taken by each of these methods also, aided by the fact that blacktails have rather small home ranges and will be found in the same location each day, unless pushed out by heavy pressures.

Spotting and stalking is best used in areas that had been burned or logged off a few years prior, and are now growing up to new brush – but where the brush is not yet high enough to completely hide the deer.

Hunters can sit on a ridge, with the morning sun at their backs, and glass other east-facing slopes. Once deer are spotted, stalking is aided by the same brush and the vertical nature of the country.

Still hunting is probably the way most hunters hunt most big game. It's a one-on-one situation then, the hunter depending on his slow, silent, careful movements to get him within range of his quarry before the quarry spots, smells or hears the hunter and gets out of the way.

Because of the heavy brush, much still hunting for blacktails is done along the many old logging roads and skid trails of this region. The Pacific slope is timber country and most of it has been logged at least once. The old roads remain, giving the still hunter a more silent path to follow.

Driving is an excellent way to outwit the black-

Hunter looking over once-logged area that is now growing up to brush and young trees.

Hunters dragging out small blacktail from typical brushy country.

Blacktail doe.

Hunters using a deer cart to haul out a blacktail from typical hunting country.

Typical logged-over area of blacktail habitat.

Hunter in the jumble of trees and logs that is typical blacktail hunting country.

Joe Clerget of Sumner, Washington, with good four-point blacktail.

68

Average four-point blacktail buck.

tail, for naturally he will be moving away from the drivers and unaware of those waiting in ambush. Correct use of such a method depends on having areas of brush that are isolated by roads, open logged-off areas or other clearings. The shooters need to be posted where they can cover these openings, ready for fast shots at deer sneaking across, headed for new cover.

The former world record blacktail deer, a huge specimen measuring 170⅛ Boone and Crockett points, was taken on a drive. Woodrow Gibbs of Sweet Home, Oregon, was hunting just out of town in 1963. He and several others decided to drive a patch of brush and timber, resulting in a new world record being driven to Gibb's waiting gun. This former record has now been topped by two others, including heads of 170⁶⁄₈ points and 170²⁄₈ points.

Sitting on a stand is part of driving of course, but can also be used as a very successful hunting method alone, when deer are moving about.

In general deer will move at three times – early morning, evening, or when pushed out of their beds in the daytime by hunters or other disturbances.

Deer don't see color but rather merely shades of gray. They do see movement very quickly though, so have the advantage over a hunter who is moving. A stationary hunter, one sitting motionless on a log, stump, rock or the ground, or one leaning against a tree, is almost impossible for a deer to spot – assuming there are no shiny objects flashing in the sun.

So stand-sitting can be one of the most productive ways to hunt blacktails. Again some pre-season scouting is necessary for the best success. Study your hunting area, look for trails of heaviest use, note the directions any deer go that you jump, consider wind and sun direction, and draw up a map for yourself. Then opening morning be on stand and motionless well before shooting light. Some deer travel about just as a result of their natural movements in the early morning, but if the area is heavily hunted you will find more deer moving as the result of other hunters.

The hunting method used will depend, of course, on the type of country, how heavy the brush is, the number of other hunters, how well you know the area, your own opinions on the subject, and even the weather. On the rare day when it isn't raining, and so rain gear need not be worn, still hunting is much more successful than when noisy ponchos or raincoats are used. Fog, also a common weather condition here, greatly limits any spotting and stalking.

Probably the most important piece of hunting equipment is your rain gear. A good suit of pants

Good 3-point buck. Tail shows.

and coat will make it possible to spend the day out in the drizzles.

If you doubt the stories of how much it rains along our Pacific coast, consider these official weather figures on precipitation from selected west-coast points, all in typical blacktail deer country:

Ketchikan, Alaska, 150; Quinalt, Washington, 128; Glenora, Oregon in Tillamook county, 130; Crescent City, California, 76. Each of those figures is inches per year!

Compare that with more logical weather in Chicago with 31 inches, Denver with 14, or Los Angeles with 15 inches of precipitation per year.

The picture is even more bleak – and wetter – when you consider that much of this precipitation is seasonal. At Glenora, for example, during November – a blacktail hunting month – the official average is over 25 inches of rain for the month. That's nearly an inch per day, every day.

Altough scope-sighted rifles are by far the most common for most species of big game, iron sights are commonly seen on the rifles of blacktail deer hunters. The ranges are short, the shooting often very fast, and scope sights tend to fog up in the rain unless they are the top of the line scopes guaranteed to be fog free. Even then I've seen expensive, positively fog-free scopes completely useless after a couple days of Oregon mist.

Although most of my hunting has been done in Oregon, the same general techniques apply in California, Washington, British Columbia and Alaska. Where you hunt will depend probably more upon where you live than anything, though non-residents of blacktail areas might want to consider other matters when choosing a place to hunt.

The trophy hunter should study the Boone & Crockett and Pope and Young Record books. For instance, the new 1977 Pope and Young book lists 60 entries in the blacktail deer category. Of these, 31 are from Oregon, 17 from Washington, 10 from California, 1 from British Columbia and 1 unknown.

Of the top 14 heads, 13 are from Oregon – and 10 of those listed are from Jackson County.

Other considerations are seasons, bag limits, non-resident costs and guide requirements.

Young hunter with average 3-point blacktail buck.

W. J. Pomeroy of Tacoma, Washington with a typical forked horn.

Sitka blacktail hunters in Alaska will find several seasons and bag limits, depending on the area. The most liberal areas include the mainland from south of Juneau to Cordova, Valdez and Whittier; the offshore islands such as Chichagof, Baranof and part of Admiralty; and part of Kodiak Island. The season in those area runs from August 1 through December 31 and the bag limit is 4 deer.

Alaska has an estimated 200,000 Sitka blacktails and many ranges are at maximum population levels. Severe winters or wolf predations are the main limiting factors, or herds sometimes suffer from overpopulation, depending on the area. The future of deer hunting in Alaska is excellent.

Residents pay $ 12 for a hunting license and nothing additional for deer tags. Nonresidents pay $ 60 for a hunting license and $ 35 for each deer tag. A guide is not required for a nonresident to hunt deer.

For the complete regulations or other information, contact the Alaska Department of Fish and Game, Subport Building, Juneau, AK 99801. Phone (907) 456–4100.

British Columbia also has extensive seasons and liberal bag limits. Seasons generally run from mid-September until October, November or December, depending on the area, with limits ranging from 1 to 3 deer. On the Queen Charlotte Islands however, the season runs from June 1 through the following February 28, with a bag limit of 10 deer.

British Columbia's deer population is not broken down into species, but is estimated at around 600,000 for Sitka blacktail, Columbian blacktail, mule deer and whitetails. However, the annual kill runs about 25 to 30,000 total deer, of which about 80% are blacktails. Deer populations and hunting should remain excellent in this province for both the Sitka and Columbian blacktails.

Residents pay $7 for a hunting license and $4 per deer tag. Non-residents pay $75 for a hunting license and $50 per deer tag. In addition, non-residents must be accompanied by a licensed guide when hunting any big game.

For complete hunting regulations, contact the British Columbia Department of Recreation & Travel Industry, Fish & Wildlife Branch, Parlia-

Antlers of blacktail deer taken by Clyde Cochran and his sons, Ed & Jerry, of Eugene, Oregon. The largest set in the center was taken with a rifle while the others were taken with bow and arrow.

Ed Cochran, Eugene, Oregon, with blacktail antlers of deer he took with bow and arrow. Will be in top 20 in Pope and Young record book.

Antlers of record book blacktail deer, taken by Jerry Cochran of Eugene, Oregon.

Woodrow W. Gibbs, Sweet Home, Oregon, with the former number one ranked blacktail. In the 1977 edition of "North American Big Game," the Boone and Crockett Record book, this head is ranked number three.

Forked horn blacktail buck.

Hunter glassing logged-over area for possible deer.

Hunter checking for tracks in mud of old logging road. Note rifle with iron sights, rain gear, wet ground.

Average four-point blacktail buck.

ment Buildings, Victoria, B.C. V8V 1×4. Phone (604) 387-6409.

Washington's season for deer in the western counties (blacktail deer country) is usually mid-October to mid-December. Bag limit is one buck. There are additional archery and muzzle-loader seasons however, so those interested should check the complete regulations.

The state's total deer herd, counting blacktails, mule deer and whitetails, is an estimated 470,000. The 1976 kill was 48,800 of which 50% were black-

Young hunter with blacktail forked horn. Tail shows.

tails. The future of blacktail deer in the state is excellent.

Residents pay $7.50 for a hunting license and $5 for a deer tag. Nonresidents pay $60 for a hunting license and $5 for a deer tag.

For further information, contact the Washington Department of Game, 600 N. Capitol Way, Olympia, WA 98504. Phone (206) 753-5700.

Oregon usually has a general blacktail deer season from October 1 through November 6 in the northwestern portion of the state and from October 1 through October 30 in the southwest. There is also an extended season, usually in late November and early December, in much of the Willamette Valley and adjoining foothills. Archery and muzzle loader seasons are available too, so check the regulations. Bag limit is one.

Oregon's total deer population, counting blacktails, mule deer and whitetails is estimated at over 1,000,000, with 650,000 of these being blacktails. The 1976 kill was 36,670 blacktails. Potentially the only problem of significance to the blacktail is overpopulation and under Oregon's good management the future of both the deer and the hunting is excellent.

Residents pay $7 for a hunting license and $4 for a deer tag. Non-residents pay $75 for a license and $35 for a deer tag. For complete information, contact the Oregon Department of Fish & Wildlife, P.O. Box 3503, Portland, OR 97208. Phone (503) 229-5551.

California has several deer seasons, by areas, from early August to mid-September, or from late September to mid-October or early November. Bag limit is either one or two, depending on the area. In addition there are archery seasons beginning as early as July. Check the regulations for full details.

California's 1976 total deer kill was 30,700, of which about 60% were blacktails. Although California has limited deer range and a tremendous human population, the future of blacktail deer hunting in the state is good.

California residents pay $10 for their hunting license and $3 per deer tag while nonresidents pay $35 for the license and $25 for a deer tag.

For complete details contact the California Department of Fish and Game, Resources Building, 1416 Ninth Street, Sacramento, CA 95814. Phone (916) 445-3531.

Chapter 7

COUES DEER

Known by at least three popular names and another half dozen lesser ones, the Coues deer is the whitetail of the Southwest. Commonly called Arizona Whitetail, Sonora Deer or Fantail, the Coues (Odocoileus couesi) is frequently referred to as Desert Fantail, Flagtail, Cactus Fantail, Apache Deer, and even on occasion Small Mountain Deer, Gazelle Deer and Cheneche. Which comes to nearly a dozen. Quite a load for a little whitetail.

But he carries it well. Extremely well.

Believing that to get the right job done one goes to a lawyer for legal matters, a watch maker for timepiece work (on and on ad infinitum), this writer took his Coues deer questions to George W. Parker. George was born in the heart of Coues deer country, is more than seventy years old, and has never lived anyplace else. He's traveled a lot, over most of the world, but never having discovered any other place more to his liking, he always returned to his Arizona border home.

George Parker killed his first Coues deer when he was eleven years old, which means he has more than six decades of experience in hunting this little whitetail. Experience well used: he has seven heads in the Boone and Crockett record book.

To my first question: "How do you pronounce Coues?" Parker said the deer was named after Lt. Elliott Coues who was stationed in Arizona, at Ft. Whipple. A surgeon, Coues was also a recognized ornithologist and had requested an assignment where he could practice in that field along with his military duties. This was in 1864. George said he feels the name can be pronounced Cooees (like in dove or pigeon) or Cowees (as in milk) but your correspondent noted that he used the Cooees version.

Owning the usual whitetail characteristics the Coues is a small deer of graceful proportions with a somewhat larger than ordinary tail. (Obviously the reason for Flagtail, Fantail, etc.) The antlers are typical whitetail, but smaller than eastern and northern deer. Actually, they are completely in keeping with the body size which runs to the short side of 100 pounds. Parker knows of one that field dressed at 140 pounds, but it was an admitted exception. Mrs. Parker won an annual deer contest in Tucson only a few years ago with a buck that field dressed at 109 pounds.

George Parker is a careful observer. A man who sees everything on the mountain as opposed to another who might see only what he's looking for. He's a man with a fabulous memory for details. A man who every writer on wildlife in the Southwest should seek out. He has hunted extensively over North America, as well as Central and South America, not to mention his African safaris. He knows game. When asked if Coues deer were hunted in the same way as whitetails everywhere, he commented, "They're a real foxy deer – I think killing a big, mature, Coues deer is the equivalent of killing a big horn ram because they are just that smart – maybe even smarter than a sheep and their hearing is superior. I think their eyesight is probably just as good."

George W. Parker

Parker describes this as one of his best Coues deer.

I took this to mean Coues deer hunting was basically a long shot situation and so stated. George replied, "I've had them lay where I almost stepped on them – they are like whitetail anywhere. I think they are one of the best trophies in North America." Continuing on, "I hunted one big buck for two years and finally almost stepped on him on a little grassy knoll and killed him at less than 50 yards".

Getting back to size – Parker compared Coues deer with Central Texas whitetails (the author places these at 70 to 80 pounds, average field dressed weight) with the horn structure possibly a little bit different but so close as to be difficult for anyone but an authority to tell them apart, and just maybe he couldn't, either. Most Tucson deer contests are won by weights running between 109 and 118 pounds. Which compares closely with Texas Hill Country whitetails.

When asked about the range of Coues deer George said he had seen them as far north as the Mogollon Rim in Arizona on south into the Sierra Madres, Sonora and Sinaloa (in Mexico) then east to beyond Silver City, New Mexico. It is known they also inhabit a segment of West Texas known as the Davis Mountains – or at least one authority places them in that area at any rate. Parker feels the true range of Coues deer in Mexico hasn't really been defined. He has killed them farther into that country than the 250 to 300 miles south of the border mentioned by some authorities.

"I've seen them from sea level, up to 7,000 and even 8,000 feet," Parker said, when asked about their altitude preference. "Some of the biggest heads come from the Apache Reservation", he added, as an afterthought.

Seeking out other authoritative sources the author learned the deer was given the name "couesi" by Dr. H. C. Yarrow, a colleague of Dr. Elliott Coues. Dr. Yarrow named it in his honor. That same authority, in "Mammals of North America,"

Parker's daughter, Paige, killed this typical Coues deer when she was 12 years old.

describes the range as southwestern Arizona to the Big Bend area of Texas and south through Chihuahua and eastern Sonora into Durango. Which coincides closely with the findings of Parker and his in-the-field experience.

One reference book I found told of seeing hundreds of the deer in the Chisos Mountains in the mid 1800's with a particular mention of one shipment of 600 skins, with the carcasses left to rot on the ground.

Another mention, almost poetic, "If we can imagine a Cottontail Rabbit crossed with a Whitetail Deer, we shall have a fair idea of this elegant creature." This description went on, "The Sonoran Deer is the most beautiful species known to me.

George W. Parker with a record book Coues. Bucks like this are downright ▶ *scarce nowadays.*

When surprised in thickets bordering streams, it sometimes evinced more curiosity than fear."

Still another late 1800's description telling of its rabbit-like ways reads. "In the Sierra Madre of Chihuahua one summer, I found these little Whitetails occupying 'forms' like rabbits, located in the sheltering matted tops of fallen pine trees which had been overthrown by spring storms. In these shelters, they rested during the day, secure from wolves and mountain lions which prowled about the canyon slopes in search of prey".

All of these comments came from the book, "Game Animals and How They Live."

"Mammals of New Mexico" offers another almost poetic discourse in describing the little deer. "They are a graceful little deer with large ears and long bushy tails that spread when erect in great white fans, blending with the white of the inner surface of the hams and the belly until, as the deer go bounding away through the brush, the gray body is often lost to view in a series of white flashes that seem larger than the whole deer. From the stubby-tailed mule deer of the same region they are easily distinguished, even at long range, by their small size and long white tails."

That the Coues deer made an impact on early day hunters and zoologists is obvious.

Sort of lost in the shuffle of modern day living the fantastic little deer seems to be seldom sought by trophy hunters. Maybe that's best — I don't know — but from what I've found in researching this chapter I'm sold on the idea of trying for one at the first opportunity. My walls include good mule deer, fair-to-middlin' desert mule deer and run-of-the-mill whitetail. Before many more seasons pass they will also be graced with a Coues, a blacktail from Oregon or Washington, and a life-size Brocket from the southern reaches of Mexico, with no attempt at a record head. My efforts in collecting trophies is directed towards an average specimen for the species. Representative, if you will. Should a record happen in front of my sights I will thank God for that added blessing.

As mentioned in Chapter 11, my feelings about "trophies" is deeply rooted. To me, a trophy is something by which to remember a specific hunt, be it in a new state, section of a state, country or whatever. Or a different species. Record book proportions, while fun to take, all too often become an obsession, thus destroying the enjoyment of the great out-of-doors and the sport of hunting. Hunting is a reason to get outdoors. Killing is harvesting. When done under fair-chase conditions killing is the culmination of that fair-chase. Not an act in itself that is particularly enjoyed by most hunters. It is getting "to" that shot where the enjoyment is really found. In fact, many of us have a definite "let down" feeling immediately after a kill. I have never taken particular pride in killing any animal, but have often had a proud feeling over the achievement of placing myself in the position to make that killing shot. Abiding by the rules of "fair-chase," in the manner of all true sportsmen, it isn't as easy and as much of a "sure thing" as some of our anti-hunting opponents would have their constituents believe. Without a doubt, there are those among us who enjoy blood-letting. God has placed all kinds on this earth with a purpose for each in mind. All the anti-hunters I know eat meat purchased from a market. That's just hiring someone else to do your bloodletting for you. There is no other way to look at it.

But let's talk more about Coues deer. As to how they are faring today as compared to even 20 years ago, Parker said, "We've had so many coyotes, and hunting pressure has been so heavy in Arizona, it is very hard to find a good buck anymore. One or two big ones are brought in every year, but going out and finding them and passing up bucks looking for that good one is almost a thing of the past. It might be possible in some areas, but they're very rare." George paused for a moment, then went on, "If you see one nowadays with a decent set of horns you kill him — if you expect to kill one"!

How would a hunter go about getting a Coues deer? Mexico might be good — then it might not. Mexico hunting is very much a so-so thing. Read Chapter 10, then make up your own mind on this one. Arizona has good hunting but it's on a drawing basis. One must go through the game department for the permit. If lucky, and that's of prime importance, a guide or rancher can be found with very little effort. Some are better than others, same as anyplace else, so care is the watchword.

I heard of a man named Ollie Barney, in connection with Arizona lion and deer hunting, on several different occasions. Asking Parker about him brought forth, "He's probably as good a whitetail hunter and guide as there is in Arizona. Chances would be pretty good if you went along with him." I'm not selling guides and am real gun-shy about recommending them, but will do so on occasion and this is one of those occasions. After all, that's what this book is for, to help the deer hunter get his game. Having been burned more times than not, with guides and outfitters around the country, you will find only two listed in this entire book. Along with one rancher and one ranch. These I know are trustworthy and can be depended upon. You will find Ollie Barney's address at the end of this chapter.

Then there is New Mexico. But only the southwestern portion is of any consequence. Jesse Williams, Chief of Information and Education for the New Mexico Game Department, said hunter success on Coues deer runs between 15 and 20%. Licenses are available to one and all and there are no added charges – just the non-resident license requirement. Jesse is himself a bit of an authority on Coues deer in New Mexico having become interested to the point of seriously hunting them. He hunted three years before finally shooting one – as he had set record-book size as his goal. On that third year he did squeeze the trigger – and killed a record-book Coues. It is listed as number 17 in the current Boone and Crockett book of North American records.

Hunting Coues deer might prove to be a bit more involved than hunting other whitetails. They are available in only this very tiny portion of North America. Permits are on a drawing basis in their primary stronghold of that tiny portion. A Coues deer hunt might well be classified as a threefold undertaking – the permit – the hunt – and finally the kill. Each a project unto itself.

But then – almost everything really worth while comes at added expense of time, money and effort. Should Coues deer hunting be any different?

The late Herb Klein, with a better-than-average Coues buck taken while hunting with George Parker.

Addresses important to the Coues deer hunter:

Ollie Barney
Star Route, Box 296
Benson, Arizona 85602

Arizona Game and Fish Department
2222 W. Greenway Rd.
Phoenix, Arizona 85023

New Mexico Department of Game and Fish
State Capitol
Santa Fe, New Mexico 87801

Director General de Fauna Silvestre, S.A.G.
Aquiles Serdan No. 28-7 Piso
Mexico 3, D.F.

Jesse Williams and his record-book Coues deer killed in the Peloncillo Mountains in the Coronado National Forest in extreme southwestern New Mexico. Jesse got his trophy in 1975.

Chapter 8

MULE DEER

Mule deer, those gray ghosts of the mountains.

THE deer of some 15 states in the western United States. On a line running through West Texas, New Mexico, Colorado, Western Nebraska, South and North Dakota, everything from there into the sunset is their homeland.

Early days saw mule deer over much of the plains of the west and central part of our continent, but like the buffalo and elk "progress' forced them out. Forced them out to the extent they almost became extinct, even in much of the land they now inhabit so abundantly. Another feather in the cap of hunter/conservationists.

Mulies, though all classified together by Boone and Crockett standards, except for the blacktail of the far northwest, do vary in size and conformation, and especially in head adornment.

Desert mule deer of far west Texas, New Mexico (the southern part) and likewise in Arizona can't compete with their big rocky mountain brethren antler-wise – nor by body weight, for that matter.

An average weight, from personal experience, for desert bucks would strike close to the 140 pound mark. I've seen lots that wouldn't top 125 pounds and a few that would hit 180. Very few of the latter, let me point out, in spite of what some hunters might "guesstimate."

Rocky mountain bucks will probably average close to 200 pounds though I believe 185 would be a better bet. Many have been guessed at weights far exceeding this, of course, but scales have a horrible way of deflating stories. The biggest this writer has

ever seen on scales weighed 265 pounds, field dressed and with all four legs cut off at the first joint. Undoubtedly bigger bucks have been brought in but for an average weight my figures won't be far off.

As this chapter is written several really good bucks have been taken in west Texas this season, heads measuring up to that of good rocky mountain bucks. Better than usual by far. I consider 22 to 24 inches very good for the spread of a desert mule deer. A 20–21 inch spread with heavy, high, antlers makes a fine, typical trophy. Most desert bucks sport antlers of very attractive symmetry, but usually not of unusual massiveness. In other words, they are normally lighter bodied than their mountain relatives.

On the same day two were seen, dead and in hand, and they measured 27 and 27½ inches in horn spread. Both were extremely heavy and would do credit to any Colorado hunt.

Desert bucks are like gold, wherever you find them. If there are any high places in the area chances are bucks inhabit the rocky ledges and outcroppings during the day if only for bedding purposes.

If there are none, try the draws. I'll never forget a jack rabbit hunt in New Mexico years ago. We were, three of us, spread out and walking across a pasture with cover sufficient to hide a jack rabbit here and there. We were getting running shots, what we wanted, often enough to make it interesting. As we approached what appeared to be a ditch but turned

The Mescalero Apache Reservation was the site of this horse camp. It was vehicles to here then horseback the rest of the way.

Stan Chee, Mescalero Apache Conservation Officer, points to a spot for Dr. Gerald Swiggett to check out with his binoculars. Deer hunting requires lots of looking at far off spots. ▶

out to be a draw, or ravine, maybe three feet in depth and five or six feet in width, out came a buck with antlers big enough to make any deer hunter mighty nervous. As we watched him disappear in the distance two more, apparently trying to wait us out but finally losing their nerve, came out of the same location. One was bigger than the first and the other smaller; three desert mule deer bucks in cover barely up to jack rabbit quality.

The same thing can happen with mountain bucks. My favorite site for trophy bucks is in some heavy sage brush country in northwestern Colorado. Way down off the mountains. Some of this sage is head high to a six-foot man. Draws work their way through this country. The biggest mule deer buck of my career came from here. Thirty-two-and-a-half inches from one side to the other. He was taken at high noon, five minutes to twelve, to be exact, after hunting high mountains for five days and seeing no really top trophies.

Though this took place 20 years ago it still happens. Look for big bucks in the most unlikely spots.

◀ Riley Chino heads up the Game Department on the Mescalero Apache Reservation, one of the better mule deer hunting spots – and they have some impressive whitetails too. The Reservation is located in South Central New Mexico.

Several mule deer bucks have been killed over the years by watching these beaver ponds from the high side. Try the same tactic wherever you hunt.

Charlie Cockerell, a New Mexico Conservation Officer, killed his high-horned trophy with his .264 Winchester Magnum at close to 200 yards.

Going down a mountainside is not so bad, but getting up the next one gets to be gut-wrenching work.

Hunters hit every place that looks like deer country. This scatters them out to those out-of-the-way places. Little pockets of cover might hold a real "bull-of-the-woods" who has selected it as a bedroom because it didn't look quite like buck country.

Deer, even mule deer, are a lot smarter than many hunters want to give them credit for being. I say "even mule deer" because they will never go down in anyone's book as being blessed with an overabundance of brains. Dyed-in-the-wool mountain hunters who have never hunted whitetails tend to believe differently, but should they ever try to outsmart a trophy whitetail buck they are in for a post-graduate course in deer hunting.

With a stiff-legged gait, that to me at least defies their being hit with a bullet, mule deer often pogostick their way out to 150 or maybe even 200 yards then stop, turn broadside, and look back to see what they were running from. It gets them killed too, unless the hunter is so green he spooks them into full-fledged flight by shooting all around them as they hop off.

Many bucks will be jumped in lowlands or near the base of a mountain. In every case they will go to the highest point. There is that odd exception, now and then, but money can be made by betting that every mulie jumped goes uphill. As they stiff-leg it, trot, or sometimes just walk, they will, at least 99% of the time, stop just before they top out and look back. This, too, gets them killed with regularity.

A whitetail buck that has reason to leave a spot isn't about to stop and double check the situation. Neither is he about to depart up the open side of a hill or across bare ground, unless caught with nothing else around and your chances of bagging him are two — very slim and none, because any whitetail like that is not blessed with a full head anyway and won't live long enough for you, nor me, to find him.

I've already said mulies aren't very smart, but some of them do have their days. One such instance saw me sitting high on a ridge watching a "quakie" pocket another hunter was walking through. There was six or eight inches of snow on the ground so everything in those trees stood out plain against that stark-white background. I saw a buck and four does move out ahead of the hunter. Not paying any particular attention to them I moved my attention to an area farther ahead.

When I looked back only the four does were to be seen, still moving ahead of the hunter. Searching the area I soon spotted the buck. He was slinking along in an almost crouched position and angling

Hunting is fun – until the successful shot. It is then the work begins.

This is the sagebrush draw from which Swiggett killed his biggest mule deer. These deep draws down in sagebrush flats are favored hunting spots for the author.

himself around the hunter. In a matter of a few moments he was again bedded down – almost in the same place he had been earlier. The hunter was far beyond and convinced no bucks were in that pocket.

Whitetails do this all the time but that is the only instance I can prove where a mule deer outsmarted a hunter by circling him. Undoubtedly it happens, but more often bucks of this species charge out and over the mountain.

The different parts of the country actually make little difference in the way mule deer are hunted.

These four bucks came off the same mountain on the Mescalero Apache Reservation. The little one, second from left, was shot for meat by the young Indian holding him after the others had passed up the little buck.

A wagon load of deer. Eleven bucks killed by a party of six in northwestern Colorado a good many years ago when two bucks were legal; the second even at a reduced price for the tag. One hunter failed to take his second deer because he held out to the end for a real biggie.

I've killed them in Texas, New Mexico, Colorado, Wyoming, Idaho, Arizona and Montana; in every instance hunting was similar.

Seek out the highest rocky ledges, bluffs, outcroppings in the area and chances are there will be bucks lying under the edge of a big rock watching you.

In the far northern reaches of Colorado I've spent far more dollars than I could afford trying for a record book head. There is a high peak in an otherwise flat section of that country that literally comes to a point. There are several huge rocks near the top. There isn't another high spot for nearly a mile in two directions and over half a mile any other way. There are some draws etched-out across the flatland making it possible to get in, and out, without being too obvious. One bright sunny morning, about 10 o'clock, my guide and I were moving to another location when I thought I saw something near a rock on a peak. Getting the guide to stop, I found a buck was laying up there surveying everything for miles around. I guessed him to measure 25-inches. My guide claimed him at 27 or maybe even 28 inches.

The contest became an argument. I didn't want him, but there was no way we could settle our differences without killing him – so – we went out to the highway, flagged down a car with a deer hunter in it (this took a while because the first three we stopped were convinced I was crazy – a Texan trying to get someone else to kill a deer so he could measure it) and took him back to the peak.

He shot the buck in his bed and was tickled to death. It was the biggest deer he had killed. I had misjudged the size but so had my guide. It measured 25¾ inches which made me a fraction closer than he.

The point here is simply that I can't help but wonder how many other hunters in that area had driven by while moving from one spot to another, as we were, but had never bothered to look up into those rocks.

The best way to kill a really good trophy mule deer is to get at least one mountain removed from other hunters. This really isn't hard to do because, unfortunately, most hunters aren't interested in working at their sport. A great majority never leave their vehicles and of those that do, most never get more than a few hundred yards away. To get beyond them one has only to cross the first mountain.

Vernon Scott, a member of the Mescalero Apache tribe, used to be in charge of all hunting on the Reservation. He is a fine guide, a pleasure to hunt with.

Bob Brister, Shooting Editor of Field and Stream Magazine, says riding horses is a lot easier than walking.

Much of mule deer hunting is at very high altitudes. What this sign doesn't say is that Ridge Trail goes up still higher.

89

The author killed this buck in Wyoming more that two decades ago. He's in Colorado for the picture but the state line is in the center of the road 50 or so yards behind. It was a good buck even then and it's hanging in his office being looked at as this is typed. Fran Marsh was his guide.

Quaking aspen (quakie) pockets are prime spots for mule deer bucks to hang out. Search the edges, just back in far enough to be out of plain sight but still close enough to see, from inside, what's going on outside.

Mule deer hideouts galore. Tough country to hunt but very productive for the willing worker.

A group of friends asked me to help set up a hunt on the Mescalero Apache Indian Reservation in New Mexico, near Ruidoso, because they knew I had some very close friends on the reservation. I'm always hesitant to do such a thing because the success of any hunt is dependent upon how much is put into it in the way of effort. The Mescalero range, like many other prime hunting locations, is often criticized by hunters as being "shot out" because they make a two or three day hunt and don't see any deer while driving the roads. In fact, I had recommended this same area to two "hunters" a couple of years earlier and they left mid-morning of opening day "because I had misled them and there were no deer in those mountains," to use their exact words. They "knew" because they drove nearly three hours without seeing any.

I finally helped this group set up the hunt with the understanding that all hunting would be walking, vehicles used only to get into an area. Eight of them camped out – drove to areas selected by their two guides for the hunt – parked their four-wheel-drive vehicles and started walking. Eight bucks came out with them when the hunt was over. Their biggest problem was in deciding which buck to shoot because they saw so many they couldn't make up their minds.

Why?

Because they were willing to "go that extra mile" by walking over a mountain and hunting where there were no roads.

Sure, it's work. It isn't for the weak-hearted nor is it for the lazy. But it pays off for the man taking his deer hunting seriously.

Another similar experience occurred in Montana. My oldest son, Gerald, and I were hunting only a few miles north of Yellowstone Park. It was a two deer season which might help you date the hunt. My interest was entirely in getting a couple of good bucks for him as he was fresh out of college and hadn't been able to hunt for several years while getting his doctorate.

We did a good deal of mountain climbing. Finally a fair-to-middlin' buck offered a shot at about 150 yards. The .270 Winchester spoke one time and the work started. It was about a mile and a half to a spot that could be reached by pickup. On the other side of the mountain, naturally. It was several hours later before he was finally aboard the Ford.

The following two days we walked, and hunted, and looked, and saw deer, but Gerald wouldn't shoot, he was always muttering something about

A keeper. High-horned, wide enough to be respectable along with being almost hog-fat which means a trophy for the wall and good venison for the table.

Donna Swiggett grins happily as she poses with her daddy's first mule deer trophy. Her father, Dr. Gerald Swiggett, got this buck about 45 minutes into his first hunt on graduating from graduate school.

Binoculars come in mighty handy in places like this. Miles and miles of seemingly nothing yet every inch possible mule deer country.

It's down hill from here with the vehicle in sight.

Toasted sandwiches and hot coffee make for a mighty good mountain lunch.

Mule deer buck and doe.

A light snow on the ground makes mule deer much easier to spot. Completely covered is even better. It's binocular time for this hunter.

What's known as being between a rock and a hard place. The pickup had been backed up against the hillside to load a deer. The ground was frozen and the snow icy. As a result the pickup skidded against this downed tree. Could go neither forward or backward. A chain saw solved the problem.

"not big enough." Finally, after turning down a buck that seemed big enough to me (and I've killed a lot more then he has) I asked if he was going to shoot his second deer or not. His answer proved the "smarts" he gained in college: "Not unless he's standing in the middle of a road."

We headed back to Texas.

Since I'm story-telling let me lay one more on you – four flat-landers walked back about three mountains and found a herd of good bucks. Three of them layed down a barrage and put down three good bucks. Real honest-to-goodness trophies. The fourth, when the shooting finished, calmly remarked, "now, how are you fellows going to get them out?"

Walking-in finds deer – but they also have to be gotten out.

Hunting mulies can be dangerous. Weather can change in an instant in the high country. On a hunt in the Sunlight Basin country near Cody, Wyoming, a snow storm came up that literally blinded us to the point that we were extremely lucky to get ourselves out. We had walked way back from the vehicle and almost missed it in the storm. Had we passed it, only the good Lord knows what would have happened.

It isn't at all uncommon to be snowed in on a deer or elk hunt in the high country. Always take plenty of groceries for an extra few days – just in case. Being snowed-in isn't all that bad IF there is plenty to eat and sufficient heat. Short yourself on either and you might become a statistic.

Same goes for physical condition. High elevations are not the place to get in shape. Flat-landers or desk-oriented hunters need to do a lot of walking, climbing, running and getting-in-shape BEFORE the hunt.

I'll never forget a Wyoming hunt where I shot a fair-sized buck across a canyon with my .300 H & H. The shot wasn't all that long as maybe I try to make it sound – close to 250 yards at best. The deer went down at the shot, then got up and staggered to the edge of a sheer drop-off, about 50 feet straight down. I was about to shoot again to try to keep him from going over the edge when he dropped.

Feeling good about the shot and knowing there was a road on the other ridge I turned to work my way around to my buck. Something caused me to look across towards my deer just in time to see him kick his back feet hard against a rock – and shove himself over that drop-off. It was a dying muscular reaction but that didn't help me any.

And sometimes it's lunch in the snow.

When you get a chance at a buck like this it pays to have your rifle properly sighted in. Much mountain shooting takes place at 200 and more yards. This buck was taken at 275 yards with a .30-06.

My companion and I spent two hours getting him back up that 50 or so feet. I've always claimed that if I was going to have a heart attack it would have happened right then and there. We were at about 9,000 feet. Physically I was up to it.

As to where the best mule deer hunting can be found, this writer can only suggest general areas. I know for a fact there are some mighty good mule deer bucks in New Mexico, Colorado, Wyoming, Montana, Idaho and Utah. These I've seen, and often enough to know one can pop up most anytime. I'm sure the same is true of other mule deer states.

The secret is to get out and HUNT them. Go that extra mile. Get in shape, physically, mentally and

Fran Marsh ponders the situation. That's his home way down yonder in the near center of the picture. This photo made from Squaw Mountain, one of the better hunting areas in Northwestern Colorado – and Southern Wyoming. That home on the left is in Wyoming. The road in front of Fran's home is the state line.

A good mule deer hunter spends lots of time with binoculars whether the hunting is by foot, horseback or 4-wheel drive vehicle.

Rudy Real with a 27 inch spread West Texas mule deer. A mighty big desert mule deer. So big, in fact, he would look good on any mountain muley, Colorado, Wyoming or Utah style.

Dan Klepper with an early season mule deer shot on top of the Continental Divide out of Pagosa Springs, Colorado. This was billed as a "trophy hunt". Since it was actually late summer hunters had to go to the top, where the bucks spend those warm months.

97

These fellows aren't moving that beaver cut tree for fun. The beaver had dropped it across the barely visible road going up the mountain.

shooting-wise. Often bucks are found, then lost, because the hunter misses.

In chapter 16 we'll go over the guns best suited for this type of hunting. The main thing is to carry one you can shoot. The most powerful rifle in the world isn't worth a hang if you can't hit anything with it.

Also, I've talked a lot about "good" bucks. If you aren't a head-hunter your job is easier. Young bucks, and does where legal, are much easier to take. Besides that, they taste better. Much of the time "eatin'" deer can be found within easy walking (dragging) distance. In fact, it is downright foolish to get very far off the beaten path for a meat animal. The farther he has to be dragged the dirtier the carcass gets. I encourage this type of hunting, really, because, after all, we intend to eat what we kill. I've never been a meat hunter for the simple reason I've always been more interested in what animals wear on top of their heads.

For those who hunt because they truly like venison I can only say "Praise the Lord!" I wish I could. I do like it and none ever goes to waste, but seldom do I get really good meat because of my lack of interest in shooting those younger animals. I've often wished I could, and I've even gone so far as to go on hunts intending to shoot the first legal deer I see, but it never works out.

And I've been the loser for a lot of years.

I once went on seven successive, expensive, mule deer hunts in northwestern Colorado without firing a shot, simply because I was holding out for that "big one." Truthfully it can be said I have never gone on a hunt where I couldn't have killed a deer. That's why it bothers me when others tell of hunts where no deer are seen. Deer are everywhere, literally. It's all in how they are hunted. True, some areas and some states offer more than others, but all have good deer populations — all have bucks that can be found by the hunter working at his sport.

Try to find a spot just beyond where other hunters go. If this can't be done get as high as you can before daylight. Pick a spot where a large area can be watched, then wait out those bucks coming up for their day's siesta. If you picked the right spot a buck will be yours before the sun gets very high. Mule deer bucks almost always go up. Keep that in mind. The bigger the buck the higher he goes ... normally.

Should this not be available to you seek out little spots of cover that might be overlooked by other hunters because of their size, or maybe because they're hard to reach. Sometimes little pockets close by get by-passed in the rush to "get back where the deer are."

Try them all.

Another tip: if you see a little buck but want antlers instead of prime meat, take plenty of time and glass the area carefully. Seldom ever is a mule deer

Swiggett killed this buck mule deer with a running neck shot using a 7 mm Weatherby Magnum. Note how the bucks nose plowed a furrow in the soft dirt. The shot was about 150 yards but wasn't as good as it sounds. He missed a much closer shot at the buck running straight away. Hal tells this on himself.

buck by himself. Often two or three will be together. Even more in some instances. Make sure the one you kill out of the bunch is the one you want. This works both ways. If a 4-pointer is spotted and steaks are the object look around for a fat forkhorn.

Mountain deer are like any other animal: shoot them through the lungs and they won't go very far. Neither does it ruin much meat. Head and neck shots are out for the trophy hunter. Since I always give my deer away rather than bring them home, I hate to destroy any meat unnecessarily, so am a religious follower of the lung shot. I believe in it thoroughly and have never been let down in some forty years of big game hunting.

The only exception I make is on elk and bear. If possible I break shoulders to lessen the chance of a chase. Same for moose. Bears are not, as a rule, all that good on the table. Elk and moose are big enough to soak up a broken shoulder without going on to other meat damage from shattered bones.

Deer, without exception, are dropped with lung shots if I have a choice.

One more item: when dressing out a deer, the species makes no difference – clean it out real good. If available, use plenty of water to wash it out. Some folks say not to wet a deer inside. That's a bunch of malarkey. I've never known any meat to be damaged by washing it. Sometimes snow can be used.

Remove the blood, and particularly any gunk from a hit "a bit too far back", as soon als possible. When skinning don't let the hair touch the meat. Simple little things – mostly common sense – but each has a role in taking home "sweet" meat.

Same goes for cooling out. Open the body cavity with a stick shoved crossways to let the air circulate. Hang the carcass if at all possible.

If slaughter houses handled beef in the manner some hunters handle game, beef WOULD NOT be the most popular meat in this country.

I find mulies more stimulating than whitetails because of the country. Mountains are awesome, true works of God. Beautiful in every sense of the word yet rugged, rough, almost impenetrable in many cases.

There is nothing in this world, and I've hunted a lot of game in a lot of places, that can top the sight of a majestic mule deer buck skylined at daybreak or dusk. Maybe not the smartest animal in the world, maybe not the toughest, but he holds a place in my heart no other animal can touch. I'm still new at mule deer hunting, barely more than thirty seasons behind me but, I'm still learning, still looking, and if the good Lord wills it, some day I'll hang a record book head on my wall.

If it doesn't work out that way I'm still the winner, because I tried.

Chapter 9

CANADIAN AND ALASKAN DEER
by Jerome Knap

Canada, along with Alaska, has always been a mecca for hunters. What hunter has not dreamed about making a trip after Dall sheep in the Yukon or Alaska, Stone sheep and goats in British Columbia, moose in Newfoundland, or caribou in northern Quebec?

There is no doubt that Canada and Alaska have a monopoly on the best big game hunting on this continent – except, that is, for the most popular species, deer.

Deer hunting in much of Canada and Alaska is generally not as good as in the lower 48 states. The reason is that much of Canada and Alaska lies too far north for good deer range. The winter temperatures are simply too severe, and there's too much snow. Winter kills in Canadian deer herds, particularly on the fringe of deer country, are not uncommon.

All this does not mean that Canada and Alaska do not have good deer hunting – in places. But it does mean that a deer hunter planning a trip to Canada should plan carefully.

Canada has all three deer species – whitetails, blacktails, and mulies. Alaska, on the other hand, has only blacktails.

As in the lower 48 states, the white-tailed deer is the most abundant and most widely distributed in Canada. It is found from Cape Breton in Nova Scotia, westward through all of New Brunswick, southern Quebec, across a good portion of Ontario, and from there all the way across the prairie provinces of Manitoba, Saskatchewan, and Alberta. It has even expanded its range into the valleys of eastern British Columbia.

The black-tailed deer is restricted to the western slope of the coastal range of British Columbia and Alaska. The Alaskan blacktail – the so-called Sitka race – is the smallest and darkest of the blacktails. It is found in the Alaska panhandle, the coastal islands, plus the northern coast of British Columbia. It has also been introduced to the Queen Charlotte Islands off the British Columbia coast.

The slightly larger Columbian blacktail is found along the remainder of the British Columbia coast, Vancouver Island, and extends down into Washington, Oregon, and northern California.

The mule deer is found from the valleys and foothills of the interior of British Columbia, eastward across Alberta, areas of Saskatchewan, and even into southeastern Manitoba. Its north-south range in Canada runs from the Canada-U.S. border right into the southern Yukon, and up to Great Slave Lake in the Northwest Territories.

Theoretical ranges, however, are only of limited use to the hunter. Just because an animal is found there, doesn't mean it's abundant enough to hunt. For example, deer are fully protected in the Yukon.

A hunter needs more specific information. He needs to know where the hunting is good; in what areas the deer are most abundant. The best way to cover this type of information is province-by-province.

Deer have difficulty moving through deep snow.

Let's begin with Alaska's deer story, and from there work eastward right to Canada's maritime provinces on the Atlantic coast.

Deer hunting in Alaska is overshadowed by the bigger, more romantic game species.

As mentioned earlier, the only deer found in Alaska is the Sitka blacktail, a relatively small deer. Does generally weigh about 100 pounds, with bucks averaging about 120 pounds. But bucks up to 150 pounds have been taken.

The Sitka is native to the coastal rain forest of southeastern Alaska. Through transplants, it has also been established in the Yakutat area in Prince William Sound, and on Kodiak and Afognak Islands.

Alaskan deer herds fluctuate, depending on the severity of winters. The annual deer harvest in Alaska ranges between 10,000 and 15,000 animals.

With over 25,000 square miles of deer range, much is reachable only by boat or float plane. Thus the hunting pressure on the Sitka blacktails is fairly light.

The best deer hunting area is probably on Admiralty, Baranof, and Chichagof Islands, with Kodiak and Afognak Islands running a close second. The mainland, including Prince William Sound, does not offer hunting that is as good.

The deer season opens in August in some areas and ends in December. During the early part of the season, most hunters try to hunt on the alpine meadows. But the best hunting comes in November, when the blacktails have moved down to lower elevations to escape the snow.

One unique way of hunting Sitka blacktails is the Indian trick of calling. Calls are made of a rubber band between two pieces of wood. The call is a high-pitched bleat, much like the sound of a lost fawn. Even bucks respond to this call. But so do Alaska brown bears once in a while, so Alaskan deer hunters tend to use rifles chambered for fairly hefty calibers for their deer hunting.

A non-resident deer license is $35, and no guide is needed for deer hunting. For more information on Alaskan deer hunting, write to the Alaska Department of Fish and Game, Subport Building, Juneau, Alaska 99801.

British Columbia probably has the best deer hunting in Canada. In a number of areas, residents are allowed to take more than one deer. In some areas of this province, the deer season opens as early as June 1 for bucks and runs until the end of February. September to November, however, are the main deer hunting months.

Because deer, particularly blacktails, are quite abundant, British Columbia is a real good bet for non-resident deer hunters. A non-resident deer license costs $50.

According to Lee Straight, outdoor writer for the Vancouver Sun, some of the best blacktail hunting spots in British Columbia are found on Vancouver Island. The Nimpkish Valley is one hotspot. But areas around Cowichan-Duncan-Copper Canyon, Northwest Bay-Nanaimo, and Oyster-Quinsam-Campbell-Mohun on the east coast of the island may be even better.

The islands in the Strait of Georgia also have blacktails. But some have no deer season. Others have seasons, yet access is more difficult because the islands are all privately owned. On others, deer hunting is with shotguns only.

It is in this area that the European fallow deer is found. These animals were introduced some years ago onto James Island, and are abundant enough to be legal game.

The southwestern side of the Sechelt Peninsula, Texada Island, and the area around the Powell River also have good deer populations, but the terrain is hilly and hard to hunt.

The best blacktail hunting in British Columbia is on the Queen Charlotte Islands. The deer there have no natural predators such as wolves or cougars, and are incredibly abundant. At one time there were no bag limits on deer in the Charlottes. Even today, residents enjoy an incredible 10-deer limit.

Some of the top mule deer hunting in British Columbia is found in the Similkameen Valley, particularly between Whipsaw Creek and Princeton, and

Typical whitetail cover.

south of the Similkameen River toward Copper Mountain.

Good mule deer hunting also exists in the North Thompson Valley in late November when the deer have migrated down into the valleys because of snow in the mountains. Further to the west, the Empire Valley and the Gang Ranch also have good mule deer hunting. The deer migrate down from the high Chilko and Chilcotin country. The west bank of the Fraser River, just north of Sheep Creek and Riske Creek also has a good reputation with local mule deer hunters.

Mulies in British Columbia are additionally found around Prince George, the Skeena, the North Coast right to Prince Rupert, around Kitimat, and even near Bella Coola on the coast.

Mulies and whitetails are found in good numbers on either side of the Kettle Valley east of Osoyoos.

Ontario whitetails are plentiful in the southern portion but no gun seasons are allowed in this farming area. Bowhunting is the big thing here. Traditional deer country herds are declining.

The steep hills of Castlegard are a productive place to hunt mule deer. Most of the lowland country around the Canal Flats, Kimberley, Cranbrook, Elko, Warden, and Fernier offer reasonable hunting for mule deer and whitetails.

For more information on deer hunting in British Columbia, contact the Department of Recreation and Conservation, Parliament Buildings, Victoria, British Columbia V8V 1×4.

Moving eastward, Alberta also offers good deer hunting. Mule deer are largely found in the foothills of the Rockies, whereas whitetails predominantly live in shelter belts and small woodlots on the prairies, and in park lands further north. This, however, is not an ironclad rule.

The best white-tailed deer hunting in Alberta is on the Camp Wainwright military base, where two deer per hunter are allowed. However, hunting on the Camp Wainwright base is restricted to residents only. This holds a clue, though, for non-resident hunters. The area *around* Camp Wainwright is open to non-residents, and is, in the words of Bob Scammel, "superb whitetail country." Scammel, the outdoor writer with the Calgary Herald, also recommends the areas around Provost, Hardisty, the area along the breaks of the Battle River, north and east of Castor, and the vicinity of Pine Lake east of Red Deer as being top whitetail hunting spots.

Top mule deer spots are found around Pincher Creek in the northwestern corner of the province. The Milk River Ridge near Milk River, Raymond, Magrath in the south-central portion of the province are also good mule deer country, but hunting there is limited to trophy bucks only.

The breaks of the Red Deer River and the South Saskatchewan River near Empress in eastern Al-

A mule deer buck doesn't have to be big to be impressive, especially when his antlers are velvet-covered as this late summer photograph indicates. Alberta allows non-residents to purchase licenses for both mule deer and whitetails.

berta also harbor good mule deer populations. Hunting there would be a good bet.

Non-resident deer hunters in Alberta must hunt bucks only. Residents, however, may take antlerless deer in some areas. The non-resident deer license is $50 for either mule deer or whitetails, but non-residents are allowed to take out licenses for both species and bag both a mulie and a whitetail.

Alberta has several special archery seasons for deer. Like archery seasons in other places, these generally run earlier than gun seasons. A non-resident bow hunter after deer has to possess a non-resident deer license plus an archery license costing $3. The archery season begins as early as late August. Gun seasons open later and run in some areas until the end of November.

For information on Alberta's hunting seasons and regulations, write to the Alberta Department of Recreation, Parks, and Wildlife, Fish and Wildlife Division, 10368-108th Street, Edmonton, Alberta T5J 1L8.

The neighboring province of Saskatchewan was, a decade ago, a deer hunter's paradise. Whitetails were so abundant that even non-resident hunters were allowed three deer per license in some areas. To boot, there were hunters who bagged their three bucks in a day.

Things have changed. Number one, Saskatchewan's deer herds have declined some. But the deer hunting is still pretty good by eastern standards. However, even worse is the fact that much of Saskatchewan's deer country is closed to non-residents.

During years of high populations, many hunters were attracted to Saskatchewan. Some were less than good sportsmen. This, coupled with the fact that most of the deer hunting in the southern third or even southern half of the province is on private land, led to conflict with landowners. Landowners complained to their government representatives, and hence the closure.

Today, non-residents can hunt deer only in game management zones 24 to 36. These zones, particularly the ones in the far north of Saskatchewan, do not have deer hunting as good as the zones farther south. However, zones 24, 25, and 26 in east-central Saskatchewan, along the Manitoba border, do have fair numbers of whitetails.

"The main problem", says Red Wilkinson, editor of the Fish and Game Sportsman, "is that these northern zones are thickly forested, which makes deer hunting much more difficult than in the small woodlots and shelter belts of the prairie country."

This is true. But whitetail hunters from Michigan and Minnesota who are used to deer hunting in thick woods and have the know-how should do fairly well in the forested country of Saskatchewan.

One thing about Saskatchewan's deer country is that it produces outstanding trophies. A quick glance at the 7th edition of the Boone and Crockett Club records of North American big game will confirm that Saskatchewan pops up in the entries with disproportionate frequency.

Saskatchewan also has some mule deer, but mule deer hunting has always been by permit only and for residents only. The best mule deer hunting in the province is found in the southeastern corner, including the Cypress Hills.

The deer season in Saskatchewan begins as early as August 30 in the far north. But the season in zones 24 to 36 generally opens in late October and stays open for two or three weeks. Both residents and non-residents may bag antlerless deer.

A special archery season is open before the gun season, but is limited to residents only. There was a time a decade or two ago when Saskatchewan welcomed non-resident deer hunters with open arms. No more. Yet non-residents are not discouraged from hunting in the middle prairie province. The non-resident deer license is $60.

For more information on Saskatchewan deer hunting, write to the Fisheries and Wildlife Branch, Department of Tourism and Renewable Resources, 1825 Lorne Street, Regina, Saskatchewan S4P 3N1.

Manitoba's deer story, in a way, parallels that of Saskatchewan. The Manitoba deer herds are only a shadow of what they once were. In fact, a few years ago deer herds declined to such low levels that all deer seasons were closed.

Manitoba's deer herds are on the increase once again, but hunting is still restricted. Only 500 deer licenses are available for non-residents. Hence the best advice for the non-resident hunter is to avoid Manitoba.

However, should a non-resident hunter be lucky enough to get a license, the whole province is open to him. The 40,000 resident hunters hunt mainly around the large population centres. Non-residents would be wise to go further afield.

The best bets are areas around Riding Mountain National Park, Duck Mountain Provincial Forest, and Dauphin Lake, all west of Lake Manitoba. The north and central area of Manitoba between the southern arm of Lake Winnipeg and the Ontario border is good as well. The hunting pressure here is light.

A non-resident deer license for Manitoba is $40. Deer seasons start in late October and end in late November.

For more information on deer hunting in Manitoba, write to the Wildlife Branch, Department of Renewable Resources and Transportation Services, 1129 Queens Avenue, Brandon, Manitoba R7A 1L9.

Ontario's deer story is a mixed bag. Deer herds in the farming counties of the southern part of the province have never been higher. But unfortunately there are no gun seasons in these counties, partially because farmers are afraid that too many hunters would descend upon their farms. The anti-hunters of course, have also had a hand in this. They oppose any expansion of hunting seasons.

However, the southern Ontario counties do have a bow season on deer. As a result, interest in bow-hunting has mushroomed.

On the other hand, the traditional deer country of Ontario, from Georgian Bay to the Ottawa River, harbors a declining deer herd. Hard winters coupled with maturing forests are largely to blame.

This area is close to Ontario's large population centers and hence has been a popular place to hunt. It is an area with organized deer camps, some of which have been in operation since the turn of the century. It is in this area that deer hunting with hounds is both legal and heavily practiced. It is the only place in the north where deer may be hunted with dogs.

The best deer hunting in Ontario is found in the northwest, from about Fort Francis on the U.S.

A .30-30 and a hound. Both good for whitetail in Ontario.

Canadian hounds and hunters. Note the guns. Both shotguns and rifles were used on this hunt.

border right up to north of Kenora on Lake of the Woods. Some of the islands on Lake of the Woods have good deer hunting as well. This is the area that non-residents should keep in mind when planning an Ontario deer hunt. More and more resident deer hunters are taking advantage of the northwest's prospering deer herds as well.

A good bet for black-powder deer hunters lies in the Aulneau Penisula. This is the only place in Ontario where a special primitive weapons hunt (including bows and crossbows) exists.

The deer and moose seasons open at the same time in early October, and both species are legal game for the black-powder hunter. The Aulneau has a good deer herd and a thriving moose population. No big game hunting with modern center-fire rifles is allowed in this area whatever.

Ontario's deer season opens in early October in some areas and closes in mid-November. A non-resident deer license, which is actually a license for deer, small game, game birds, bear, and wolf, costs $40.

There are plenty of commercial deer hunting camps in Ontario, particularly in the northwestern part of the province. These offer guided hunts and are a good bet for non-resident hunters.

For more information on Ontario, write to the Public Relations Branch, Ministry of Industry and Tourism, Queen's Park, Toronto, Ontario M7A 1T2.

Quebec's deer picture is likewise not very bright. "The only real deer hunting hotspot in 'La Belle Province' is Anticosti Island at the mouth of the St. Lawrence River," says George Gruenefeld, out-

Whitetail hunting and canoes go together in Ontario along with much of the rest of Canada.

door writer with the Montreal Gazette. About 1,200 deer are killed annually on the island.

Anticosti Island is probably the only place in the northeast where a hunter may bag two deer of any sex. The hunter success rate runs almost 100 percent. The hunts on Anticosti are done from government-owned camps. Applications for the hunt must be made to the Quebec Department of Tourism, Fish and Game.

"Only 1,200 bucks are bagged annually in the rest of the province of Quebec," says Gruenefeld. "The best areas are Argenteuil and Papineau counties north of the Ottawa River, the Eastern Townships along the U.S. border, and the area south of the St. Lawrence River from Rimouski to the U.S. border."

A non-resident Quebec deer license costs $75 and includes a black bear tag. An Anticosti Island

non-resident deer license is also $75 and includes small game and upland game birds.

The deer season starts at the end of October and continues for two or three weeks in some areas. There is only one area with a special archery season for deer, and that's near Hull on the Ottawa River. The archery season begins in early October, two weeks before the gun season. A non-resident bow-hunting license for deer is $50.

For more information on Quebec deer hunting, including how to apply for the controlled hunts on Anticosti Island, contact the Tourism Branch, Department of Tourism, Fish and Game, Parliament Buildings, Quebec City, Quebec G1R 4Y1.

Of the four Canadian maritime provinces, only two – New Brunswick and Nova Scotia – have deer hunting. There are no deer in Newfoundland. Even the island's moose are not native. Prince Edward Is-

Whitetails in camp.

British Columbia probably offers the best deer hunting in Canada. Blacktails, mule deer, as photographed here, and whitetails are hunted along with European fallow deer in some parts of the Province.

land has a small herd of whitetails at the western end of the island as a result of an introduction made in 1949.

New Brunswick's deer herd has been faring quite well in recent years. The annual harvest is around 6,000 deer. Hunting in New Brunswick is much like that in Maine. It is steeped with local tradition, and the deer season is still a big event in small towns and rural villages.

The best deer range lies in the southwestern portion of the province, with Charlotte, Kings, and Queens counties having the highest deer kill. Victoria county in the northwestern corner of the province is also good deer country. This county has been the traditional center of deer hunter outfitting, with a number of lodges catering to non-resident deer hunters.

The deer season in New Brunswick runs from about mid-October to mid-November. A non-resident license costs $50.

For more information on deer hunting in New Brunswick, write to the Fish and Wildlife Branch, Department of Natural Resources, P.O. Box 600, Fredericton, New Brunswick.

Nova Scotia, like New Brunswick, is a tourism-oriented province. The deer herd in Nova Scotia is also thriving, except perhaps on Cape Breton Island. But even on Cape Breton deer are again on the increase. Provincial wildlife authorities believe that in a few years, Cape Breton will be a good bet for deer hunters once again.

Right now, the south shore counties of Queens, Lunenburg, Halifax, and Guysborough offer the best deer hunting. But Cumberland and Colchester counties in northwestern Nova Scotia are good as well.

Nova Scotia does not have as many commercial deer hunting camps as New Brunswick, but guides and lodging are easy to find in all small towns. Maritimers are among the friendliest people in the world. The non-resident hunter will be made welcome and won't lack a place to hunt, even if he's a complete stranger.

The deer season in Nova Scotia has always been the whole month of November. A non-resident deer license is $50.

For more information on deer hunting in Nova Scotia, write to the Wildlife Division, Department of Lands and Forests, P.O. Box 516, Kentville, Nova Scotia.

Ontario whitetail country.

Chapter 10

MEXICO

"There isn't a deer, or anything else edible left," some stateside hunters will tell you in referring to the land of tomorrow known as Mexico. Others say the hunting is fabulous. The truth lies somewhere in between. Bird hunters, true, will find this great country bordering the United States from San Diego (California) to Brownsville (Texas) a literal paradise. Whitewings, parrots, ducks and geese are plentiful. Generous seasons allow visitors ample shooting on any given trip.

Mammals — well, that's another story.

Mexicans are like folks anyplace in the world. It takes food in their bellies to sustain life. With a nationwide economy not even within shouting distance of that in the United States citizens get food wherever they can. Quail can easily be trapped. Animals such as deer can be killed one way or another by a hungry man more easily than most hunters realize.

As a result, big game hunting in Mexico ranks right along the bottom, by most any set of standards one might select for comparison. Desert sheep are there, but not legally for Norte Americanos. Bear hunting, a popular sport of the past, is mostly gone. Coyotes, javelina, all varmints for that matter, along with small game, have a season and a bag limit as do most all game birds. Mexican officials are trying to control the killing, but if a group ever faced an uphill battle it would have to be those Mexican game wardens.

Since deer are the subject of this book, let's stick to deer and see what we have. Mexico is a hard country to find out about. Getting information from one of their government offices is closely related to pulling teeth out of a chicken. It can't be done — but should you luck out on occasion — the very next person willing to talk will give you, as gospel, an entirely different version.

Laws have been known to change rather suddenly too. Like in the middle of a hunt, as some from this country could attest. But much of that is changing for the better. The day of "Mordida" has hit its peak I believe. While still in effect throughout the land, buying your way in and out of things and places is slowly giving way to general law and order.

Forgive me for getting involved in their politics, but then no one can go hunting, or even enter the country for that matter, without becoming somewhat involved.

Background information for this chapter was obtained from that great book "Deer of the World" by G. Kenneth Whitehead. Mr. Whitehead lives in England and is the acknowledged authority on the subject of deer throughout the entire world. Not the hunting of them, don't be misled, but on the many species, subspecies, where they live, sizes, etc. I would encourage anyone deeply interested in this subject to obtain a copy.

According to Mr. Whitehead there are, in North, Central and South America, fifteen species of deer which are further broken down into 93 subspecies. This includes Moose (4 subspecies); Caribou (5); Wapiti (4); Mule deer and Black-tailed deer (11); White-tailed deer (38); Brocket deer — Red (14),

Inside measurement of this buck is 33 inches. The bases measured 5¼ inches around. Deer was killed 50 miles below the border.

Little Red (2), Brown (10) and Dwarf; Huemul; Marsh Deer; Pampas deer (3) and Pudu (2). I'll bet you didn't have any idea there were so many. I know I didn't. Maybe you didn't even know moose, caribou and wapiti (elk) were deer – but they are. Big deer, granted, but deer nevertheless.

Still referring to Mr. Whitehead's book, he tells us mule deer in Mexico cover six subspecies and do not generally inhabit much of that country. One extends its range south of California into Baja where it is joined by another. Two are located on tiny islands east and west of Baja California (which is in Mexico). The other two subspecies run over from Arizona, New Mexico and West Texas and extend as far south as Zacatecas in Central Mexico.

Given the name of desert mule deer or burro deer the subspecies from Arizona south into Sonora is replaced by another subspecies farther east, according to Mr. Whitehead. We in the Southwest still call it desert mule deer, it's the one from southern New Mexico and West Texas on south into central Mexico; a subspecies I've campaigned for many years to have included in record books as a separate listing. More on this in Chapters 8 and 11.

Whitetailed deer in Mexico, according to Whitehead, include the Coues (see Chapter 7) spilling over into the coastal regions of the Gulf of California, then the Carmen Mountain whitetail in the more mountainous area. He states the ranges of these two do not apparently overlap.

Further south "Deer of the World" lists 10 subspecies recognized in Mexico. Then, as mentioned earlier, whitetails range on through Central America into South America. I have been dove hunting in Colombia and was told of big whitetails, but was not privileged to see any. The whitetail in Mexico, by the way, is called "Venado." I believe that really means "deer" but whitetails were under discussion when the term was used.

An exceptional whitetail that scored 203⅛ via Boone and Crockett. Bucks like this, according to Naquin, are usually found in agricultural areas where there is a low deer density.

It's the next one mentioned in my English friend's book that really fascinates me. So much so, I am already making arrangements to hunt, kill, and mount, life-size, an average specimen of a Brocket deer, if, of course, it can be done legally, importation to the States and all. From what I can find out, this is possible. The Brocket deer not only is not included on the endangered species list, but both authorities I approached on the subject (questioning the legalities of importing either the hide and horns or a fully mounted animal) had never heard of it. Could be that's why it isn't endangered.

The Brocket is only in southern Mexico and is represented by two species, though the Red Brocket is far and again the more abundant. The Brown Brocket is limited to the Yucatan Peninsula. The Red Brocket, the largest, stands about 28 inches high at the shoulder. Little is known of these animals, except that they inhabit dense thickets, usually weigh less than 40 pounds, live weight, and

have spike antlers seldom measuring more than 4 to 5 inches in length.

I've gone into this background information as a prelude to relating my conversations with two men, one a Texan and the other from Arizona, who probably know more about deer hunting in Mexico than anyone else. Neither of them has read "Deer of the World" which makes it almost exciting to hear them relate their experiences and the various locations of those experiences. The findings of these two men confirms what was written by Mr. Whitehead.

George W. Parker was born within a stone's throw of Mexico and is now in his seventies, having lived all those years in the same area. Much of his hunting was done across the border and all the way down to Campeche, which is as far south as you can go in Mexico. There is more about George Parker in Chapter 7.

Gene Naquin is a young fellow dedicated to finding out all he can about deer. Whitetails, primarily, are his bag. Gene lives in Laredo and is a graduate of Texas A & M University with a degree in Wildlife Science. He has become deeply involved with the propagation of quality deer herds on both sides of the border. He is working with the Mexican Agricultural Department in Nuevo Leon and with the tourist departments in Sabinas Hidalgo and Monterrey. Tourism folks are interested in hunters because they spend money. Hunters aren't interested unless there is plenty of game, hence Gene's involvement. He is working with Mexican ranchers in upgrading their herds with the help of the Agricultural Department. Much is being accomplished. Mexico is not the backward country thought of by some, but more appropriately a country that simply hasn't been developed to its fullest. Education is the answer. The government is interested and many ranchers are interested, particularly the younger ones taking over family holdings.

They can see where game animals, deer in this instance, are in fact a renewable resource to be harvested the same as cattle, sheep, goats and horses. As a result, they are fencing in ranches and closely watching poachers. Bag limits are enforced. Seasons are honored. Deer are the winner because they now receive protection. Hunters are, too, because they get to harvest the crop. In spite of what conservationists (some of them) and all preservationists would have us believe, game still has to be controlled and harvested if it is to flourish. It can not do it on its own with civilization as its primary enemy.

Once man set foot on the face of the earth the ecological soundness of wildlife surviving on its own went down the drain. Man is the enemy – not the hunter. Habitat destruction is responsible, in most every instance, for declining populations. It is not the killing of a few animals during a hunting season.

Gene has flown over more than half a million acres of northern Mexico in government-owned helicopters, so he can speak with authority on the whitetailed deer situation in that part of the world.

Other than in this particular area: Falcon Lake (south of Laredo) along the Texas-Mexico border to Del Rio and south into Mexico some 50 miles (and in far western Mexico) there is no whitetail hunting worthy of the name. We are talking about a measly 10,000 square miles in a country listed at 760,373 square miles. Most ranchers throughout this country feel deer compete with livestock and not only couldn't care less about having them on their land, but actually have stated that they wouldn't care if they were wiped out.

Ted Gorsline, from Ontario, Canada killed this Brocket deer with his shotgun. It was his first. Taken in deep southern Mexico.

Poaching is the big problem; night hunting basically. Does, fawns, little bucks, all look alike under a headlight spotting eyes. As a result most of those landowners have their wish, few deer are left.

A few ranchers have seen the light in the western portion of northern Mexico and their land, while not included in that 10,000 square mile figure, is on the upswing so far as deer hunting is concerned, but only on ranches where landowners value deer as a crop to be harvested are the animals protected. Again, we are back to education.

Just to show the possibilities – Naquin started working with a ranch eight years ago that had NO deer. It now has a population of one deer (including bucks, does and fawns) per 34 acres. The last hunting season produced 20 bucks for harvest, or one for every 1,200 acres. From zero to 20 in only eight years.

Naquin was asked his opinion of spike bucks. This subject runs rampant throughout Texas with many for and many against shooting them. I believe Gene's thinking coincides with that of most learned individuals. He feels a spike buck is an inferior buck if it is an area offering plenty of

Gene Naquin with a few heads from Mexico. They are typical of the heads he allows taken where he controls the hunts.

nourishment. However, where insufficient nourishment is available he feels it could be caused by lack of nutrients. In other words, each ranch, in Naquin's opinion, has to be considered on its own merits as to the killing of spike bucks — but — where nutrition is available spikes are definitely inferior and should be taken off the land. A quality deer herd can't be realized with inferior bucks doing the breeding.

Naquin also has strong feelings about predators. He claims one ranch under his jurisdiction in Mexico has one deer per 44 acres and coyotes so thick a man has only to throw his hat to hit one. Also, five mountain lions were seen there in one hunting season. He calls the herd on this ranch well-balanced. Generally he feels coyotes and lions have little or no effect on a deer herd other than to help keep it under control, all else being in favor of the deer of course.

About hunting farther into Mexico, Gene feels there is little because of population problems. He does think, however, that where one is beyond the reach of those populations, so far back in the mountains as to take three or four days by burro, there could easily be some mighty good deer hunting. Places, I might point out, that are almost impossible to reach.

Good whitetail country in Mexico is similar to the terrain north of the border, according to Gene. He says Webb, Zapata, Duval and Maverick counties in South Texas are identical to ranches he is working on in Mexico. And the deer are the same size, in other words — really of trophy potential.

A foreigner, meaning us, going into Mexico on his own might have a good hunt, but the odds are against it, Naquin feels. Obviously, this is not the thinking of a commercial hunter trying for clients, as Gene plans to take only 30 deer a season off all the land previously described. He does not have any trouble getting those 30 hunters. More on this later from my other source, George Parker. Once the gun permits, licenses, etc. are obtained, which can be done by anyone with perseverance, the hunter will find himself at the mercy of landowners who don't know whether they have any deer or not. Some will say they have lots of animals because they saw two or three the last time they crossed the place, but huntable numbers are almost unheard of other than on the protected ranches.

If you can't speak the language fluently stay out of Mexico. Cities and larger towns offer no problem, but back in the interior where a hunter would have to go, few, if any, Mexicans speak English.

Now let's talk about George Parker a bit. His experiences are oriented more towards the western portion of Mexico all the way to the southern border, then on into South America, for that matter. He tells of some fine desert mule deer, right down to the beaches; in fact, Parker killed one from a boat. Well, not really, but the buck was seen from a boat, the boat beached, he walked about 50 yards, shot the buck, then dragged it back to the boat. Close enough to be counted as boat hunting on the beach in this writer's opinion. This was south of Puerto de la Libertad on the Gulf of California in Sonora.

There are whitetails in this same country, according to Parker, and he has seen evidence of the two crossing, whitetail and mule deer. His collection of mounted heads includes one that is obviously a cross. A Texas biologist, Rod Marburger, is working on this very program in West Texas. He claims he can prove whitetail-mule deer crosses.

There are lots of whitetails in the western portion of Mexico on ranches bordering the United States, says Parker. He has seen up to 100 in a single day; all on protected ranches and carefully controlled.

Brocket deer killed in southern Mexico. *Photo by Ted Gorsline*

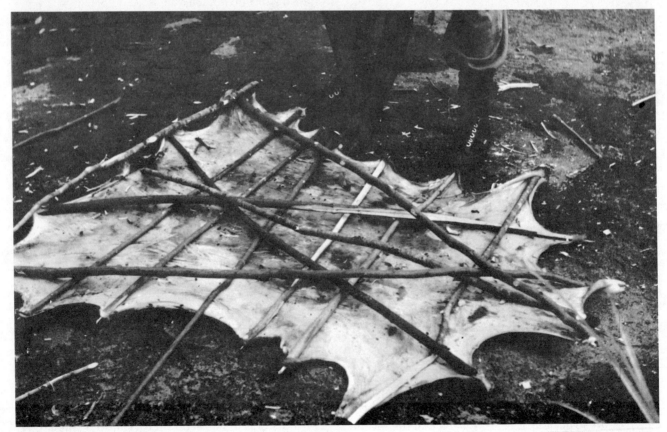

Stretching the hide of a Brocket deer. *Photo by Ted Gorsline*

118

Brocket deer as exhibited in the Field Museum of Natural History, Chicago.

Open, uncontrolled land offers no hunting possibilities for the deer hunter, in Parker's opinion.

Mule deer *might* go as far south as Sinaloa, Parker told me. He knows they are in Sonora, but that they do not go on down the coast. He feels they are in Chihuahua, which places them south of New Mexico and West Texas, but also feels they do not go so far down as Guadalajara. At best, he says, "Any deer more than 300 miles into Mexico would probably be a whitetail."

"Desert mulies are seldom found high up in the hills, that is, the higher mountains," Parker said, "I've seen very few more than 500 feet above sea level."

"There are mule deer in lower (Baja) California, but no whitetail," Parker went on, "on the peninsula of lower California . . . these look like desert mule deer but might be a little smaller." George Parker has seen enough desert mule deer in his life that he knows for sure what they look like, so this writer accepts his statement as fact. He told me he also saw a spotted fawn in April, in lower California, where just across the gulf, in Sonora, they usually have little ones in July.

A few claims have been made that there are whitetails on the peninsula but George has been up and down and across about every foot of that land and has never seen a live one nor any antlers from a deer killed by someone else in that area. He also added an interesting note – that there are no javelina in Baja California.

All this boils down to the fact Parker feels mule deer range in Mexico is limited to an area south of Yuma and El Paso and going into the country maybe 300 miles.

When asked about Brocket deer, Parker said he thought something should be written about them and that they should be included in North American Big Game records because they are a game animal on this continent. His only experience with the little deer, which he described as maybe weighing 25–30 pounds and real fine eating, was the few he and friends had killed while on other hunts in Campeche and Tabasco. He said they lived in pretty thick cover in the jungle.

On this subject, it seems natives kill the little Brocket deer for food . . . sometimes with shotguns and occasionally with a rifle . . . but more often catching them with dogs.

When asked about a "gringo" going into Mexico on his own, George said it could be done, but agreed with Naquin that it would be impractical. "Mexi-

Jerry Johnston, founder of the Texas Trophy Hunters Association killed this heavy-horned 10 pointer with an 18 inch spread on his first Mexican hunt.

cans do a lot of hunting, have guns and ammunition – and Jeeps. They drive all over and they hunt hard," said Parker in referring to public land possibilities.

His parting shot: "I can only encourage stateside hunters to go into Mexico under the right setup;" meaning have everything in the way of paperwork done far in advance and a good solid contact down there before ever setting foot on their soil. He added one more comment, "If you talk 'Mexican' you might make out all right, but chances are you won't find it easy."

Mighty good advice, and from a man not involved with commercial hunting as opposed to exactly the same advice from Naquin who is a commercial hunter and could conceivably be accused of favoring his profession.

I know this sounds discouraging on Mexican hunting, but it is straight from the mouths of two men who, in my opinion, know more about hunting in Mexico than anyone else this side of the border.

George Parker does not hunt commercially so his address is not being given. Gene Naquin does and like I've said earlier, this is not to tout him as your single source for hunting in Mexico. It is to give you someone to write to who'll give you an honest answer. To contact him write to: Gene Naquin, Wildlife and Land Management, Inc., P.O. Box 2955, Laredo, Texas 78041.

I seldom ever give an outfitter's or guide's name, but Gene is just as apt to tell you hunting is lousy and that it's best to stay home and save your money, if that's the way he sees it at the moment. He's much too honest to ever be a rich man.

"Deer of the World' by G. Kenneth Whitehead is the most thorough book on the subject ever written. To get a copy write to: Constable & Company Ltd., 10 Orange Street, London WC2 7EG, England. They are the publishers.

As for myself – I've hunted whitewings and quail a few times in Mexico and have had no trouble. I fully intend to make a Brocket deer hunt as soon as possible. Gene can't help me with this. Brocket deer are far south of his domain. But I can guarantee this much – I won't set foot in Mexico until my papers are in hand and my thoroughly checked-out guide booked. Mexico not only is a foreign country – it is the most foreign of any I've ever been in – in spite of the fact it borders us.

Should you wish to try for information directly from Mexico write to: Director General de Fauna Silvestre, S. A. G., Aquiles Serdan Nr. 28 – 7 Piso, Mexico 3, D.F.

Gene Naquin grins as he told the author it would be great if all the heads he gets out of Mexico were this good.

Jerry Johnson killed this better than average whitetail only a few miles south of the Rio Grande. On ranches where game is managed heads like this will come more often. But then that's true whether it is in Mexico or stateside.

Chapter 11

TROPHY DEER

What is a "trophy deer"?

The author disagrees with the general use of the words "trophy" and "record". I continually mention "good bucks" and "real trophies", even "trophy" and "record" on occasion, but always in the context of the true meaning of the words. Let's go directly to the horse's mouth and see where we stand. Webster's New World Dictionary puts it this way; trophy (many listings, of course but one applying directly to this chapter) 5. a lion's skin, a deer's head, etc. displayed as evidence of hunting prowess; nowhere does it mention size.

The word record is described as; 7. the best performance, as the highest speed, greatest amount, highest rate, etc., reached and publicly recorded.

In other words many, far too many, confuse the word "trophy" with "record". There is a vast difference between a trophy buck and a record buck. It might be one and the same to some, but if it is, that person is beating himself out of lot of enjoyment that comes from happy thoughts of a hunt in some distant place where a "record" was unobtainable.

I maintain a trophy is simply something by which to remember a particular incident or place. It can well be, in the case of deer hunting, the first deer killed by the hunter. That one will always remain a trophy by anyone's standards. Or at least it should. Another trophy might be a head from a state not hunted before and possibly never again. Whatever the size, a buck tagged in a far off place is a trophy of such a trip.

So many deer have dropped to my guns I do not kill for the sake of killing anymore. Not that I ever did, simply for the sake of killing, but I used to put a lot of emphasis on the importance of bringing something home. Since the meat has dropped in importance my thinking, today, is directed more towards a top head or nothing. Meat never goes to waste: normally it is promised to someone before the hunt ever gets underway.

Even when I succumb to the impulse of firing at an animal smaller than one killed in the past, it is always at least an average size animal for the area. This, then, becomes my trophy for that hunt. And I sincerely mean this – any average head taken from a new hunting spot (meaning a particular state or section of a state, not necessarily just another ranch down the road) is an honest-to-goodness trophy.

Don't ever let anybody try to convince you otherwise.

My walls hold antlers of deer from 13 states and one Canadian Province. None of them are in any record book, yet I consider all of them trophies. Most would not rate a second look from a "record book" hunter.

Among my many "trophies" are two that came mighty close to record book proportions: a mule deer that scored 183 points back when 185 made the book and a black bear that fell $7/8$ short, back when the minimum was lower than at present. Had they made it, both would be out now by reason of the increased minimum scores. Nevertheless, they are still top trophies in my book and always will be.

World Record Typical Mule Deer killed by Doug Burris, Seguin, Texas in Dolores Country, Colorado in 1972. It scores 225 ⁶/₈ in the Boone and Crockett Records of North America.

(PHOTO COURTESY OF WM. H. NESBITT, HUNTER SERVICES DIVISION, NATIONAL RIFLE ASSOCIATION.)

Far too much emphasis has been placed on record book heads. These are all but unobtainable. Seldom, ever, does the hunter bagging such a deer do it intentionally. Most are just deer hunting. For some reason known only to our Creator, "just plain deer hunters" happen onto the majority of the bigger heads. Could be He is trying to tell us something.

At any rate it is great sport, seeking out a head of antlers far larger than "average." I encourage any who have taken a number of normal-sized heads to give real "trophy" or "record book" hunting a try. It's different! It requires a new set of ideals. An entirely new outlook on hunting. Different methods in some cases. Even to changing rifles on occasion.

About those ideals – new deer hunters are excited, or should be eager to "get a buck." I like this and wish I were still capable. To them any legal buck is where it all is. These hunters can hunt and be successful in country other hunters, seeking bigger heads, wouldn't venture into. Young bucks make up the majority of their kill; which isn't bad, believe me. They are by far the best eating.

As years go by this hunter develops a bit more control. He starts holding out for six and eight pointers. When this happens he changes tactics a bit because here he is hunting deer a little older. Maybe only a year older, but hence a little smarter.

The next step is holding out for the real "biggies".

It is here the hunter changes many things. First he has reached the point where just seeing a buck doesn't excite him at all. Even average-sized deer have little, if any, effect on his blood pressure. Oh, he enjoys looking through binoculars at eight and ten point whitetails with heavy horns and spreads of

124

Vernon Swiggett walks up to his first whitetail buck. A 6-pointer that should have had eight except that he grew no brow tines. Every first deer is a life-long trophy. Size means nothing.

17–18 inches, but seldom ever shows any change of expression until those antlers reach 22–24 inches across. Even the coolest nerves twinge a little then.

By the time the spread reaches 25 inches, and the tines are long, things start to liven up. Could be the deer might even get shot. But only by the beginning serious hunter. Next year he'll be even calmer.

Hunters for mule deer quality heads don't normally get up tight until the spread reaches 27 or 28 inches. Long tines, the secret of high scores, give even steel-hearted hunters a case of the shakes around this point. Spread, while highly thought of in the telling, doesn't count much towards records. It's the weight of the beam, the length of the main beam and the length of those tines that make the score.

I like to see a hunter try for a bigger head each time he hunts. Bigger than the last one killed. That way, unless lady luck has really smiled on earlier successes, hunting gradually progresses to true hunting rather than killing. Then the real fun begins.

Good average heads can be found any place there are deer, because all that is being sought is average for the area. Going on to higher quality means being more selective of hunting sites. A good way to start is by checking taxidermy shops as you travel about the country. While vacationing during the summer, for instance, stop in at small shops and see what sort of deer were brought in last season. This is a favorite pastime of mine. Besides keeping up with what comes from a particular area it helps one meet a lot of nice people. On occasion, even a hunt can be arranged, one that would never have come about had the shop not been visited.

125

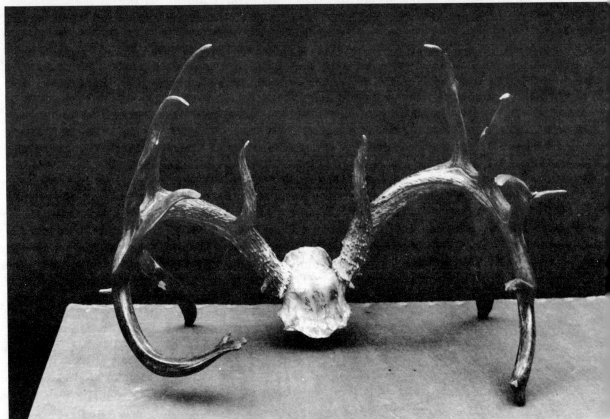

Linda Swiggett, the author's daughter-in-law, shot this "tiniest 8-pointer I've ever seen," to use the author's description. Her rifle was a Model 722 Remington .222 Rem. The ammo was handloaded 20.5 grains of 4198 under a Hornady 55 grain bullet. Linda was turkey hunting and this little buck got in the way. And got shot at 40 yards.

Hal Swiggett and high-horned Mescalero Apache mule deer buck he killed with this Remington Model 700 7 mm Rem. Mag. Hal declares magnums not needed for deer hunting except that he condones them for the record book hunters or those seeking out-sized heads. Stan Chee, well-known Mescalero Apache guide, led Swiggett to this trophy.

Another trick is to watch ranch and farm buildings and fences during travels. Antlers nailed to barns and hung on fences are generally what that landowner has killed. Sometimes bass and catfish heads can lead to a new fishing spot which some deer hunters (I'm thinking of myself) would find mighty hard to pass up. Farmers and ranchers hang them on fences too.

Sporting goods stores I take with a grain of salt. These are always tops for the area, trophies hung for exhibit I mean, and sometimes not even local.

If taking record book hunting seriously, one must check out Boone and Crockett's North American Big Game Records. This is the book listing all records for each species. It won't take long to select the spot producing the most big heads. The still newer source for this same information is Burkett's

Trophy Game Records of the World. It is also more accurate as it keeps records in a computer on an annual basis.

Just for kicks, let's go through the North American Big Game book. In alphabetical order (that's the way they list them) Columbian and Sitka blacktail deer are listed as one. Three states and one province are listed as sites where a record buck was killed. A total of 225 heads make up the "book." Of these 44.4% came from California, 28% from Oregon, 23.1% from Washington and 4.4% from British Columbia. Obviously the Columbian and Sitka deer inhabit the northernmost west coast. There is no non-typical listing for this species.

Coues (typical) deer, those little beauties from deep in the Southwest and Northern Mexico provide 117 heads for the "record book;" these from

Lin Nowotny, life-long San Antonio taxidermist, and an official Boone and Crockett scorer, poses with two sets of antlers he had just scored. Both from South Texas. The left set at 185⅝ and those on the right 194⁴⁄₈. Unlike the game of horse shoes, close doesn't count for "book" records.

two states and one country. Arizona is tops with 80.3%. New Mexico holds 17.9% and Mexico the remaining 1.7%.

Coues (non-typical) lists 14 heads. Arizona claimed 92.8% and Mexico 7.1%. Numerically, it was 13 to 1.

Mule deer (typical) lists 227 heads from 10 states, two provinces and Mexico. Percentage-wise it reads: Colorado 44%; New Mexico 13.6%; Utah 9.6%; Idaho 7.4%; Wyoming 6.6%; Arizona 4.8%; Montana 3%; Oregon 3%; Nevada 1.7%; British Columbia 1.7%; Saskatchewan 1.3%; Mexico .8% and Alberta .4%.

Mule deer (non-typical) heads, 203 of them, came from 13 states and three provinces. Front runner is Colorado with 25.6%; Arizona 13.7%; Idaho 13.3%; Utah 9.8%; Wyoming and Montana

6.4%; Saskatchewan 4.9%; New Mexico 3.9%; Washington 3.4%; Nevada 2.9%; Oregon 2.9%; Alberta 2.5%; British Columbia 1.4%; Nebraska and California .9% and Kansas .4%.

Whitetail, the most popular big game animal in North America, lists 299 heads in their typical book. Twenty seven states, six Canadian provinces and Mexico contribute to this list. This reveals more than half the states in the "lower 48" have produced a record book whitetail deer. Like I said, they are everyplace.

Specifically: Saskatchewan 17.3%; Minnesota 7%; Nebraska 6.6%; Wisconsin 6.3%; Manitoba 5.6%; Arkansas 4.3%; South Dakota 3.6%; Alberta, Missouri and New York 3.3%; Montana and North Dakota 3%; Pennsylvania 2.6%; Iowa and Ohio 2.3%; Georgia and Illinois 2%; Michigan

1.6%; Washington, Kansas and Virginia 1.3%; Tennessee and Kentucky 1%; Idaho and British Columbia 6%; West Virginia, Mississippi, Wyoming, Maine, Louisiana, Ontario, New Brunswick and Mexico .3% (one record from each state, province or country).

Whitetail (non-typical) recordings reveal 203 heads at minimum or above. These are from 26 states and six Canadian provinces. As they are listed: Saskatchewan 18.2%; Wisconsin 11.3%; Nebraska 7.3%; Washington, Montana 5.9%; Texas 4.9%; Ohio 4.4%; South Dakota 3.9%; North Dakota, Wyoming and Alberta 2.9%; Manitoba and Michigan 2.4%; New Brunswick, Minnesota, Idaho and Pennsylvania 1.9%; Iowa, Nova Scotia, British Columbia, Maine, Michigan, Louisiana, Arkansas and Illinois 1.4%; New York .9%; Kansas, Georgia, Virginia, Oklahoma, Kentucky and West Virginia .5% (one deer each).

Going back over these figures we soon see that the most logical place to hunt for a record book Columbian and Sitka blacktail is California since almost half of those listed came from that state.

Coues deer hunters would head for Arizona since they hold more than 80% of the record in typical and all but one of the non-typical listings.

Mule deer hunters, if we can go by the records, should seek out the high spots of Colorado since that mountain state holds 44% of the typical records and one-fourth of those rates as non-typical. It might be good to note, here, that New Mexico rated as number two in typical heads, but dropped to eighth place with slightly less than 4% of the non-typical, category. Along the same lines Arizona rates number two in non-typical but only sixth in typical heads. Idaho comes to the front here by taking third spot in non-typical whereas they ranked fourth in typical listings.

One item in the mule deer listings caught my eye. A single non-typical buck made the book from Kansas. KANSAS! A state where mule deer seem far off base. One map I've seen shows a tiny northwestern corner as mule deer country. I'll bet it was made after this buck was killed.

Whitetails? Well, it's sort of pay your money and take your chances. Saskatchewan leads typical heads with 17.3%, with Texas claiming a little over half that at 9.6%. Non-typical ratings change that picture somewhat, except that Saskatchewan still leads with 18.2% while Texas drops to sixth spot with only 4.9% of the top heads. Wisconsin moved into second place here with 11.3% of the records.

We might digress a moment and discuss what it takes to make Boone and Crockett. The BC method is a negative system insofar as I am concerned. It is based primarily on symmetry. If a head is wider than the longest main beam it brings about a deduction. If tines don't match – deductions. An extra tine is a deduction. Anything that takes away from the symmetrical appearance is deducted from the total. To make the book, Columbian and Sitka blacktail deer must score 130. Coues (typical) deer lists 110 as minimum. For a non-typical head this jumps to 120. Mule deer start at 195 points for typical and 240 for non-typical. Whitetail minimum for a typical head is 170 and 195 for non-typical.

Archers have their own system known as the Pope and Young Club. It is basically the Boone and Crockett method except that minimums are much lower. For instance: blacktail 90; Coues (typical) 68; Coues (non-typical) 78; mule deer (typical)

From Nova Scotia this whitetail has 26 points with a 33 inch spread. From the collection of Dr. Charles T. Arnold.

From the collection of Dr. Charles T. Arnold this New Brunswick whitetail has a spread of 27³/₄ inches and wears 33 points.

This Nova Scotia whitetail has 40 points more than 1-inch long and 27³/₄ inches of spread to go with the 28 inch main beams.
From the collection of Dr. Charles T. Arnold.

131

Now it's getting close. Plenty of width, tines reaching high and a heavy beam. This whitetail should score high though not making the "book" in all probability. Could be close. An outstanding whitetail, no doubt about it and one the author would have trouble passing up.

140; mule deer (non-typical) 150; whitetail (typical) 125 and whitetail (non-typical) 135. Though the minimum is lower it is just as hard, possibly even harder, for an archer to "make the book".

There is a new scoring system as this book is written. Dr. Joe Burkett, a veterinarian, spent nine years perfecting the method now known as Burkett's Trophy Game Records of the World (BTGRW). It is based on volumetric displacement; a positive system. Dr. Burkett feels that if an animal grew it, he should get credit for it. Initially scoring was by immersement in water. Hence the volumetric displacement. Obviously it could prove somewhat impractical to haul around a tank large enough to immerse moose, elk and caribou antlers so it was back to the drawing boards for a way to measure a head and achieve the same score as through volumetric displacement. By using a tiny diameter cable and a tine origin caliper (Dr. Burkett's invention) this goal is reached.

If the sides differ by more than 5% the head becomes an "extra-typical" in the BTGRW book. In every case each trophy receives credit for the antlers as the buck grew them. And on and on for elk, moose, caribou, cats, bear, horned species – every game animal can be, and is, scored by BTGRW. Even down to jack rabbits, squirrel, ground hogs – you name it, and they will keep records for the species. Still better, where BC scores mule deer, period, regardless of where killed, the Burkett system takes into consideration the varied sub-species (in case there really are definite geographical differences) such as with desert mule deer; a category long neglected in this writer's opinion.

Whitetails from one state will compete, in the first rating, against whitetails from the same specific area, then branch out finally to an overall top for the particular species.

Another advantage to BTGRW is that every head entered makes the book for that particular year. The advantage here is for areas suffering declines, for instance, smaller than normal heads through lack of nourishment, will still have a chance at the book because each year is a listing unto itself. The overall book will list only the top 100 heads. Known as the top 100 of the species. No minimum. The 100 best heads in BTGRW make up the record book.

Called the Science of Tropaeology, it requires scorers to study at a seminar for a full week to learn the how's and wherefore's.

Binoculars play a big part in big deer hunting. Lots of country has to be looked at and lots of heads checked out.

It is the coming scoring system and it's only a matter of time before it replaces Boone and Crockett and Pope and Young, and possibly even foreign methods, as each continent goes its own merry way at the moment. It is the only scoring system that includes every animal that walks on the face of the earth.

Another advantage of BTGRW is that it separates the various methods of hunting. Archers already have their method but Burkett will keep handgunner records, muzzleloader records, bow and arrow records, all broken down to show how each hunter stands regardless of his chosen arm.

And still one more advantage. As heads are entered, data on where it came from will be entered into the computer. Once this bank grows to formulate a pattern it will provide information to hunters on the specific areas yielding the best trophies last season, by simply touching a button, for a slight fee. It won't be expensive and it will be information not available anyplace else. True, Boone and Crockett lists them – but only once each six years and the book costs many times more than BTGRW's!

Burkett's Trophy Game Records of the World is a scoring method, the Science of Tropaeology, to be considered should you have a top head and want it listed in a record book at least once. For that matter, for that single listing, it doesn't have to be of any particular size. As mentioned, every entry will be listed in the records of that year.

Now that we have talked about records, scoring methods, minimums etc., how does a hunter go about deciding on the hoof if an animal in his sights has a chance.

It's not easy – to be blunt – but it isn't impossible, either. In fact, experienced head hunters can gauge surprisingly close at 200, 300 and sometimes at even 400 yards.

Whitetail deer vary so much in size across the country it is hard to set up any set of standards that is consistent. By and large ears will measure six inches in length, but more importantly there will be from 14½ to maybe 17 or even 18 inches between the eartips on a live animal. If your average deer weighs 100 pounds 15–16 inches would come mighty close to the distance between his ear tips.

Should he weigh in at around 200 pounds make that 17–18 inches. Obviously we have here a quick measurement. If antlers appear to reach three inches beyond the ears on a 100 pound deer the measurement should come right close to 21–22 inches.

Once the spread has been determined, glance quickly at the tines and beam. Tines should be even to the side and on a heavy beam. Light, spindly antlers signify a buck that should be left to grow another year, or two, or three, even if antlers have a width sufficient to be attractive.

John Wootters, in his fine book "Hunting Trophy Deer," offers as good a method as I've heard of to try and judge beam circumference. John refers to the average pistol grip on a modern rifle as being about 4½ to 5 inches around at the smallest point. This also happens to be the figure that must be reached for a whitetail to approach "record" classification.

Mule deer, with much bigger ears, will average 17–18 inches for the smaller varieties on up to 20 inches for Rocky Mountain bucks. It is hard to measure a dead deer and know exactly how he held them in life but I have measured a good many heads and have found only two that came in close to 22 inches, and this included giving them the benefit of any doubt. I measured several at 21 inches, but the average is closer to 20–21 inches.

If a mulie's antlers appear to reach three or four inches past his ears he's a "shootin' buck" in most any camp. That will place them close to 25–29 inches, depending on the locale; a head needing no apologies, unless one is seeking a "book" head. In that case more care is needed before the shot.

On thing I have discovered, if there is any doubt at all in a hunter's mind as to size, the buck isn't big

How about this whitetail buck. Would you shoot him? He's mighty impressive but he is also only 2½ years old. Just imagine what he'll be like in four years, if he lives that long.

135

Not heavy enough of beam nor long enough of tine to be a high scorer. It's bucks like this that get shot by the excitable "trophy" hunter. A good representative mule deer head it is, maybe even a bit above average.

enough. Many bucks look big at first glance. Experienced hunters soon learn to distinguish between those making the grade and those not. Let me repeat – if there is any doubt about the buck in your sights he isn't the one you want.

It is for record book hunters that I now break a long standing rule: my contention is, and always has been, that magnums are not necessary for any deer that ever walked the face of this earth; nor most other game either, for that matter, but here deer is our subject.

Hunters seeking records, hunters with the experience to shoot only when they are sure the head will score highly enough to qualify, can use magnum rifles to good stead. More often than not those old bucks are spooky. By the very reason of their being record book material proves they are above average in the smarts department. Age, and only age, puts record mesurements into a pair of antlers. Sure, it takes plenty of the right nourishment too, but without age it's a lost cause.

Magnum rifles will help here because the perfect shot is seldom offered. Head and neck shots are not for trophy hunters so one needs all the punch he can get, within reason, of course. The hunter still has to be capable of placing his bullet.

No one in his right mind would take such a chance on an eating deer. First off, it could ruin a lot of meat from the shot itself, and more from the chase. Meat is not the object for book hunters, nor is it for those seeking top trophies since seldom ever does a buck of this size receive anyone's "prime meat" rating.

Too, hunters who have reached this classification are usually blessed with long experience so rarely is an animal lost. In 40 years of deer hunting I've never known of a top scoring head that was lost after being crippled. Thought it undoubtedly has happened.

One more comment about really big trophies or record book heads, whatever the species (using the two terms in their proper perspective). Once an animal has grown to these proportions, since we know age is the controlling factor, he has outlived his usefulness. Often we are criticized for taking "the best the species has to offer." Poppycock! The best, true, so far as that particular animal is concerned, but not for the propagation of the species. That big buck or bull has served his time as a breeder. Those seven, eight or even ten years it took him to reach peak growth was when he did his bit for his species. By the time he interests trophy hunters

World Record Typical Whitetail killed by James Jordan, near Danbury, Wisconsin, in 1914. The head scores 206⁵/₈ in the Boone and Crockett Records of North America. It is owned by Dr. Charles T. Arnold, Nashua, New Hampshire.

he is of little value to does. He spends most of his time fighting off the real studs, those younger bucks.

Trophy hunters DO NOT injure the species in any way, shape, manner or form. If anything, they help by removing that animal, thereby providing food for a younger specimen to make it through the winter.

If venison is your aim this chapter hasn't been your game, but one day it will be. Sooner or later most all of us reach the point where we want to better our past. The only way a deer hunter can perform that feat is to hang bigger and better heads on his wall. Which is as it should be since young folks come along behind us to take up the slack on "eatin' size" bucks.

And the circle starts over again.

For information on the three scoring methods mentioned contact: Boone and Crockett Club, 424 North Washington Street, Alexandria, Virginia 22314. Pope and Young Club, Box J, Basset, Nebraska 68714. Burkett's Trophy Game Records of the World, Route 2, Box 195-A, Fredericksburg, Texas 78624.

Chapter 12

MUZZLE LOADERS

We will not attempt to discuss the intracacies of muzzle-loader shooting in this chapter. There are lots of good books on the subject: Lyman's Black Powder Handbook, edited by C. Kenneth Ramage; Black Powder Digest, published by Digest Books and "Shooting the Muzzle Loader" by Jolex Publications. Nor are we to be concerned with brand names of rifles.

Our goal is to show how muzzle loaders are used for hunting deer. Calibers. Loads. Preferred ranges and the like.

Many of you may have read some of my black powder writings over the years, dating back to the very beginning of this current enthusiastic reincarnation of things smelly and dirty in the gun line. My stand was, is, and always will be, that .45 caliber rifles are inadequate for the killing of deer. Granted, lots of venison has been put in the pot through their use. No one knows how many deer have been crippled by the lightweight round ball before one was brought to the knife.

Round balls for a .45 caliber muzzle loader measure, give or take a bit, about .440 inches and weigh, according to that exact measurement, in the vicinity of 128 grains with a top of about 133 grains for a .445 round ball. Coupled with this light weight there is ballistically nothing, short of a 2'' x 4'', that is less efficient than a round ball. Put the two together and you have a first class crippler at much beyond spitting distance.

For kicks let's do a bit of figuring Using Lyman's Black Powder Handbook as a guide. Two thousand feet per second (fps) is well within reason for a .440 round ball from a .45 caliber rifle. At 100 yards it is moving at 1057 fps and the muzzle energy of 1137 ft/lbs has dropped to only 318 ft/lbs, less than one-fourth of the hitting power at 100 yards of the .30-30 Winchester which is looked down upon by many as a crippler of deer.

Please bear in mind that many so-called "authorities" have gained their claim to fame by doing most of their hunting from a comfortable chair in a warm living room. Don't get overly excited about any touting of light caliber rifles, meaning .45's, for such hunting.

True, it was done in the old days, but IT WAS NOT DONE once heavier calibers became available.

That's all I'm going to say about round balls in .45 caliber rifles. You be the judge. If the facts and figures you find will allow you to shoot deer with such a load, with a clear conscience, that's all the authority you need.

If you have a good shooting .45 caliber rifle and won't be doing a lot of hunting I suggest you work up a good load for either Thompson/Center's great Maxi-Ball which weighs about 230 grains or one of the several .45 Minie's which go from 265 to 300 grains in weight.

These develop enough authority to drop a buck should the occasion present itself.

The .50 caliber, in my opinion, is the minimum to be considered by the serious hunter. Round balls measuring .490 inches, a common size for hunting

Kodiak MK-1 double barrel .58 caliber muzzle loading rifle. Many makers offer serviceable muzzle loaders but only the Kodiak offers a fast second shot.

Good sights are a must – something not offered on most muzzle loaders. Including this Kodiak MK-1 .58. Swiggett is a great handgun fancier and likes their sights so he installed Thompson/Center pistol sights on his Kodiak.

use, weigh about 170 grains. Depending upon bore measurement some rifles can call for a ball diameter of up to .498 inches – which will weigh about 180 grains. Patch thickness is the determining factor in selecting ball diameter. To obtain optimum results the shooter will undertake a strenuous shooting session with varying ball diameters and patch thicknesses to determine the one combination best suited to his particular rifle.

Round balls in .50 caliber rifles can be started out at 1,800 to 2,000 fps with relative ease and over this 200 fps variation most rifles will single out a specific charge that demonstrates superior groups. When found, this is the one to hunt with. The animal has never been born that can rise up and tell you whether he was hit with a ball moving at 1,800 fps or 2,000 fps.

Let's use 1,900 fps, right in the middle, for the sake of argument. The .50 caliber round ball hits with 47% more authority at 100 yards than does the miniscule .45 caliber round ball. It's the weight that makes the difference.

Still greater devastation can be achieved with .50 caliber rifles by shooting the Thompson/Center Maxi-Ball at 370 grains. Loads developing 1,500 fps are well within reason. Potent, but safe, in any rifle in good condition. This one churns up 85% more ft./lbs. of energy at 100 yards than the .50 caliber round ball and 2½ times what the .45 caliber round ball does at that distance.

The .50 caliber Maxi-Ball at 1,500 fps hits with 860 ft./lbs. at 100 yards. This is still only 66% of what the .30-30 Winchester does at the same distance. From personal experience with both I have to say the .50 caliber muzzleloader is considerably more deadly under this set of circumstances. The combination of bigger diameter with more than twice the weight, in spite of a velocity lower than that of the .30-30, gives it a solid advantage. Between the two my choice would be the muzzleloader and I'd never look back.

Getting into the more than half-inch diameter bores puts real authority into hunting rifles and these are the rascals this writer likes. Probably the most near-perfect caliber for muzzleloader hunting of big game is the .54 caliber. It shoots round balls of about .530–.535 diameter weighing from 220 to 230 grains, Maxi-Balls at 400 grains and Minie's weighing 410 grains.

Round balls can be started at 1,800–1,900 fps with safety in any well-made rifle giving them about

Raymond Rhodes killed this 8-point whitetail buck with the author's .58 caliber Texas Carbine using 90 grains of GO FFg and the standard 505 grain .575 Minie. That spot on the tree in the background is where the Minie whacked it after going through the buck.

25% more "oomph" at 100 yards than the .50 caliber. Maxi-Balls can be pushed to 1,400 fps, or a tiny bit more, and hit with almost the identical ft./lbs. at 100 yards as the .45 caliber round ball does at the muzzle – about 1,100 ft/lbs. I don't like to push Minie's over 1,300 fps. Less is often better. The skirts don't seem to me to be strong enough to withstand more velocity which, when they fail, causes erratic accuracy. Even at 1,300 fps a .54 caliber Minie zaps its target with about 1,000 ft./lbs. of energy. This borders on .45–70 ballistics with even greater efficiency due to the increased diameter. Bullet weight is comparable.

From here we move on to what I consider the Lord and Master of muzzle loading hunting rifles. Just as I consider the 12 gauge shotgun the ultimate

in shotguns, I place .58 caliber rifles right alongside in their field. Each normally provides an efficiency against which all others are compared.

Though I failed to mention it, I see little reason for round balls in either the .54 or .58 caliber. Since we are in true big bores I feel the added weight of Minie's and Maxi's (Minie's in .58 and Maxi's in .54) are what it is all about.

But – for the sake of record – round balls will be mentioned. In the .58 caliber round balls measure, usually, around .560-inch in diameter and weigh, again give or take a little, 260 grains. Still this seemingly inefficient monstrosity can be made to start out at about 1,400 fps which drops to only a little over 900 fps at 100 yards. Even at that, it hits with almost half a thousand ft./lbs. of energy which

141

Not every black powder shooter is going to want a scope on his rifle. The man with aging eyes or the hunter wanting more precise ball placement will look kindly towards this Leupold M8 2X long-eye-relief scope and the Buehler one-piece base holding it on this Thompson/Center .50 caliber Hawken.

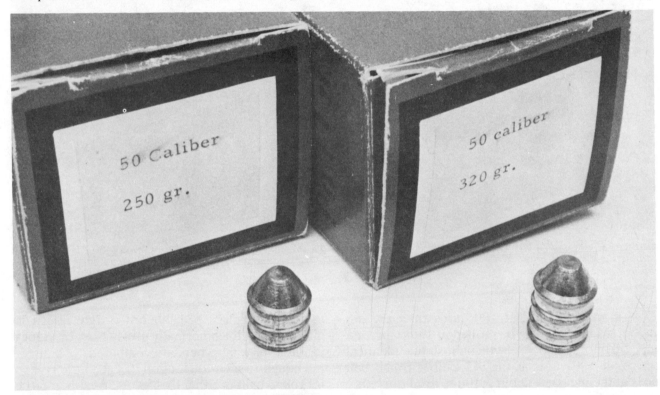

Lee's R*E*A*L* .50 caliber bullets. Both shoot good in the author's rifles but he prefers the 320 grain as being ballistically superior.

Poly-patches by Butler Creek are handy to use and at least equally accurate when compared to the usual patching material.

In using Poly-patches the ball must be small enough to fit well into the cup yet large enough to be a tight fit so as to stay in place. Sometimes rifles require a different diameter ball than the one usually used with conventional patching.

Caliber .50 round balls, Lee's R*E*A*L* 250 grain and 320 grain bullets and T/C's 370 grain Maxi-ball. All have a place in deer hunting. Hal prefers the heavier projectiles over round balls.

The author prefers Minie's in .58 Caliber. On the left is Lee's contribution and on the right Lyman's heaviest. Both are larger diameter than the standard .575 by two and three thousandths and shoot better in all four of Hal's .58 caliber rifles.

James Rigdon took this trophy buck with his muzzle loader in the Fairforest Creek area of South Carolina. It was a special primitive weapons hunt for archers and black powder shooters. (SCWMRD photo by Ted Borg.)

BIG GAME CHECK
STATION

S.C. WILDLIFE
RESOURCES DEPT.

makes it close to the .54 caliber in potency except that as with the .54-over-the-.50 it increases in deadliness because of the still larger diameter.

Several Minie's are available for .58 caliber rifles. One of the most popular is Lyman's number 575213 weighing in at 505 grains. Bearing this same number but with the "old Style" added, is a 460 grain projectile. In my rifles I seem to do better with still heavier versions listed as number 577611 at 530 grains and the 57730 at 570 grains. These are also slightly larger in diameter. Each barrel is a law unto itself, so only by trial and error will you be able to determine which will work best in your rifle.

As to the efficiency of these big hunks of lead I once shot a buffalo (American bison) with the 505 grain version and 90 grains of FFg which churned up only a little more than 900 fps at the muzzle. At the distance I shot this particular bull it thumped him with about 800 ft./lbs. of energy and it got his attention right suddenly.

There are a couple of lighter missiles offered, but I can't recommend them for hunting since the reason for going to bigger rifles is to get heavier bullets.

Muzzle loader hunters have to be a special breed, for several reasons. First, not only are they limited to a single shot (which can be the case in centerfire rifles too), but it takes them a heck of a lot longer to clear the bore, drop in a powder charge, dig in a pocket for a container holding pregreased Minie or Maxi balls, thump one down the bore, seek out and install (usually with at least one or more dropped in haste) a percussion cap, then try to find the animal not knocked down with the first effort.

Then there is the problem of cleaning. I know, as I'm sure you do, many centerfire rifles that never get cleaned. Black powder guns HAVE to be cleaned daily if they are fired. It makes no difference how cold, how tired, how hungry the hunter is, nor does it make any difference how late it is. If the gun isn't properly taken care of it can be totally useless the next day.

Then comes the effectiveness of black powder rifles. Deadly, that's for sure, but at nowhere near the ranges considered commonplace by many centerfire hunters.

Though I've hunted with black powder guns more than half a century (my grandfather was using a double shotgun to help feed us in the early 1920's) I've never come to think of even the best as a long range possibility. Just the opposite, in fact. When asked about distances my reply usually sounds

Mike Powasnik, a Colonel in the Texas Army and a dedicated muzzle loader hunter, loads up for a test shot on the range.

Most any muzzle loading hunter would like to get a shot like this. Few whitetail bucks stand so picturesquely during hunting season at this fellow did in late summer.

Raymond Rhodes takes a test shot before embarking on his deer hunt with this .58 caliber Texas Carbine made by Mowery for Trail Guns Armory.

something like "get just as close as you can, then move in another ten steps".

Trajectory is the bugaboo for muzzle loading riflemen. Sighted in to hit the point of aim at 100 yards most guns will have a 4–5 inch mid-range trajectory. Put another way – if shot on a level the ball will drop something like 8 to 9 inches at 100 yards. And from there on out it really gets bad. Here we are referring to sensible velocities safe in any well-made rifle. This becomes almost 2½ feet at 150 yards. Here I'm talking about my favored .58 caliber rifles and ordinary loads. You get the idea.

If you feel confident of placing a ball in a killing spot I'd say shoot. If at all doubtful – get closer.

I have seen a good many animals fall to muzzle-loaders, but only one that fell to a shot exceeding that often referred-to 100 yards, and it by only 15 more; a good many in the 60 to 80 yard bracket, but by far the majority have been less than 60 yards.

I am not a believer in long range shooting at flesh and fur with black powder guns, nor any other gun for that matter, though excessive range for a fine centerfire with a good scope is a far cry from excessive range with open sights on a muzzle-loader.

It is still bullet placement that gets game. Good hits come from knowing your rifle; knowing it well and being downright personal with it. A rifle should be a part of the hunter. If it isn't, he needs to spend more time with the tool that stands between him and the success of his hunt. All else can go well: lots of game, beautiful weather, fine companions, good food, warm comfortable sleeping bags, but all is for naught if the hunter doesn't have a top-quality relationship with his rifle.

Lots of little problems can come up with black powder guns that centerfire hunters never encounter. Like the time in Tennessee when I missed a shot in some very dense cover – and in a very wet rain. I

Smoke pours from the muzzle of Swiggett's .50 caliber Thompson/Center rifle as he takes a shot in the Tennessee woods.

had been walking all morning with the breech of my rifle under my coat trying to keep water away from the nipple. My effort had been successful because the shot fired perfectly. The problem came with the necessity to reload. My ramrod had swelled in the rain and couldn't be removed from the thimbles. Period. End of morning hunt. I had to go back to camp and use pliers to get it out.

Moral of this story? — hunt with fiberglass, brass, well-waxed, varnished or oiled ramrods.

I've often put a small piece of plastic over the nipple and held it in place with rubber bands. Saran Wrap is very good for this. A similar piece over the muzzle, held in place with a rubber band, will protect the charge from inclement weather conditions.

There are several handy items on the market that make it a simple matter to carry extra charges in the field. One of my favorites is the Lizzy-Loader — a plastic tube capped at both ends. One end holds the

Swiggett feels .50 caliber should be the minimum for deer hunting. Here a .22 rimfire bullet lays in the muzzle of a .50 caliber rifle to somewhat show bore size.

147

Anne Snow took an immediate liking to this little Hopkins & Allen "Buggy Deluxe" .45 caliber rifle.

powder charge, the other, the ball and a couple of caps. Half a dozen of these in his pocket and the hunter is set.

Round ball shooters can do little better than a loading block with half a dozen holes into which patched balls are seated ready to be rammed into the muzzle of the rifle. Plastic vials, available from most drug stores, are great powder containers.

I've never been a buckskin and fringe black powder hunter. Neither do I carry a powder horn or bullet bag. My interest is entirely in shooting the guns, not in the fuss and falderal that goes with costuming. When seen in the woods, the only way anyone will know my gun is a muzzle loader will be to look at it. They will never know from my dress or my accoutrements. Powder charges, caps, balls and a nipple wrench with a pick are usually all I carry, and these in coat or vest pockets.

Buckskinners can do their thing as they see fit—it doesn't bother me a bit—so long as they stay downwind.

In my vehicle, or in camp, one will find all sorts of things, such as: extra nipples, another wrench or two, at least one extra ramrod, ball and patch paraphernalia, plus cleaning supplies in quantities far exceeding what is actually needed for the trip.

Be sure to have ball-pulling equipment handy, JUST IN CASE. Charges can be destroyed in all sorts of ways. Grease from patched or lubed Minie's and Maxi's has been known to kill charges, especially in hot weather. Moisture is the most common threat. Then there is always the possibility that the chamber wasn't completely dry before the charge was put in. But, most often, bullet-pulling comes about when a ball is rammed home hurriedly just before it is remembered that no powder charge was loaded.

When this happens, it is often possible to shoot the ball out by removing the nipple and trickling powder into the that tiny hole. Get in all you can then replace the nipple, *shove the ball down as far as it will go,* put on a cap and fire. Usually the ball will come out with this first effort. In case it doesn't, go over the same routine again and again, each time pushing the ball back down as far as it will go before trying to fire. Always make sure the ball is fully seated before *any* shot is fired.

Normally this will remove balls and fouled charges from barrels. If not—pulling is the only other alternative.

Some unload and clean their rifles every night when no shot has been fired. I don't do this. Every precaution is taken before I load to make sure the chamber is clean and dry. I'm a firm believer in lighter fluid for this purpose. Once loaded I only remove the cap when I come in and I have never had a rifle fail to fire when subsequently called upon.

I use Saran Wrap on the nipple and let the hammer down. Saran Wrap is also used over the muzzle.

About that lighter fluid: I wipe the barrel out with a thoroughly soaked patch, usually a couple of them, then I squirt lighter fluid into the bore through the removed nipple hole. Blow through the barrel a few times and the stuff dries almost instantly. When it evaporates the oil is gone and the bore is bone-dry.

I've had my share of hangfires and no-fires, that's for sure, but not under the circumstances mentioned above.

Often I'm asked how I arrive at a specific charge for a given rifle. It's a personal thing, I guess. Every shooter has his own little quirks. First, I want a rifle to crack when it goes off. A dull boom does little for me. Next, I want it to sort of snap back against my shoulder. Black powder never, in sensible loads at least, develops recoil like smokeless powder, but it can head in that direction.

Both of these criteria come about, usually, when proper powder charges are achieved. When seeing a lot of sparks in the smoke directly in front of the muzzle I know I've used too much powder. Then I'll back off a few grains at a time, usually in five grain increments, until only a few sparks are visible. This to me is the best charge for that particular rifle. By then the "crack" is there along with the proper recoil and I know most of the charge is burning in the barrel.

A final thought on muzzle loading rifles for big game: if you feel in any way handicapped while carrying one you should consider taking up some other form of hunting. Only by knowing your rifle well and having confidence in it will you have any chance for a successful hunt. Never, under any circumstances, should you attempt to carry both a centerfire (for those long shots) and a front loader (in case you get close). It doesn't work, and besides, it's often illegal.

A good many states offer special muzzle-loading seasons. Included in this list are: Alabama, Arizona, Arkansas, Colorado, Connecticut, Delaware, Florida, Georgia, Idaho, Kentucky, Maryland, Massachusetts, Michigan, Mississippi, Nebraska, New Hampshire, New Mexico, New York, North Carolina, Ohio, Oklahoma, Oregon, Pennsylvania,

149

This Thompson/Center .50 caliber rifle has taken 19 head of game including the whitetail doe shown here. Seventeen of those with Maxi-balls. This doe and an exotic deer were killed with .490 round balls over 120 grains of FFg.

South Carolina, South Dakota, Utah, Virginia, Washington and Wisconsin.

Most of these restrict hunting to a minimum caliber, usually .44, though a few legalize .40 caliber. Illinois allows the use of .38 caliber as does Mississippi. North Dakota says .36 caliber is o.k. with them and South Carolina goes even lower with .35 caliber legal in that state.

Several other states have legislation pending, so by the time you read this more states might be offering special privileges to hunters carrying front-stuffing rifles.

There are a few other peculiarities worth mentioning. Pennsylvania allows only the use of flint-lock rifles. Colorado, Delaware, Idaho, New Jersey, South Carolina and Virginia say NO TELE-SCOPIC SIGHTS PERMITTED. I disagree with this violently because it discriminates against the middle aged and older hunters along with the hunter wanting to be sure of a clean kill. It takes young eyes to see open sights competently. Hunters beyond that are forced to hunt with a rifle knowing they can't do the job right, or else give up the sport. Neither alternative is desirable.

Just imagine – states allow the use of squirrel rifles for deer, then turn around and bar the one way to be sure of placing that tiny ball in a vital area, at least more sure than with open sights. It proves, once again to this writer, that a man doesn't have to know anything to get a political-patronage job as a state game department official. It's all a matter of being in the right place at the right time.

"This is the trigger," Phil Chase, center, seems to be saying as Chuck Adams, left, and Scott McMillan look over the CVA Mountain Rifle to be used on a deer hunt.

Besides those states offering special seasons, a few others provide special black powder hunting areas during their regular seasons.

I hesitate to encourage anyone to take up black powder hunting for the sake of an extra season. Same goes for archery. To me either is a sport unto itself and should be practiced as such. If sufficient ability can't be achieved to instill confidence in the use of a muzzle loader or bow, then they should be put aside until that plateau has been reached.

Sportsmanship is hard to define except that fairness is the essence of it. This includes being fair to animals. While harvesting is what they were put here for (one has only to go to the first book of the Bible, the book of Genesis, to affirm this) it does not give us the right to cause undue suffering.

Learn to use your choice of hunting medium to the best of your ability, then take shots at whatever range that proven ability justifies, be it muzzleloader, bow, or centerfire rifle.

You will enjoy the hunt more – because you played the game fairly.

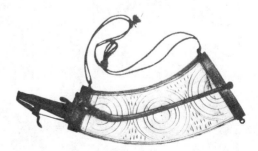

Chapter 13

BOWHUNTING
by Judd Cooney

It wasn't too many years ago that a few dedicated hunters, looking for a way to put more challenge in their hunting, managed to persuade their state game and fish agencies to have a "bow and arrow only" deer season.

These individualists took to the woods with their yew wood bows, cedar arrows and camouflage suits, oftentimes accompanied by the good natured jibes of their gun hunting buddies.

As these early day bowhunters began scoring on game, they intrigued their gun toting companions with stories of the thrills they had in getting that trophy buck and they soon converted more and more of their brethren to the ranks of those bowhunting for deer and other big game.

Today most all states have a special bow and arrow season, and archery hunting is one of the fastest growing outdoor sports in the nation.

For the hunter and outdoorsman who is looking for a way to spend as much time in the woods as he can, bowhunting is a natural. Most of the states offer bow seasons that are very liberal in length and the sportsman can still hunt (in most states) during the rifle season. This two-season hunting allows the ardent sportsman twice the amount of time to enjoy his favorite outdoors pastime.

As deer bowhunting became popular, and more and more hunters were taking up the bow, there were constant improvements being made in the equipment. The hunter in the woods today is far better equipped than was his predecessor of not too many years ago.

Comparing the bowhunter of a dozen years ago with the bowhunter of today, as far as equipment is concerned, would be like comparing the first plane to a modern jet. No longer is the bowhunter carrying a yew wood bow that must be unstrung after each day's hunt to keep it from taking a permanent set, nor is he using mismatched wooden arrows that have a tendency to change point of impact from day to day depending upon the moisture in the air.

The bowhunter of today is more than likely using a compound bow, which uses the mechanical advantage of pulleys and cables as well as superstrong fiberglass and wood laminated limbs. This combination allows the bowhunter to hold less weight at full draw and yet still shoot a heavier bow. This in turn gives the arrow faster flight with a correspondingly flatter trajectory, which results in better overall accuracy.

To match his compound bow, the deer hunter of today is in all probability using aluminum or glass arrows that are warp resistant, straight to within several thousandths of an inch and identical as to weight or spine. Much the same as the rifle's accuracy is determined by the quality of the bullet it shoots, the best bow in the world cannot be made to shoot well with warped, out-of-spine arrows.

Feathers for arrow fletching is another fast fading phenomenon. Today most arrows are being fletched with modern space age plastic fletching called vanes. These plastic vanes give the arrow more consistent flight, are almost wearproof and completely weather resistant.

A small whitetail buck.

Whitetail hunters from South Dakota discussing how a buck gave them the slip by crossing a river.

Another major change in the equipment of the modern day bowhunter is the type of broadheads available. To make a clean kill, a broadhead *must* be RAZOR SHARP, anything less should not be allowed in the woods. Most bowhunters are simply not patient enough to learn the technique of getting a broadhead RAZOR SHARP. By this, I mean a broadhead that will shave you as well as your TRAC II razor does.

Several manufacturers have come to the bowhunter's rescue however, and quite a number of broadheads on the market now come from the factory RAZOR SHARP. Some of these hunting heads, such as the Savora Super S, use razor blade inserts that are disposable and are easily replaced when they get the slightest bit dull. Bear Archery Co. also has brought out their famous Bear Razorhead, presharpened to a razor's edge by the factory. In my opinion this is something that should have been done years ago by all the broadhead manufacturers. No matter what type of broadhead you use for your deer bowhunting, make sure that it is RAZOR SHARP.

Another little innovation that goes along with broadheads and the newer type of shaft materials, is the screw-in adapter. This device allows the bowhunter to change broadheads in a few seconds. No longer must the bowhunter in the field take time to sharpen his broadhead after each shot. With the screw-in adapter, a bowhunter can simply screw out the dull broadhead, screw in a new head (presharpened at home and taped up to protect the edge) and he is ready for another shot. He can also switch from a broadhead to a field point or Judo head or a blunt for small game or "stump" shooting, without any fuss or bother. It is a simple matter to carry a quiver or tube full of shafts with screw-in inserts and a case full of RAZOR SHARP broadheads separately and with no danger. When you are ready for the hunt, simply screw in the broadheads and you are ready to go. The screw-in adapters can be used with all types of shaft materials including wood, so there is no reason to be without them on a deer hunt.

There are so many makes and types of bows and arrows on the market today that it would be impossible to pick the one best combination for each and every deer bowhunter. However, there are a few tips on equipment that might prove helpful to the beginner.

J. E. Jones, Jr., and M. N. McNeill pose with their whitetail bucks.

Author getting arrows out of ethafoam target.

Target and arrows from 40 yards.

Bill Clemens got himself a 16½-inch 8-point whitetail on the Y. O. Ranch near Mountain Home, Texas.

Spotting scopes can be brought into play glassing high country for big muley bucks . . .

. . . but good binoculars are more valuable for this type of hunting.

A bow is a very personal piece of equipment that you must have full confidence in; it must fit you and you alone. A bow of 45–60 lb. pull is sufficient for deer bowhunting, and whether it is a recurve, two-wheel compound or four-wheel compound is strictly a matter of personal choice. Try several different makes of bows and choose the one that you can handle the best and the one that feels and shoots the best for you. Match the arrows to the bow as to length and spine. The next step is to practice with your outfit until you feel confident that you can do a reasonably good job of shooting. Only the experience of actually hunting deer will tell you how good you really are as a bowhunter.

With all the modern equipment, there is one basic ingredient in bowhunting that hasn't changed over the years and that is ... YOU STILL HAVE TO BE A DARN GOOD HUNTER TO GET CLOSE ENOUGH FOR A SHOT.

The bow is different than a rifle, in that a rifle can easily kill a deer at 100, 200 or even 300 yards. With a bow, you are going to have to get closer. Most deer are killed by bowhunters at ranges from 5 to 40 yards and when you get this close to the game you are hunting, you have accomplished something. At these ranges it is the little things that become extremely important to the success or failure of your hunt. Such things as a slight change of wind direction, that at 200 yards wouldn't have made any difference, now sends the deer bounding out of range without a backward glance. A glint of sunlight off a button or uncamouflaged bow does the same thing. A stick or branch cracking underfoot might go unnoticed at rifle ranges, but it will now bring that deer's head up with both ears and eyes glued to you like radar needing only your slightest twitch to put him in full flight.

These are the little things that make bowhunting frustrating and oftentimes seemingly impossible, but they are the same things that make deer bowhunting extremely challenging and rewarding along with making you a better hunter.

Whether armed with a modern compound, aluminum arrows and razorbladed broadheads or an old yew bow with cedar shafts, fletched with turkey feathers and tipped with flint arrowheads, it is going to take a HUNTER to get his game with a bow and arrow.

Although the task of getting close enough to a deer with a bow and arrow, and then actually stick-

Bear compound bow with aluminum arrow shaft and new Bear Razorhead.

Binoculars play an important part in mule deer hunting. Particularly for the hunter seeking big bucks.

Author in high country screwing out dull broadhead and replacing it with a fresh razorsharp one.

Tree stands are a vital part of whitetail hunting and can be used by mule deer bowhunters in some instances.

Author making use of tree during drive for whitetails in South Dakota.

159

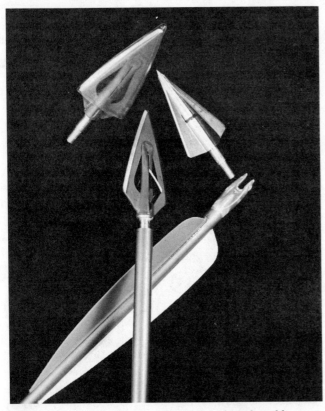

New type Savora Super S. head on left with replaceable razor blade inserts. New Bear Super Razorhead on right and on shaft now comes from factory with blades and insert sharp enough to shave with. Upper arrow shows new type vanes used on most arrows. Heads and shaft also show the screw-in type of head that makes change of heads a simple task.

Safety belt.

ing him in a vital spot, seems impossible, it isn't. Each year there are thousands of deer taken from Maine to Florida, from Texas to the Rockies of Colorado and into the coastal mountains of California and rain forests of Washington.

There are several basic ways of hunting deer with bow and arrow that have stood the test of time and are pretty much the same east or west, north or south.

The most successful method of deer hunting with a bow and arrow is to use a stand, either in a tree or on the ground. Stand hunting requires that the bowhunter make use of his knowledge of the deer's habits. Frequent trips to the field during the off season watching deer feeding, watering or moving between feeding grounds and bedding areas will help determine the best spot to place your stand.

Stands should be placed where the wind is in your favor and so that you are not going to be shooting directly into the sun during the morning or evening hours, nor that the sun be outlining your shape for the deer to pick out. When placing your stand, do so

well in advance of the season and let the deer get familiar with it. Spend some time in the stand just observing the deer and their habits. After all, this is the best part of hunting, getting close to your quarry. Measure distances to various points from your stand and then practice at your home range, shooting from a mock stand at these distances. Do some actual shooting from your stand or blind to make sure that there are no branches or limbs in the way. Prudent trimming may be necessary to give you a clear shot. Every hour spent in preparation for the moment that big buck walks out and stops 10 yards from your blind, will make your chance of sticking him in exactly the right spot that much better.

Not all species of deer are easily hunted from tree stands, however, and there are many areas in the west where a mule deer simply will not come under a tree stand. The muley is a little gun shy of anything above him and will look up without hesitation, whereas a whitetail in most areas will seldom, if ever, look up. The exception to this being South Texas, where the whitetails are constantly hunted

160

A trophy muley buck during late season, the kind that any bowhunter would gladly take, if he could.

from tree blinds or tower blinds. I have had them look at me perched in such a blind and even though they came in, they were watching my every move out of the corner of their eye.

Still-hunting and stalking are my favorite methods of hunting as this is what bowhunting is all about. Still-hunting, contrary to what the word implies, is not standing still, but moving slowly through the hunting area, in search of game. Once the game is spotted, you make your stalk, or if you are close enough when you spot that old buck, you simply shoot without making a stalk.

The key to this type of hunting is to spot the game *before* it spots you. The western U.S. is much better country for this type of hunting, with its canyons and ridges and more open terrain. A good pair of binoculars is essential for this type of hunting, as you are going to be doing lots of looking and little moving if you are to be successful. It is not uncommon to spot a good buck a mile away and then take all day to work within bow range of him. Here you have to plan your stalk with the precision of an army

Winter camouflage is as important as fall for the bow hunter.

The name of the game, getting close for a good shot.

Charles Selsor and his extremely long spike whitetail.

Plenty of backyard practice at varying ranges is essential before going after deer in the field. Note author's target is only a deer silhouette that blends with background making the bowhunter pick his spot on a natural type of target.

general, taking advantage of the wind direction and cover possibilities along your route. It is always a good policy to try to make your final approach from above the deer, if possible, as a deer will seldom bed down looking uphill. This particular method is not as good for hunting whitetails as the "flag tails" inhabit brushier country where visibility is severely limited, making the spotting of deer, first, much tougher. Stalking a muley buck in the alpine valleys of the Rockies, whether you score or not, is an experience that will be long remembered and often told around the hunting fires.

Driving is the next most common method for bowhunting deer, both whitetails and muleys, although it is used much more with whitetails, especially in late season when they move into the brush patches and river bottoms during the winter months.

A thorough knowledge of the country and the habits of the deer in the area are essential to success in this venture. The standers can be spaced along known escape routes, either on the ground or in trees, as the case may be. The most successful method for driving deer that I have found, is for the drivers to actually hunt through an area with the greatest of stealth. An old buck will many times lie in hiding and let a noisy driver move past him as long as he can hear him and keep him pinpointed. In fact, I have seen whitetails, mule deer and elk stay bedded down while a man walked within 100 feet of them. This same old buck, however, will try to sneak out ahead of you if he thinks you are hunting him or if he can't keep track of you in the woods. Driving for mule deer is much the same except that in most cases, where the terrain is up and down, the muley will have a strong tendency to move uphill on the drivers. Standers should pick trails at the heads of the valleys and above the oncoming drivers. A muley is a much easier animal to get a shot at if he is moving uphill toward you, and more than likely, if you are above him, the winds will be in your favor during most of the day.

Whether you choose to hunt mule deer, whitetails or blacktails with a bow and arrow, or whether you hunt from a tree blind, stalk your buck or drive him, you are going to get your money's worth, you can bet on that. The thrill and challenge of hunting with the bow and arrow for deer is one that will make you a better hunter and give you a whole different outlook on the sport of hunting.

Chapter 14

HANDGUNS

Short guns, those designed to be shot with one hand but usually held firmly by both when game shooting, are the most demanding of all hunting firearms. I say this without reservation.

More practice, more perserverance and far greater discipline are the trademarks of every successful handgun hunter. It is not only unsportsmanlike and unethical for the unpracticed to squeeze the trigger on a game animal; it amounts to an almost criminal situation, in this writer's opinion. Crippled animals, as a rule, die within a few days; some within hours; few, very few, where they can be found by the hunter. Thus, they are wasted. To me this is criminal negligence.

Handguns demand more perserverance than shoulder arms because it takes down-right stick-to-it-ness to practice long hours, then hold back when shots are uncertain. Which brings out the self-discipline: only by having this trait will anyone truly become a successful handgun hunter.

Luck will take care of a few. But only a few. It certainly cannot be depended upon.

Handgun hunters are a special breed. It seems to me they are sometimes a bit calmer, a bit more sure of themselves, yes, maybe even a bit superior on occasion. Not that they should be, but somehow gaining sufficient ability to go afield with only six or eight inches of barrel spewing out a bullet that, at best is minimal for the job at hand, lends them an aura of self-confidence.

Some long gun hunters get carried away with advertising and the words of a few inexperienced writers. They know their rifles will kill "way-out-yonder" because they saw it printed in ads or in some amateurish article. Most, without sufficient practice, place their faith totally in the capabilities of their rifles and often shoot when hits, if taking place at all, are sheer luck.

Handgunners are guilty on occasion, too, but not as often. Having studied calibers, bullets, velocities, muzzle energies and drop tables galore, even the rankest of handgun hunters knows the capability of his gun is limited to only a fraction of what a rifle can do. He also knows his chances of a good hit are a lot slimmer under identical conditions. As a result he has disciplined himself to get closer and wait for near certain shots. Since nothing on the face of this earth is certain except death and taxes he can only shoot when he feels there is a better chance for a hit than a miss. Even then there will be misses, unfortunately.

There is a good deal of erroneous information printed on handguns and game. In spite of what some would have us believe, light calibers are not big game killers. Bullets have to get inside game to be effective. It can't be done from the outside. Neither can it be done with the shock from a handgun. There is no way sufficient velocity can be obtained to produce a kill from the shock of a handgun bullet hitting flesh.

There are those who feel the .357 magnum is a good deer cartridge. It is certainly the minimum to be considered. It is adequate, in some instances, even in this writer's eyes. My home state of Texas

Though factory loaded .45 Colt cartridges aren't up to hunting big game handloaders can bring them mighty close in this new Model 25-5 from Smith & Wesson. While it will never equal .44 magnum potential deer-sized game would never know the difference.

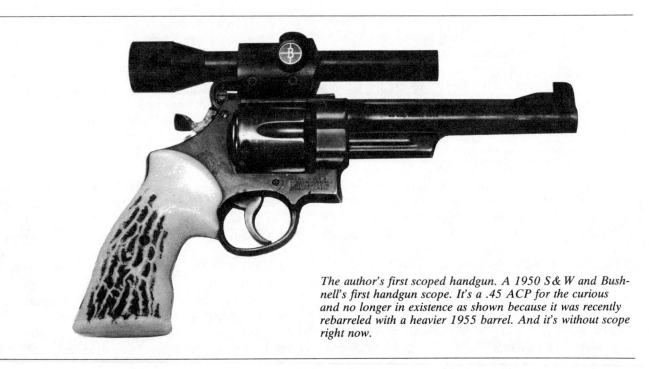

The author's first scoped handgun. A 1950 S&W and Bush-nell's first handgun scope. It's a .45 ACP for the curious and no longer in existence as shown because it was recently rebarreled with a heavier 1955 barrel. And it's without scope right now.

A typical Hill Country 8-point buck.
The author dropped this whitetail with a customized Ruger Super Blackhawk .44 magnum.

produces whitetails hard-pressed to weigh 100 pounds on the hoof over most of the state. At sensible ranges the .357 is a good whitetail killer where animals of this weight are the consideration.

I will never concede that the .357 magnum is adequate where any game animal weighs more than 100 pounds on the hoof, live weight.

Though the deer are small the bullet still has to get inside. Light, fast, bullets expand, which keeps them from getting in very deep. Bullets of the 110–125 grain weight offer impressive figures on ballistics charts but, unfortunately, few game animals are killed with printer's ink.

Most handgun hunters are handloaders, but for the sake of numbers let's quote a few factory statistics: an average factory-listed velocity for a 158 grain projectile fired from a .357 magnum revolver runs about 1,550 fps. Using a test barrel, of course. Firing this same cartridge in a revolver reduces it to more like 1,235 fps. Producing a muzzle energy of about 550 ft./lbs. Doesn't sound so bad does it? . . .

not until those figures are compared with those produced by rifles of proven killing power where deer-sized game is concerned. Rifles such as the .32-20 Winchester listed at 645 ft./lbs.; the .32-40 listed at 760 ft./lbs.; the .38-40 at 705 ft./lbs.; the .38-55 at 985 ft./lbs. and the .44-40 Winchester at 760 ft./lbs.

All of these rifles have killed a lot of deer but every one has been replaced over the years because they were felt to be inadequate for the job. Yet all are more efficient than the .357 magnum! How can I say more!

If the hunter who feels he has to use a .357 magnum for his deer hunting, will practice self-discipline to the point where no shots are taken at more than 50–60 yards, licenses would be filled with relative ease, especially on small whitetails. In fact, I'd go so far as to say *only* on small whitetails. Mule deer will weigh anywhere from 125 pounds to near 300 on occasion. Big whitetails will weigh every bit as much and occasionally more. These animals are

*The Auto-Mag –
the finest to be had for the
handgunner wanting to use an
autoloader for his hunting.*

not fair game for the .357 magnum so far as I'm concerned. Under closely controlled conditions, with shots under 50 yards, and with bullets directed into the heart or lungs, venison will be taken. This I will concede.

I will skip over the .41 magnum because I have no practical experience with it in the field. Ballistically it is far superior to the .357 and should be a fine hunting cartridge. My reason for avoiding it is purely personal. Anything the .41 caliber bullet can do, a .44 caliber bullet can do better – in my opinion. Except for bullet diameter the .41 magnum should rank close to fully-loaded .44 Specials in killing power. And that is certainly adequate for deer hunting. Bullets are lighter, naturally, so it might be harder to get them through muscle and bone. I admit to no experience with this caliber.

The .44 magnum was introduced in 1955 and touted as "the most powerful handgun in the world". Immediately great things were accomplished with it, many on the order of stunts, most in

Swiggett's big Auto-Mag rides comfortably in Bianchi's shoulder holster.

One of the author's favorite rests is the hood of his pickup.

fact. It has cost the handgun hunting fraternity more aficionados than any other single thing. Of that I am convinced. Inexperienced shooters, some never having owned a handgun before, thought immediate success was to be theirs by simply owning and shooting the powerful .44 magnum at game.

Some of those guns were fired only once, a few two or three times; a few more – a whole cylinder full. The nerve-shattering, arm-wrenching, teeth-rattling recoil soon separated the would-be's from the want-to-be's. The would-be's put their big revolver on the shelf and practiced with smaller guns and or lighter loads through handloading, until they could again take on the big wrist-cracking behemoth. These were the people who became handgun hunters.

Those want-to-be's stopped by the sporting goods store on the way in from the range and sold their guns for a fraction of what they had paid for them, sometimes only hours later.

These are the handgun hunters we lost.

Obviously, the .44 magnum is only a blessing to those making the effort to handle such power, effort that comes with long hours of practice and the firing of hundreds and hundreds of rounds; fully-loaded rounds, not pip-squeak loads barely coming up to factory .44 Special figures as is often seen at public ranges where the shooter rares back and says, with his actions, "see me, I'm shooting a .44 magnum." He is only fooling himself and those other inexperienced shooters around him.

I like the big gun. In fact, I own several. To be truthfully blunt, I don't think anything smaller is worth carrying.

The big .44 Auto-Mag is truly a worthwhile hunting handgun, as is the .357 Auto-Mag for that matter. The smaller bored one is sufficiently more potent than the .357 magnum as to make it downright devastating on game. Both are fine long range hunting handguns.

So far as ballistics are concerned I find the Auto-Mag a little more potent than the .44 magnum.

169

Swiggett's first T/C .30-30 pistol. This handgun has taken more head of game than would be believed if mentioned, but it recently earned retirement. Hal got himself a newer Bull Barrel in the same caliber and put this one away, scope and all.

Thompson/Center's Contender single shot pistol is the easiest to scope and often turns out rifle-like accuracy. This is an old favorite of the author – T/C's newer scopes are called Lobo.

Thompson/Center Super "14" – designed for the silhouette shooter it should serve superbly for the handgun hunter. This one is chambered for the powerful .35 Remington cartridge.

It's main claim to fame is its ability to digest such potent loads in a semi-automatic action.

There are a few others worthy of note: Thompson/Center's great single shot pistol, the Contender, is chambered for several rifle cartridges making it a top "contender" in any handgun hunting situation. Specifically I'm referring to their .30-30 Winchester and .25-35 Winchester chamberings. A pair of wildcats, the .30 Herrett and .357 Herrett might be considered as well. This writer can't get very fired up over the .30 Herrett, because it is simply a bit faster than the .30 carbine round, which we all know has been proven useless throughout the world as either a game killer or man killer. In fact, most states have it outlawed for big game hunting; the .30 carbine I mean, not the .30 Herrett.

The .30 Herrett moves the same little 110 grain bullet, ballistically the worst in the .30 caliber line, at some 300 or so feet per second more than the .30 carbine. Let your conscience be your guide. I've found the standard .30-30 chambering far more efficient because it takes more powder and can use heavier bullets. The .30-30 Winchester in a T/C barrel loaded to maximum with a fast burning powder under Speer's 130 grain hollow pointed bullet will do deadly things to deer out to 150 yards, almost equal to a rifle.

At this writing Thompson/Center has just released a heavy bull barrel that is 14 inches long and chambered for the .35 Remington cartridge, probably with silhouette shooters in mind. However, I can't imagine they would care a bit if one of us hunters ordered a barrel and decked a few head of big game with it, a feat well within the .35 Remington's capabilities.

In essence, this is close to the .357 Herrett, but with a factory cartridge and heavier bullets. Both Herrett wildcats are off-spring of the .30-30 Winchester. Steve shortened the case, changed the shoulder and made himself a .30 and .35 cartridge. The only fault with the .357 Herrett is in having to make the cases, it's a laborious job at best.

Then, of course, the T/C is chambered for the usual handgun cartridges with the .44 magnum and .45 Colt best suited to big game hunting. There are others, a few at any rate, that could be considered, but basically it's a sport for the .357 magnum, .357 Herrett, .357 Auto-Mag, .41 magnum, .44 magnum, .44 Auto-Mag, .30-30 Winchester or .35 Remington.

There is one special "oldie" worthy of note: the ancient .45 Colt will take a lot of game with good

Another of the author's favorite hunting handguns – his Thompson/Center Contender chambered for the popular .30-30 Winchester cartridge and topped with Leupold's fine 2 X long-eye-relief scope. Conetrol mounts hold the two together.

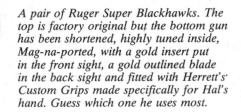

A pair of Ruger Super Blackhawks. The top is factory original but the bottom gun has been shortened, highly tuned inside, Mag-na-ported, with a gold insert put in the front sight, a gold outlined blade in the back sight and fitted with Herrett's Custom Grips made specifically for Hal's hand. Guess which one he uses most.

Hunting chores not calling for those longer shots made easier with scopes are usually handled by one of three revolvers – the customized Super Blackhawk shown above, the Model 29 S&W at the left or the Virginian Dragoon below. All are .44 magnum. All are favorites of the author.

Colonel Jack Cannon's Deadeye Pistol Stock is a right handy gadget for the handgunning hunter. Perfectly legal since it does not attach to the gun it provides almost rifle-like steadiness for the shot.

handloads. In modern handguns. Even a Colt single action of late manufacture can be safely loaded to close to 1,000 fps with 250–255 grain bullets. Ruger Blackhawks are a different breed. They can be safely loaded to 1,200 fps without danger to the gun or the shooter. Nearing .44 magnum potential they have the added blessing of the slightly larger diameter bullet. Not at all a bad way to go, particularly if you already own a .45 Colt-chambered Ruger or T/C barrel.

We won't get into specific loads here because there are numerous good handbooks on the market supplying more information than could be included here at best. Speer, Hornady, Lyman and Hodgdon might be named as the most popular. All are reliable if used as printed. None are reliable if you decide you know more than they do. By this I mean if

you go by the book, you will not run into any trouble. If you decide you can better their efforts by switching primers, amounts of powder and bullet weights, then you are on your own and may God help you every inch of the way.

Over the years I've found handguns more than adequate for deer hunting. I'm not a long range shooter with rifles, by choice, so have no trouble waiting for close shots with handguns. I've always been a lung shooter which is where handgun bullets should be placed. Unless I'm confident there is a better chance for a hit than a miss my trigger never gets squeezed. This again fits perfectly with handgun hunting. Common sense is probably the best word for it.

Of the 48 states, 23 list handguns specifically as legal hunting guns for big game – deer, so far as we

173

Bill Richardson, the pro-gunner politician from California, is an Auto-Mag fan. Bill shoots the .44 AMP.

Mag-na-porting a handgun helps hold back in the recoil department but more importantly, to the author, it helps hold the muzzle down for faster second shots. Here the port can be seen alongside the front sight. There is another on the other side.

are concerned. Some restrict the choice of guns by naming calibers; others, anything above a certain caliber, usually .357 magnum, is legal. Some won't allow handguns to be used under any circumstances, yet approve muzzle loaders and archery. Since handguns are at least equally effective as muzzle loaders, and considerably more effective than bows and arrows, this is hard to understand, but that's the way it is.

Specifically, Alabama legalizes handguns for hunting with no mention of caliber, only that a permit to carry is necessary. Arizona says .357 magnum or larger is o. k. for big game and smaller calibers receive their blessing for small game, nongame and predators. California allows the use of the .357, .41 and .44 magnum on bears and hogs but not other big game. Florida says we can use any centerfire handgun for big game. Idaho gives us blanket authority to hunt the game of our choice with handguns. Kentucky simply says, "Certain handguns permitted for deer."

Louisiana makes it easy. They say it the way we like to see it printed: "Handguns permitted for hunting." Same deal in Maine. They say, "Handgun permitted for hunting big and small game, predators and unprotected wildlife." Maryland allows the use of .44 magnum handguns wherever rifles are legal. Michigan posts a confusing situation by stating, "Handguns may be used for small game and deer except prohibited in southern Michigan during deer season." I take this to mean we are legal only in northern Michigan.

A true negative note is sounded in Minnesota where the law reads, "Handguns not legal for hunting any protected wild animal, including finishing shots." Mississippi legalizes us across the board. Missouri allows "Pistol or revolver not smaller than .357 magnum." Montana makes no restrictions on handguns. Nebraska specifies legal calibers as .44 magnum, .41 magnum, .357 magnum and .44 Special with Keith magnum handloads.

New Hampshire allows the use of handguns for big game hunting wherever rifles are allowed. New Mexico says the use of .357 magnum, .41 magnum and .44 magnum is o.k. with them. New York allows any centerfire handgun where rifles are permitted. Oklahoma lists centerfire handguns as legal so long as the barrel is at least 3½-inches in length and the soft-nosed bullet of at least 75 grains delivers a minimum of 500 ft./lbs. of muzzle energy.

Pennsylvania outlaws semi-automatic pistols. Revolvers or single shot pistols are legal. Rhode Island has no law against hunting with handguns, but they negate their generosity by their restrictive handgun-carrying attitude. South Carolina allows handguns in game management areas only. Tennessee says at least four inches of barrel is needed on .357, .41 and .44 magnums.

Utah allows the use of .357 magnum or larger. Wyoming legalizes handguns in a somewhat restrictive manner by stating, "Handguns that meet rifle specifications may be used, but going by the cartridge length requirement, most handguns are disqualified." Under rifles it reads, "at least .23 caliber and chambered for centerfire cartridges not less than two inches long overall, including soft or expanding bullet normally seated." This would allow the .25-35 Thompson/Center barrel along with the .30-30 and the .35 Remington. The .30 Herrett and .357 Herrett might sneak by with careful bullet seating.

Handguns can be used for all sorts of things. On a South Texas deer hunt Dr. Gerald Swiggett was using a rifle — but had his .38 Spl handily tucked in his trouser waist. Note the headless rattler. High performance 110 grain factory ammo did the trick.

175

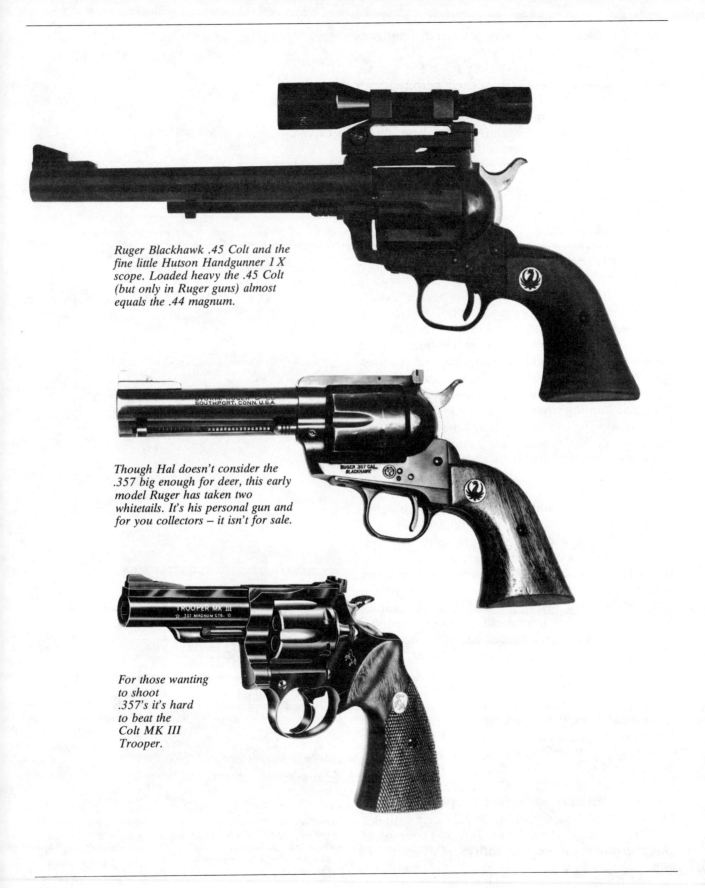

Ruger Blackhawk .45 Colt and the fine little Hutson Handgunner 1 X scope. Loaded heavy the .45 Colt (but only in Ruger guns) almost equals the .44 magnum.

Though Hal doesn't consider the .357 big enough for deer, this early model Ruger has taken two whitetails. It's his personal gun and for you collectors – it isn't for sale.

For those wanting to shoot .357's it's hard to beat the Colt MK III Trooper.

Clyde Fischer believes in using rests for handgun hunting. Wherever they can be found.

Alaska allows the use of any centerfire cartridge in handguns and Canada prohibits handguns entirely.

There are a good many states allowing the use of handguns on small game, non-game and predators, so more may be added to this list as time goes on, particularly if local hunting groups get behind the action. Those allowing handguns for some forms of hunting should be receptive to big game hunting with proper guns if the idea is presented in a logical and forthright manner.

Not listed in those 23 states legalizing handguns for deer is the Lone Star state of Texas. The regulation on firearms reads: "limited to rifles, shotguns and other legal firearms". In checking with a game warden this writer was told any handgun shooting centerfire ammunition was legal for deer in Texas anywhere the hunter had a legal right to be. Ex-

plaining his statement, the warden cited an example: if a hunter trespasses and kills a deer with a handgun he can be arrested for illegally carrying a handgun along with killing the deer illegally since he was on property he had no right to be on. This could be a confusing statute and one that should be cleared by regulation. Handguns are permitted for hunting in Texas or many of us have been breaking the law for years and most of us do it within eyeball range of wardens with regularity.

There may be other states in this same category so, even if your state doesn't list the handgun as legal for hunting, it might be a good idea to check it out with your local game warden, unless they are specifically mentioned as being illegal.

Handloaders are at their best in hunting situations. They have at their disposal a greater variety of bullets and velocities thereby obtaining the very

Bill Jordan of handgun exhibition shooting and Shooting-Editor-fame tries a few shots with Swiggett's .357 Auto-Mag.

best the handgun will produce by way of accuracy and killing potential. Sometimes accuracy gives way a bit for the sake of velocity (that which produces muzzle energy), but a super accurate load barely reaching the target would prove useless.

Even though I mentioned earlier that we would not get into details, so far as handloading is concerned, I feel called upon to list a few favored loads that have served me well over many hunts. All of these are *MAXIMUM* and should *not be LOADED* for your particular handgun until they have been approached from below and proven o. k.

Though I've not killed any game with the .30 Herrett, mine shoots well with 22.5 grains of either H110 or 296. The latter powder produces a bit more velocity, but the former seems to be more accurate in my barrel. Use only 110 grain jacketed bullets over these charges.

My .30-30 T/C barrel likes 27.5 grains of 4198 under a 150 grain jacketed bullet or one grain more under my favorite, the 130 grain Speer H.P.

Revolvers chambered for the .357 magnum round are loaded with 18 grains of 296 under a 146 grain jacketed bullet. If you shoot either 158 or 160 grain bullets reduce the charge by one grain.

The .357 Auto-Mag likes 137–140 grain bullets and can produce about 300 fps more than the standard .357 magnum. I've found 296 a good powder and like 23.5 grains.

I've been shooting a .44 magnum since shortly after it made its debut and as far back as I can remember my load has been 23.5 grains of H110 under a 240 grain jacketed bullet. It's hot but I haven't damaged any handguns with it yet and it has dropped a lot of game.

I use this same charge in the .44 Auto-Mag with the same bullet.

The .45 ACP is not a hunting handgun but with either Remington or Federal 185 grain h.p.'s in factory loads it will do an adequate job out to 50 yards or so on the smaller whitetail deer. Handloaders can also work over their guns and shoot Keith-type bullets to good advantage. A 250 grain bullet over 6.8 to 7 grains of Unique does a great job. I wouldn't recommend this as a steady diet for any Colt autoloader but a hunting gun it will make.

New Colt revolvers chambered for the .45 Colt cartridge, sometimes mistakenly referred to as the .45 Long Colt, can, if the gun is in good shape, go to 10 grains of Unique under a 250 grain cast bullet. *Do not try this in an old black powder-numbered single action.* This is a stout load and neither this author, nor the publisher, stands responsible should you try it. Two New Frontier Colt's with 7½-inch barrels owned by the author have digested hundreds, no thousands, of rounds and are still in one piece.

Ruger revolvers are stronger and can be loaded up a bit heavier as can the great Thompson/Center Contender. A .45 Colt chambering for these guns can go to the 225 grain jacketed h.p. bullet over 26.5 grains of 296 or 19 grains of 2400 and do right well.

If you are not an experienced handloader, take these loads with a grain of salt. If you are, you will know they have to be worked up to very carefully. What one gun can safely stand might take another apart without bothering with the seams.

Care is the watchword when handloading, *always*. With maximum charges it is imperative that they be approached slowly and with deliberation.

If you hanker to handgun deer get yourself a good revolver or single shot pistol — or semi-automatic, should you like the Auto-Mag — and learn to shoot it. Start off with light loads and gradually work up to full charges. In the case of .357 magnums, shoot .38 Specials until familiar with the gun. Shooters starting with the .44 magnum should shoot .44 Specials at first.

The important thing is to learn to control the gun and hit what you are shooting at. Once that is accomplished then, and only then, should full loads be tried.

Hunting with handguns is most rewarding, especially to this writer. It might prove to be the same in your case. The only way you will ever find out is to give it a try.

Not all hunting handguns are big. This little .22 derringer has put the finishing touch to several bucks over the years. Sure beats using a knife.

Chapter 15

SHOTGUNS

This is the hardest chapter in the book for me to write. I detest the use of shotguns on a fine animal like a deer... bordering on criminal, to my way of thinking.

Unfortunately, several states demand the use of the smooth bored barrel for deer hunting. Safety measures, ostensibly, since obviously their range isn't nearly so great. A few states not demanding shotgun use sanction such goings on. Between the two, shotguns have forced their way into this book.

Using rifled slugs makes the most sense. Accuracy is a sometimes thing, compared to rifles, but is of sufficient quality to make the killing of a deer possible at 75 yards or even up to 100 yards in some cases.

Better suited to 50 yard shooting in most instances, slugs are definitely devastating at that distance. Weighing 7/8-ounce, that's 383 grains, the 12 gauge shoves out a chunk of lead almost equal to that of a .45-70 rifle in weight, but considerably larger in diameter.

Older versions of slug shells were marketed at 1-ounce per slug, but current Remington and Winchester catalogs list them at the 7/8-ounce figure. Moving at a muzzle velocity of 1,600 fps it outdoes the .45-70 which starts at 1,330 fps. At 50 yards the 12 gauge slug hits with 1,175 ft./lbs. of energy while the .45-70 thumps its target with about 1,400 ft./lbs. of authority. Considering the greater diameter of the 12 gauge slug I'd have to vote for it as the most deadly of the two at this distance. Because of its ballistically more efficient bullet the .45-70 gains

favor as distance increases, and the shotgun slug drops out of the picture rather quickly. Understand the heavy centerfire rifle bullet of the .45-70 could never be classified as having long range potential under any set of circumstances.

Sixteen gauge slugs weigh 4/5-ounce, 350 grains, and they reach that 50 yard target with 1,075 ft./lbs. of force. Enough to put any deer down.

Smaller gauges, the 20 for instance at 5/8-ounce (273 grains) and the miniscule .410 bore at 1/5-ounce (87.5 grains) should not be used on big game of any sort.

Most of the major builders of shotguns, stateside at least, market a Deer Gun in either semi-automatic or pump action. Normally with 22-inch barrels for the self-shuckers and 20-inch tubes on slide actions. All seem to be choked improved cylinder so this must be the industry favorite as best suited to slugs. It also tells us that when using other shotguns for this sort of shooting open choked barrels should be the choice wherever possible.

Deer guns as currently marketed wear traditional rifle sights, both front and rear, and usually of an adjustable nature to assure sighting-in to a specific point of impact.

These guns are described in factory literature as being for rifled slugs or buckshot which points out something I've always felt, but haven't tested enough to prove. Open choked barrels seem to pattern buckshot better than those with more constricted muzzles. It makes sense that they should, since less damage to each pellet would be in store

Soon as the doe steps out of the way this young buck becomes venison for the lucky shotgunner.

If a shotgun loaded with buckshot was ever a necessity it would probably be in a situation such as this.

Deer close to the gun are ideal targets for buckshot from an open-bored shotgun.

A deer in cover this thick could easily be a shotgun target – with buckshot.

for those emerging from the lesser choke. It's those deformed pellets that fly off into the outer reaches of someplace that cause poor patterns.

Weaver Scopes jumped on the mechanical advantage of Remington's Model 1100 autoloader and 870 pump guns by developing a scope mount that installs by simply replacing two pins with two machine screws. This makes it possible to use scopes which definitely adds to the deerkilling potential of the slug gun.

Sights of several types are available for installation on shotguns. Most are make-do at best but all are better than nothing. Without a rear sight, slug shooting is a guessing game, not one in which any sportsman would want to take part.

I have never killed a native deer with slug or buckshot. I did shoot one exotic deer, in the interest of science, and was not impressed with the results. Using 00 buckshot in a 12 gauge, four of the nine pellet load hit the animal. Two were in the kill area. This at 45 yards. I finished the deer with a single shot from my everpresent .44 magnum and vowed never again to use buckshot on game.

Targets, some 200 set at distances of 15 to 60 yards, with six shotguns choked from improved cylinder to full convinced me that 40 yards should be tops in distance for deer hunting with 00 buck. Twenty five to 30 yards seemed very deadly. Beyond that every yard took its toll. I ran these tests for this book – long after the above-mentioned deer killing episode.

I know there are those who will disagree with my thinking and they are clearly within their rights. I stick to facts as I see them, letting my comments fall where they will.

Short magnum shells contain 12–00 pellets. The 2³/₄-inch version. Three-inch magnums gain three more pellets for a 15 count. Based on the tests I made it would seem each might be good for five yards over the lesser load. Should this check out, it is possible 3-inch magnums might be good to 50 yards. Only your own tests will verify this one way or the other. The increased number of pellets should take care of the additional yardage.

I once had a man tell me, with a straight face, how his old Model 97 Winchester full-choked shotgun would put all nine pellets from a 00 buck shell in a deer's chest at 100 yards. Not being prone to embarrass a man unnecessarily, I never asked him to show me.

Another fellow, a military man, flatly told me any good shotgun would put all nine 00 pellets in a foot circle at 60 yards. I never asked him to prove it either.

I'm not certain, but I believe if I were forced to shoot deer with a shotgun I'd indelibly impress a 25-yard distance into my shooting eye and stuff my 12-gauge shotgun with a couple of shells filled with Number 4 Buck. There are 27 of these little dudes in a standard 12 gauge shell. They measure .24" in diameter and weigh approximately 20.5 grains each as opposed to .33" diameter for   00 buck at 54 grains per pellet.

With three times as many pellets per shell it stands to reason three times as many should hit the target. Multiple hits, in my opinion, will accomplish more insofar as killing power is concerned. The deer might not be any deader hit with 15 to 18 #4 buck, as opposed to five or six 00 buck, but my guess is he would be at least as dead. And with more certainty because of the advantage of more pellets hitting kill areas. And at short range penetration would be sufficient for the job at hand.

It has been proven, by police tests, that #4 buck is more deadly on human beings than 00. Distance would have to be a factor here. If shots are going to be at extreme range such as 50 yards or even more I'd have to vote for the heavier pellets for the sake

Using his 12 gauge autoloader and 00 buck this hunter bagged a fine heavy, high-horned, whitetail.

of penetration. On the other hand, I can't recommend buckshot for this distance so don't have to make that concession.

Things to avoid when shooting slugs: full or tight choked barrels (slugs won't hurt the gun but they won't, as a rule, shoot with any accuracy), double-barreled guns (because they are set to crossfire at about 40 yards) and any shotgun without sights (that front bead doesn't count – there must be a rear sight with it to know where the thing is going to hit).

Let me bow out of this with the advice that, should you live where shotguns are mandatory for deer hunting, pattern buckshot loads carefully to determine exactly how many yards you can cover to be sure of at least five pellets hitting the deer. This with 00 buck. Out of these five hopefully two or three will get into vital areas to kill your animal. Beyond this specific yardage hold your fire.

If shooting slugs put some sort of rear sight on your shotgun and sight it in to hit the point of aim at 50 yards. Should your smoothbore print good groups this might be increased to 75 yards, but not unless all those slugs are staying within 4–5 inches at the first distance. Any group larger than 7 to 8 inches is the extreme distance for shooting at game, in this writer's opinion. This, coupled with human error, could cause more cripples than kills.

Of course the ideal shotgun/deer situation would be similar to an incident witnessed by a long-time friend: he and another fellow were hunting squirrels, loaded with # 6 shot in 12 gauge pump shotguns. Deer season was open. A buck, an 8-pointer, casually sauntered past the squirrel hunter sitting at the base of a tree. And was dropped in his tracks with a charge of squirrel shot. At 12 yards.

But most of us aren't that lucky.

185

Chapter 16

RIFLES

I've heard it said there is no perfect rifle, one that can be used for any and all purposes. When this term is used I assume the reference is to caliber rather than the rifle itself. I realize there are mighty strong feelings about the country as to what is best in types of actions, as well as calibers, but I'm still not convinced the one-rifle-one-caliber-man can't take care of himself under any hunting situation he might be confronted with on this continent.

But let us not fret about that at the moment.

Probably the most publicized, most talked about, and most used of all rifles and calibers is the lever action Winchester .30-30. The first smokeless powder sporting round offered was announced in 1895 and introduced in the Model 94 Winchester. The original loading was with a 165 grain bullet over 30 grains of powder producing a muzzle velocity of 1,970 feet per second (fps).

In the 85 years of its existence it has grown to a 170 grain bullet (the one that really made it famous) at a bit over 2,200 fps and producing more than 1,800 ft./lbs. of muzzle energy.

Though out-moded it still ranks high as a deer killer. Many swear by it. Many swear at it. To most, it is the cartridge used as a basis for comparison with all others.

I find the .30-30 at least adequate for deer hunting out to 150 yards provided the 170 grain bullet is used. Lighter offerings are neither fish nor fowl since sufficient velocity can't be achieved to take advantage of a lighter missile in the form of sure expansion. With this range limitation it can hardly be classed as a mule deer cartridge though many a buck has been dropped with a .30-30 bullet. Here, success is determined by the hunter more than the cartridge. A good hunter can perform feats far beyond those most of us should attempt.

Any caliber bullet, properly placed, will drop the biggest deer in the woods. The reason for heavier and faster bullets, in most cases, is to try and make up for bad shooting.

That doesn't look so good when put on paper, does it? But it is the truth. And we all know it.

Deer aren't big animals nor do they have tough skin or heavy muscles. It doesn't take a tank crippler to put one down. Which sets me up for criticism time and time again, but I'll stick to my guns by repeating again, as I have so often before in magazine articles, magnums are not necessary to kill deer.

Magnumitis hit this country some years back through the efforts of Madison Avenue. Advertising men went to work convincing the shooting public deer have become tougher and that more powerful cartridges were now needed to kill them. Their game is to sell new guns. Mine is to be honest. I've often felt two fields of endeavor would be mighty near impossible for a truly honest man. One is advertising and the other, the legal profession.

It takes a minimum of 1000 ft./lbs. of energy to kill a deer dependably. Much less will do it, true, but to be certain, a bullet bearing this much authority, properly placed, will do away with the need to chase a cripple in all but the exceptional

A heavy-barreled Remington Model 700 .25–06 with a high powered 8 X Weaver scope. Ideally a long range varmint rig this rifle would do well on a deer hunt where shots could be at 300 yards.

case. To meet this criteria we can start with the little .243 Winchester and 100 grain bullets.

I'm of the opinion nothing less than .24 caliber should be used on deer, nor should the bullet weigh less than 100 grains.

Now, back to that .243 Winchester. With a factory listing of 2,960 fps and a muzzle energy of 1,945 ft./lbs. it conforms to my standards for an adequate deer rifle. I say adequate because from personal experience I feel better about 200 to 250 yard deer with this cartridge. Same goes for the 6 mm Remington. Both are popular but both are also borderline so far as I'm concerned. Lots of deer are killed with them each year but, unfortunately, lots of deer also get away with a .24 caliber hole punched through them.

Part of the problem is bullets. After all, it takes velocity to make them expand. Any bullet showing good expansion at 2,000 fps might come apart at 3,000 fps, or more, on game close to the muzzle. One of the folks I envy least in this gun business is the bullet designer. There is no way he can win. For example, larger caliber bullets kill better at longer ranges simply through their bigger diameter. Without expanding they produce a wound channel comparable to expanding .24 and .25 caliber bullets. Also, their added weight makes penetration more efficient thereby making the kill more certain.

Next in line are the .25's such as the somewhat new .25-06 Remington and the oldtimers in .250 Savage and .257 Roberts. Both of these oldies are great deer cartridges as is, of course, the newer .25-06. With bullets of 120 grains this newcomer

One of Swiggett's favorites for long range shooting. The Savage Model 112 single shot in .25-06 caliber with a 10X Weaver scope. Actually it is a varmint rifle and far too heavy to carry on a deer hunt but if hunting from a vehicle or stand it will get the job done "way out there."

will take deer easily out to 300 yards. The .250 Savage is a fine 200 yard outfit and the .257 Roberts, with 117–120 grain bullets can be stretched to 300 yards.

In the .26's there isn't much really popular at the moment, but those purchasing a used 6.5 Remington Magnum will find themselves owning a mighty fine deer caliber. Though called "magnum" it performs almost identically to the proven .270 Winchester with a 10 grain lighter bullet. It is a fine 300 yard deer bagger.

Many like the .264 Winchester Magnum. Used with 140 grain bullets it does a fine job though it is considerably more powerful than necessary on shots of less than 200 yards. If any modern caliber is a 400 yard deer killer, this would be it – along with

the 7 mm Remington Magnum. But more about that later.

One of the most popular of all-time cartridges, and rightfully so, is the .270 Winchester. It has taken everything from jack rabbits and ground squirrels to moose and enormous brown, grizzly and polar bear. I have to class it, with the 130 grain bullet that made it famous, as a perfect deer cartridge. Out to 400 yards or a bit farther it performs beautifully. What more does any deer hunter need? The bullet diameter here is .277, for those interested.

Moving up to .284 diameter bullets we get to the famous, or maybe it should be "infamous," 7 mm Remington Magnum which is overpowerful for any deer that ever walked on this earth. There is no way I can recommend it for such use, except for the

Dick Dietz shows Remington's Model 788 bolt action rifle. This is their least expensive line and it's available in several deer hunting calibers.

A beautifully made Dumoulin .243 Win. rifle. Many feel this caliber optimum for deer. The author feels it is minimum and only adequate in near ideal situations.

Swiggett instantly became very fond of the tiny Remington Model 600 when it was announced. He owns three. This one is the .308 Win. The short 18½-inch barrel makes for a fast-handling deer rifle and the caliber is suited to whatever reasonable distance a shot might demand.

Mike Walker, a bench rest shooter of note, sights in his Remington Model 700 7 mm Rem. Mag. for a mule deer hunt. Note the position of Mike's hand under the forend. He says this helps in getting the rifle to print the same from the bench as from offhand or sitting. The reason, the rifle is being held the same way – just gaining support from the bench.

Scopes make the difference in killing shots according to the author. Here the rifle is an Interarms Mark X and the scope is Bushnell's 3x-9x held on with Weaver mounts.

hunter insistant on 500 yard shots. But you can't have your cake and eat it, too. Closer than a couple of hundred yards and your venison will be pre-chewed.

The .280 Remington is a true 7 mm using .284 bullets and it is a fine cartridge tho it never made the grade in popularity. If you come across one at a good price don't shy away because you haven't heard of it. You have now and it's a good one. As is the .284 Winchester, which didn't make it either in the popularity polls. Either of these will fill your freezer with little fuss as long as you direct the bullets to the proper spot.

Then comes my personal all-time favorite for fun hunting. The little 7 x 57 Mauser. An old European military round, turned sporter, but never really pushed in this country. Factory loadings are deplorably inadequate in all but Federal's fine 139 grain loading and Norma's 150 grain soft-point boattail. Either of these will put meat in the freezer at 300 yards, or more, and with no fuss whatever to the shoulder or ears. Most factory loadings use the heavy military 175 grain bullet at the original military velocity... which is necessary because of the many tired old military rifles lacking strength enough to handle those loadings possible for the handloader. Those Federal and Norma rounds mentioned are still loaded to the same low pressure levels recommended for older rifles. It is lighter bullets that gives them a decided advantage over other factory ammo.

This cartridge is ideally suited to the handloader because there are lots of .284 bullets available making it a practical medium for everything from varmints to big game. In a modern, strong, action of course. If yours is one of the old military rifles turned sporter, handloading won't help to any great extent other than to go to lighter bullets. Pressure levels must be kept the same. Just changing the bullet can do wonders, though, as witnessed by Federal and Norma.

And finally we get to those .30 calibers; bullets measuring .308 in diameter. Don't be confused by the varying designations in cartridges of this caliber. Regardless of what it is called it still shoots .308 bullets if it is a .30 caliber anything. This goes for the miniscule and impotent .30 Carbine, .30-30, .30 Remington, .308 Winchester, .30-40 Krag, .30-06 Springfield, .300 H & H Magnum, .300 Winchester Magnum, .300 Weatherby Magnum or .308 Norma Magnum. They all shoot .308 diameter bullets.

This chapter isn't intended to push any specific manufacturer but two of the favorites in Swiggett's battery of deer rifles are these Remingtons. The Model 600 6.5 Rem. Mag. on the left and its later version the Model 660 in .308 Win. The Model 600 is topped with a K6 Weaver scope.

This hunter takes his shooting seriously. He's trying several loads to see which shoots best in his rifle. Sight any caliber in to print 3-inches high at 100 yards to get the maximum trajectory from it. Where shots will be at 100 yards, or less, set sights to print dead-on at that distance. This will aid in getting through small holes in brush revealed by the scope.

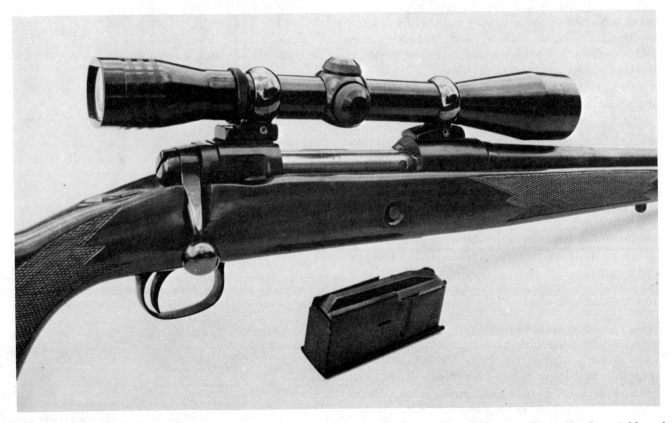

Every hunting rifle should be scoped in this writer's opinion. Here is a Savage 110 "Chieftan" with a Weaver 2x–7x variable and Conetrol mounts.

Skipping the military .30 Carbine, which no one in his right mind would use on deer and, praise the Lord, is outlawed in most states, we start with the aforementioned .30-30 Winchester, the .30 Remington (ballistically the same cartridge but rimless for pump action rifles) and go on through the .308 Winchester, the real oldie .30-40 Krag and the world's all-time favorite – the .30-06 Springfield. None above these are needed for any deer hunt. Sorry fellows, that's just the way I feel about it. Those big .30 magnums are big-boomers, both from the front and back, and a lot more gun than required to put any buck on the ground.

Extreme range hunters can use them, sure, but here we go again, close shots, such as 200 yards or less, are pretty much out of the question. Tissue destruction is unreal and most of a deer will be lost through blood-shot meat. And besides that, for every deer shot over 200 yards several hundred, or even thousands, will be taken at less. Most, according to every survey I've ever seen, are taken at less than 100 yards.

Stick to bullets in the 150 to 165 grain bracket. Any of these will do a great job for you. In the .308 my family has taken a lot of game using Speer's fine 130 grain hollow point bullet loaded to a bit short of maximum. I've also used it extensively in .30-06 and in my Thompson/Center .30-30 pistol barrel.

If I were to recommend a single caliber for a beginning hunter it would be a toss-up between the .270 Winchester, the .308 Winchester and the .30-06 Springfield. To prove my feelings here – until my two sons left home upon finishing school they used my rifles. Whichever they wanted at the time. When the older one left, I bought him a brand new Model 670 Winchester in .270 caliber, and topped it with a Weaver K4 scope. A couple of years later number two son left. He had become very fond of one of my .308's so he got a new Model 660 Remington .308 for his going away present, also topped with a Weaver K4 scope.

But back to the subject – a man could close his eyes, reach out and grab one of those three, then take off on a lifetime of hunting and never look back. My personal choice leans to the .30-06 Springfield because of the great variety of loadings available in this caliber. Bullets from 100 grains through 220 grains are available to the handloader. These same bullets can be used in the .308 but the case is a little smaller hence not quite so versatile. On the other hand, 130 grain bullets in the .270 Winchester have proven mighty capable all over the

Practice should include offhand. Jack rabbit and coyote hunting provide the opportunity for many, particularly in the Southwest. Most hunters sight in off a bench and never know where their rifle prints from offhand – nor if they can hit anything that way. And many find they can't when the time comes.

The largest and smallest bullets the author has listed as suitable for deer. Remington's 405 grain soft point .45–70 bullet compared to Speer's 70 grain .224 semi-spitzer for the .220 Swift, .22–250 Remington and .225 Winchester.

Norma .220 Swift with 50 grain soft point semi pointed bullet; Remington's .22–250 with 55 grain soft point Power Lokt bullet and Speer's 70 grain semi-spitzer. Swiggett recommends these in cartridges for the hunter feeling it necessary to hunt deer with a .22 centerfire. Hal feels 50 and 55 grain bullets are too light for deer.

world and 150 grain projectiles are factory loaded for those bigger-than-deer animals.

I guess you'd best make your own choice.

Above the .30's there is little of real use except that anyone owning a .32 Winchester can do anything with it the .30-30 will do. Same goes for the .35 Remington. Along with the .350 Remington Magnum and .358 Winchester. Neither of these succeeded along the road to fame but both are good deer killers.

Eastern hunters have come to consider some of these larger calibers, particularly in lever or pump action rifles, as "brush rifles."

Now we graduate to the infamous .44 caliber, bullets of .429 and in some cases .430 diameter, more commonly referred to as the .44 magnum. Starting out as a handgun cartridge (see chapter 18 for more on this one) it immediately caught the eye of those thinking ancient thoughts about the same cartridge in rifle and handgun. Lever guns were soon chambered for it and Ruger brought out their now-famous little 5-shot .44 magnum semi-automatic carbine. While some factory loads appear to me to be hotter than handgun loads ought to be, namely those by Federal and Norma, I've shot a lot of them and really like them, but feel they are a bit potent, especially for beginning shooters. They do an excellent job, however, in my Ruger semi-autoloader.

When it first came out I was helping with the hunting on a ranch that made hunts available to underprivileged youngsters. After letting one young fellow try a few shots at a target we settled ourselves in a blind hoping a doe would wander past. One did. She came over a slight rise which made us look up at her. At about 30 yards, my young hunter took careful aim and squeezed the trigger just like he had been instructed. When that big flat-nosed 240 grain bullet hit her square in the chest it raised her front feet off the ground and for an instant I was sure she was going over backwards. Then her back legs folded up and down she fell. Very dead.

Big, flat-nosed, bullets offer tremendous shocking power. They don't have to be setting any velocity records to do it either, since it comes from their diameter and weight. Bullets in .44 caliber and up can do the same thing without expansion that smaller calibers are struggling for with perfect performance.

Not intended as a long range deer killer, the .44 magnum rifle is mighty well suited to 100 yards and

Hal Swiggett won the trophy for the first deer ever killed with a Colt Sauer rifle with this buck. Shooting the .30–06 Colt Sauer and 180 grain Peters ammunition (that's what they furnished). Hal got his trophy-winning buck shortly after sunup on the first day of the hunt. The occasion was Colt's introduction of their new Colt Sauer bolt action rifle. The location was Cimarron, New Mexico.

even a bit farther. About as good as one can get, for that matter.

Marlin and Remington put their heads together and came up with the .444 Marlin cartridge and chambered it in a lever gun so as to prove popular with woods hunters but it, too, never received top acceptance. It was, initially, the same .44 magnum bullet loaded hotter by reason of the much longer case and powder supply. Hornady came to the rescue and designed a 265 grain bullet which aided handloaders. This is also a fine bullet for .44 magnum handgunners where deep penetration is needed. Remington recently changed their bullet to one weighing 265 grains and designed especially for

the .444 Marlin. Now the full potential of this cartridge is available in a factory load.

I own one these rifles and have killed several deer with it. The longest shot was at a mule deer at close to 200 yards. It brought him down, but from the bullet performance I'd suggest holding shots to 150 yards or less for best results. Again, this was not intended as a long range cartridge. Out to half again the length of a football field it will do a mighty good job on most anything a hunter might want to tackle, meaning game larger than the subject of this book. Particularly with Remington's new load.

There has been a tremendous upsurge of interest in things of old which has brought about the rein-

Remington .25–06 120 grain pointed soft point; Federal Premium .25-06 Remington 117 grain boat-tail soft point.

Remington .30–06 150 grain pointed soft point; Federal .30–06 150 grain soft point; Remington .30–06 "Accelerator" 55 grain pointed soft point. This latter one is not for deer. Remington offers it for the .30–06 shooter to use on varmints.

carnation of the 1873 military cartridge, the .45-70. Again, we are talking about a close-range hunting cartridge. Shooting a big 405 grain bullet in current factory loadings (of 1,320 fps) it will drop any deer instantly if shots are kept to about 100 yards.

There have been lots of tales about long range shooting with this one and some of them are no doubt true. But it is still a short range hunting load and if used sensibly will take game easily.

I've killed only one deer with this cartridge. It was a whitetail buck, an 8-pointer, that field dressed 86 pounds. The shot was at 76 steps, paced off after getting the buck, and he ran about 40 yards with a perfect heart shot. In fact, though I can't explain it, the heart was blown up as if hit by a modern, high-velocity, bullet. I was shooting a handloaded Remington 405 grain jacketed soft-point bullet at factory velocity in a replica Remington Rolling Block from Navy Arms. Using the Creedmore sight. This same rifle, and load, also took on black bear at about 80 yards. With a single shot.

The .45–70 is a fine game killer *at close range.* What about actions?

Rifles come in single shot, bolt action, pump action, semi-automatic, and lever designs. Actually, "you pay your money and take your choice."

Lever guns have received a lot of fame in the southwest as horseback rifles and in the east as "brush" rifles. Accuracy though is not up to that of single shot and bolt guns, though certainly more than adequate for deer hunting. In fact, I've seen a few that, for some strange reason, shot like they didn't know they were lever guns.

The cartridge selected will have a bit to do with this choice. None of the lever guns, except for Savage's Model 99, chamber the more potent modern calibers so are necessarily limited to close-range shooting. Savage Model 99's can be had in .243 Win., .250 Savage and .308 Winchester. If you like guns working from the bottom, don't back off because of caliber. Pick the one you like and you will be set for deer hunting anyplace in the United States, except for maybe mountain hunting, and even there a good hunter won't be in any serious trouble.

Marlin and Savage users can scope their rifles easier because of the side ejection. Winchester shooters can use a side-mount if they want a glass sight – or one of the long eye relief handgun scopes mounted in front of the receiver.

I hesitate to recommend a lever gun because I don't consider the calibers available for all-around

Remington .30–30 Winchester 170 grain soft point; Federal .30–30 Winchester 170 grain soft point; Federal .30–30 Winchester 125 grain hollow soft point (that's another one showing the point). The 125 grain load is not intended for deer but for lesser-sized animals.

Remington 7 mm Magnum 150 grain pointed soft point; Winchester Super X 7 mm Remington Magnum 150 grain soft point; Federal Premium 7 mm Remington Magnum 150 grain boat-tail soft point; Federal 7 mm Mauser 139 grain soft point. The author considers this short one, on the right, an ideal deer cartridge.

Swiggett's Ruger .44 Magnum autoloader in its current dress.

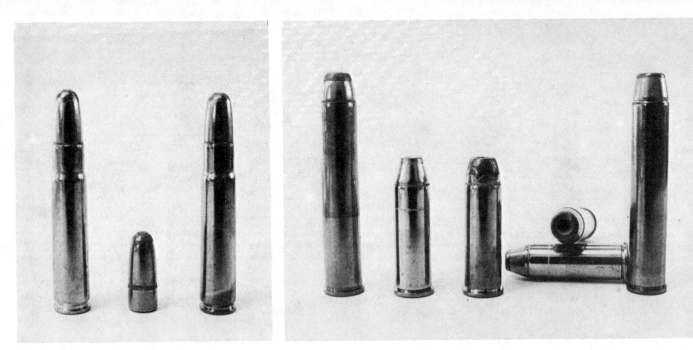

Federal .35 Remington 200 grain soft point; .35 Remington 200 grain soft point bullet and .35 Remington 200 grain soft point.

Remington .444 Marlin 240 grain soft point; Federal .44 Remington Magnum 180 grain jacketed hollow point; Remington .44 Remington Magnum 240 grain semi-jacketed hollow point; Handloaded .444 Marlin with 47 grains of 4198 under Norma's 240 grain jacketed hollow point. The author has found this handload to be accurate and a good deer killer.

Use a rest for every shot if at all possible. The rifle here is a Remington Model 600 .308 Win.

Winchester .45–70 405 grain soft point; Remington .45–70 405 grain soft point; Remington's 405 grain soft point bullet; Federal .45–70 300 grain hollow soft point (their new load) and Hornady's .45–70 300 grain hollow point bullet.

The .444 Marlin in that firm's fine lever gun is well-suited for deer out to 150 or so yards.

use, except, as mentioned, the Savage, should the owner change parts of the country or want to take up some other types of hunting. On the other hand, I wouldn't feel very handicapped with a .30-30 Winchester topped with a 1.5 x–4 x scope. And even less handicapped with a .444 Marlin outfitted the same way. Mine is, by the way.

Single shot rifles are the rage at this writing. Some of them border on super-accurate. They can be chambered for most any cartridge imaginable and scoped the same way. I tend to lean a bit towards single shots, though I own only two and one of them is a varmint rifle (in centerfires – I own and shoot a bunch of them in muzzle loaders). My reasoning here is to encourage more careful use of that first shot. There seems to be a growing tendency to spray the woods with bullets, a la military, rather than on bullet placement. It is still the single bullet that generally takes home the game.

Single shot rifle shooters aren't handicapped at all, really, because it doesn't take but an instant to open the action and drop in another round.

Pump action shooters are blessed with a better choice of calibers than lever lovers, hence are more generally better equipped for those longer shots that sometimes are the only ones offered. And pumps are easily scoped. I wouldn't select one for my own use but can understand why some might like them. Especially pump action shotgun shooters. This keeps them with the same action for all their shooting.

Bolt actions are tops for all-around use. Chambered for most every cartridge manufactured they are inherently the most accurate (except for single shots) and can be had with short barrels, a la carbine fashion, for the shooter so inclined. They can be operated faster than any hunter can carefully place shots and they are as near foolproof as a rifle can be. Weight can range from light to heavy, as the shooter desires.

In spite of what some will tell you they make a top brush rifle, especially topped with a low power (magnification) scope. Only those who have never learned to use one will tell you otherwise. Any place iron sights are good, a low power scope is better. Period.

You will note I've neglected semi-automatic rifles. This will antagonize some shooters and a couple of manufacturers, but I hate 'em. I see no place in the sporting rifle market for a semi-automatic rifle.

The author with the one magnum he really likes . . . one barely mentioned in this chapter because few, if any, factories still chamber for it. His ancient .300 H & H Magnum has brought down a lot of big game over a lot of years. Not even a Magnum by today's standards of power, factory .300 H & H ammo is much superior to the .30-06 and handloads can almost equal modern juggernauts.

They are always loaded for another pull of the trigger which makes them far too dangerous since there is NEVER any need for that sort of fast shooting. In shotguns, I can not only accept them but have grown to like self-shuckers because fast shots are the name of the game. In hunting deer, or any other big game for that matter, there is no need to spray the woods with bullets. If a buck is missed with the first shot, carefully placed as it should be, then a fast second shot, and third, and fourth, will make no better headway, unless it just happens to be that buck's time to cash in his chips.

My feelings are so strong about semi-automatic rifles I will not let one in my vehicles. Doing a bit of guiding I was assigned a hunter some years ago (in Texas hunting from vehicles is legal on private property) who pulled one out of his car, filled the clip, inserted it in his rifle and got into my pickup. As he was getting comfortable I reached over and dropped the clip into my hand. Thumbing out a single round I handed it to him. A bit upset, he asked why I had done that. On hearing my opinion of self-loaders he informed me he knew how to use it. I still kept the clip and it turned out he did know how to shoot his rifle because he got a fine buck with that single round. It might have proved something to him – at least I hope it did.

I know of two instances where excited hunters have shot vehicles by swinging with running deer and shooting as the muzzle passed their transporta-

Dr. Gerald Swiggett used his Steyr-Mannlicher .22–250 for this whitetail and turkey hunt. Shooting handloaded Speer 70 grain bullets his rifle/load combo performed perfectly.

tion. One went through the corner post of a Jeep windshield, the other through a radiator.

The same thing could happen to a companion.

The telescopic sight is the greatest aid to a hunter that's ever been invented (except for fine rifles). Unfortunately, as with "magnumitis" – "poweritis" has taken a firm hold. Some seem to think that if 4 x is good 8 x is better and 12 x is where it's all at. Here again I guess advertising has reared its ugly head.

Seldom ever is more than 4 x needed for the longest shots at big game. Power in scopes is shown by the "x" and the magnification by number. Hence 4 x means four times magnification of normal vi-

sion. Said another way, a 4 x scope will make a deer appear as if he were 25 yards away though he is standing on the 100 yard mark. Carrying this on out to 300 yards it means that same 4 x scope will make the buck appear 75 yards away. Which again points out the lack of need for anything stronger.

Greater magnification requires more careful eye-relief, that distance between the eye and the rear lens of the scope. It also magnifies movement to the same degree it magnifies animal size. A tiny, unnoticeable, movement through a 4 x scope will appear so distracting as to cause a miss through a 9 x glass sight. Seeing that movement, the shooter will try to stop it, thereby bringing himself under even more tension and shaking. A hopeless situation.

A fine rifle perfectly sighted in, a blaze orange jacket and cap, and a good deer mountain. In this instance the rifle is a Klein-guenther K-14 .30–06. Hal feels this caliber is near perfect for deer hunting anyplace on the North American continent.

Elmer Keith, left, and Tom Kocis talk over the relative merits of a single shot rifle. Tom is head honcho of Wickliffe Single Shot Rifles and Elmer — well, everybody knows Elmer Keith.

Left-handers can use bolt action rifles with little difficulty. All it takes is practice. Here Bob Adler gets in a few practice shots before a deer hunt with his Kleinguenther K-15 topped with a Weaver 2X–7X and Conetrol mounts. The Author feels 2X–7X or 1.5X–4X as ideal deer hunting scopes.

Just because you are left-handed don't shy away from bolt rifles. They are easily mastered with a little practice. A few companies offer left-handed bolts but if one isn't readily available to you don't fret over it.

205

The author downgrades autoloaders because of his personal distaste for them – but he does, strange as it might seem, have a warm spot in his heart for the little Ruger .44 Magnum carbine. Out to 100 yards it does a fine job making it near perfect as a "brush" rifle. This photo made in his younger days when he could still see iron sights. This rifle is now scoped with a Weaver V 4.5.

Practice a few shots from a sitting position. This is probably the most important position for a deer hunter. Offhand, if the animal is close, and sitting for those longer shots. Many times trees, stumps and the like are absent when most needed for a rest.

I can accept 6 x, or on occasion, 7 x for extreme long range shots but, above that, added magnification is useless.

I heartily agree with variable magnification scopes. They are the greatest. If shooting a caliber in the short-range category, meaning possibly 200–250 yard maximum, it is impossible to beat the little 1.5 x–4 x or 4.5 x scopes. Offered by most of the major makers, this is, to my way of thinking, the best all-around scope on the market. Close shots can take advantage of the 1.5 x setting which allows that brush hunter to see holes through cover he never would have known were there with the naked eye.

To take full advantage of a scope in this class one should carry it on the lowest magnification. Close shots will always be the fast shots. If the animal is farther away, requiring a bit of magnification, there is also time to set the scope.

My next choice up the ladder would be for a 2 x–7 x variable. This one will cover all fields of big game hunting from dense cover to far off game. The 2 x minimum is still o. k. for heavy cover and the 7 x a mite more than needed in all but rare instances.

The current rage, 3 x–9 x scopes, are heavier, not low enough power for close shots in dense cover and more magnification at the upper level than all but experts can hold. Not necessary in other words. Nor even good, for that matter.

Telescopic sights are not hard to learn to use and once mastered will turn mediocre shooters into almost instant experts. Nothing beats being able to see what you are shooting at. Some die-hard easterners will often try to tell you scopes are too slow to use in heavy cover. All that means is that they have never learned to use one. All of us have seen bullets slam into limbs, even small trees, that weren't even noticed as those iron sights were lined up. Scopes show the way through small openings. Even at extreme low power.

Start off with yours set on 1.5 x or 2 x, whichever is lowest. Take plenty of time. Carefully snuggle your cheek against the stock so you get the full sight picture. Do this several times. Once you find the most comfortable position for viewing through the scope you have the battle well on the way to being won.

Carefully note the position of your head, the way your neck is bent, the slant of your cheek against the stock. Further practice is then in order. Do this by moving your head into that position you've just discovered as the butt is brought to the shoulder.

In no time at all they will both be reaching the proper position at the same instant. Continue practice with your eyes closed. Bring the rifle butt to your shoulder as your head is leaned into position. As your cheek hits the stock your eye will be lined up perfectly through the scope. Open it and see for yourself.

It is easier to learn than it is to explain, believe me. And the man who says scopes are too slow had best not undertake this project unless he has some salt handy to make his words more palatable.

Reticles in scopes are varied. Modern technology has given us one called Dual-X, 4-Plex, Duplex, to mention the names used by some of the manufacturers. It features a coarse, wide, crosshair on the outside edges tapering, or turning, into a tiny crosshair in the center. This is by far the best hunting reticle on the market.

Running shots allow it to be used as a peep sight. Just put your target in the center of those four wide crosshair tips. Worry not about the tiny lines.

Careful aiming takes advantage of the finer center crosshairs. Even extreme poor-light shooting is possible with this reticle by using the peep sight method. The eye automatically centers any object in the circle. You'll have to fight to get it off center.

There are still plain crosshairs, dots and posts, but if you ever look through one of those Dual-X, 4-Plex, Duplex styles, you will throw rocks at all the others.

To what conclusion have we come?

As to caliber I have declared the .270, .308, .30-06 as "ideal" deer cartridges. Bolt action rifles win hands down. As do the 1.5 x–4 x or 2 x–7 x scopes.

In other words, there just might be a really perfect deer rifle suited for any part of the country. For size, try on a bolt action .270 or .30-06 with a .22-inch barrel and topped with one of the fine 2 x–7 x variable scopes.

I don't think you can beat it! Unless you happen to already own a bolt action .308 with a .22-inch barrel (or a mite shorter) wearing a 1.5 x–4 x or 4.5 x scope.

In that case I'll concede to a "stand off."

Chapter 17

ACCESSORIES

Accessories for the deer hunter cover all sorts of sins. What you feel necessary, or handy, could well be considered by another as weight better left at home. Some of the things generally considered in this category and in no particular order include:

Binoculars – to me are the single most important item in a deer hunter's paraphernalia. The only time they might not be needed is when shotgun hunting in dense cover. I do know thick forests can make them invaluable at times. It is much easier to determine if a spot of something that doesn't seem to fit is a hunk of deer hide with binoculars, than it is with the naked eye. Of course, my pet peeve is seeing hunters in open country using rifle scopes to scan a mountainside, or, to determine if that movement way down yonder is a deer. Whenever a scope is used to check a point of interest it aims the rifle at that point, in spite of one of the first laws of firearms safety, that being to never point a gun at something unless you intend to shoot.

I don't care who he is – if I catch a hunter using a rifle scope to check out an unknown object he and I are through. Period. I don't want to be in the same county with that type of person.

High power binoculars not only aren't necessary, but aren't even advisable; normal 6 x or 7 x is all that's needed. More magnification makes it very hard to hold steady enough to tell what is being looked at.

Spotting scopes for deer hunters are basically unnecessary. On occasion they can be put to use in the mountains, but not often enough to make the effort worthwile.

Fluorescent orange! If the state where you are hunting requires it, you are stuck. I personally despise the stuff and feel like a fully decked-out Christmas tree when so dressed. One state, New Mexico, refuses the law on the grounds they don't want hunters thinking they can shoot at anything not wearing blaze orange. All I can say to that is – Amen! Again, if I was to find a hunter depending on color to determine game I'd not want to be within shooting distance of him!

Edged ware has been well handled by Bill Hughes in Chapter 18.

Boots are maybe THE most important item, especially if it's a walking hunt. Make sure they fit well and are well broken in. That last phrase is often used, but I'm not at all sure if good boots that fit properly really need any breaking in. Wear the same socks when buying as you do when hunting. Stand up and put all your weight on the feet. Buy from a store that has an experienced salesperson, one who understands how feet can swell under the strain of long hours of walking and climbing. Boots need to be loose enough to allow for that swelling but tight enough to prevent slipping. Sounds crazy, I know, but that's what you are after.

A note of caution. Be sure the soles are for your intended use. Rock climbing soles are not wanted for timber or grassy slopes, or vice-versa. Most of us have several pairs of boots and I often take two or three pairs on a hunt. Light walking boots, heavy mountain climbing boots and, in late fall or winter, ALWAYS a pair of pacs, even if it means leaving something else out.

To go a step further – if a hunter can't sleep, he won't be able to walk the next day regardless of how well his boots fit. Buy your sleeping bag for the country you intend to hunt, with your own experience as the guide. If expecting cold, get one designed for considerably colder weather than you hope to experience. If, like me, cold doesn't soak in until it gets severe, you won't need the biggies. I have my own answer, which we'll get to in a moment. One of my sons freezes at anything below freezing, so he was outfitted a long time ago with the heaviest down bag made by Eddie Bauer. It has served him well and probably will for the rest of his life, since it only gets used about a week a year, and then not every year. Expensive, yes. A valuable and necessary investment, even a bigger YES.

I learned a long time ago to be prepared. It was on a spring bear hunt, in Idaho, a number of years ago: the outfitter said it would not get cold. For sure, not down to freezing. I took a light summer bag since, as I've said, I don't feel the cold as acutely as most. The outfitter was right about one point – the near freezing. Only he was on the wrong side. It got up to that mark during the hot part of the day but nights hovered in the 12–15 degree area, and I got cold. So did everyone in camp, including the outfitter, thank God. We slept in our clothes and I put my light down jacket (something I'm never without) in the bottom of my sleeping bag, opened towards the top, before inserting my feet. At least they slept comfortably.

My answer to sleeping bags, since that experience, is a DuPont filled large-sized bag rated at about 32 degrees. To this I've added an Eddie Bauer 1-lb. down liner, of mummy bag design. If it's cold I put the liner inside the other bag and I have slept warm and comfortable on a bed of pine boughs, under a tent, in 10–15 below zero weather. This same idea could be carried further by getting a light down bag rated at maybe O degrees, then using the liner for colder situations. It's just a thought that works for me and lets one good quality bag serve for all of my hunting.

Buy the best you can afford and, as with boots – skimp on something else if necessary, but make sure your boots and sleeping bag are top quality. No hunt can be enjoyed – better said, survived – if your feet are blistered and swollen and you can't sleep.

Much is said about a compass being necessary. It sure is, except that it is valueless unless used as you leave camp. There is no way you'll find your way back if you don't know the direction you took upon leaving. A compass will tell the direction, true, but what good is north if you don't know whether you are east, west, north or south of camp.

The best direction finder is between a man's ears. As you walk away from camp look back over your shoulder every so often. That way you will know what the country looks like from the other direction.

If hunting on your own – without a guide – in strange country, be prepared for the worst. Carry a compass, a map of the area, a waterproof container of matches, signal flares, a candle or two, a couple of candy bars along with a few boxes of raisins and a small package or two of nuts. Nothing that requires much space but enough to get you out, if lost. A small mirror could come in mighty handy for signaling purposes. With this take as big a package of common sense as you can get. If lost DO NOT PANIC. Stop right where you are until you get settled down and can think straight. Make a plan, then stick to it. Sooner or later you will get out. Fast walking or frantic running in hit or miss fashion only wears you out. No one was ever hurt by just spending a night or two in the woods when he used his head.

There's the story of the hunter who got lost and who fired three shots into the air as a signal for help. He waited what seemed like a long time then fired three more shots. After several of these efforts he really became concerned. Trying it one more time he muttered to himself, "I sure hope it works this time – I'm almost out of arrows."

On the subject of coats and jackets, I'm seldom ever caught on any sort of a jaunt without a light down jacket. I have them in several weights and in spite of how cold it is, or isn't, the lightest jacket always makes the trip. Down was, until recently, the best substance available for warmth, until science settled down to cater to our interests. No pun intended there. "Hollow Fill" is the trade name of one substitute and there may be others of a similar nature every bit as warm as down, just as light, and without the bad points of down when it gets wet. This new product does not soak up water so never gets saturated like down, and it is a lot cheaper. Also, it is better to wear two or even three lighter items such as a heavy shirt, or a sweater under a jacket or coat than one big, heavy coat. Lighter garments can be discarded as needed as the day warms.

I find 20 feet or so of light nylon rope to come in rather handy on occasion. Coiled tightly, it requires very little space.

A handy item is this portable stand made by Braden Wire and Metal Company in San Antonio. It folds up to fit in a car and weighs only 44 pounds. Linda Swiggett, the author's daughter in law, likes it because visibility is so much greater than from ground level.

Little is said about headwear as a rule, but it is an important item; very important in extreme hot or cold situations. Keep your head warm and your feet will be warm – or at least warmer. Without a good head covering valuable body heat is lost through exposure. Down caps are hard, if not impossible, to beat in severe cold. Wide-brimmed hats are by far the best in rain or heat. In the summer a good western straw can make an unbearably hot day in the sun almost endurable. In the winter, western felt hats are worn by a lot of folks, not necessarily westerners, because they have discovered their good points. They keep the sun out of your eyes and the rain off your glasses and from running down your neck. But they do get heavy if soaked. Most stores selling western hats also sell plastic hat covers. I always have two or three extras with me for friends who forget theirs.

What about gloves? Mittens are the warmest and some are made with a finger slot for the trigger finger. Here again, some need them more than others. I personally wear tightly fitted buckskin gloves most all the time when outdoors, year around. I do a lot of handgun shooting and like the feel better. It seems to me the trigger, and even the gun itself, can be better controlled with that thin covering of leather over my hand. Even in cold weather they go with me, but admittedly they are not ideally suited to cold-weather use. Wool shooting gloves are better. When I discard my buckskins it is in favor of a thin leather glove that is lined with a thin layer of foam. I've found these very warm and have never had to go to more. My interest is in wanting something on my hand that does not hinder the feel of the trigger. Again, each has to survey his own situation and wear something that aids comfort. Just be sure to include a good pair of something for the hands in your gear.

And for that woman deer hunter – God bless her – there are clothes and boots made to fit. Buy trousers, shirts, footwear, coats made for her figure. Do not, please guys, make her wear cast offs you've outgrown or worn out. If she's willing to share your hunting sport believe me, she is a jewel, and should be treated as such.

And do not forget a small pencil. It is of vital importance. This sounds silly, I know, but game laws being what they are, and game wardens enforcing them to the comma and period, a tiny little pencil could mean the difference between being in trouble or not. Filling in the blank spaces on a game tag is a mighty serious phase of big game hunting. The license in your pocket is no good if you are found dragging a dead deer (come to think of it I've never heard of anyone dragging a live deer) and a game warden happens on the scene.

I guess what I'm saying is that it would be better to wear ill-fitting boots, no coat or hat, sleep in an inadequate bag, tromp around without any survival gear and without a knife, worse, one with a dull blade, than to be without that pencil.

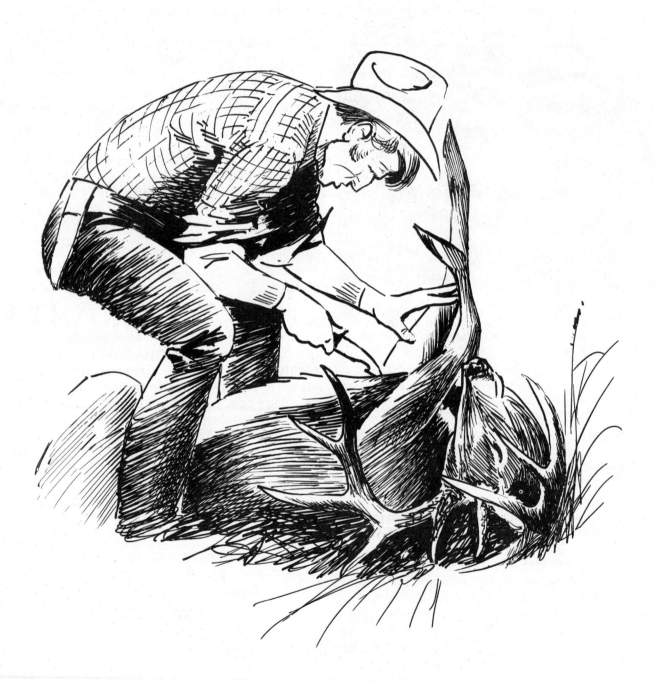

Chapter 18

A KNIFE FOR DEER
by B. R. Hughes

A North American deer can be a petite whitetail in the thickets of South Arkansas or a husky mulie from the mountains of Colorado. In one instance, you have an animal that will weigh little more than 100 pounds; in the other, there's an excellent chance that the mature mule deer will tip the scales at well over 200 pounds.

The knife that is just the ticket for the whitetail may suffice for the mulie, but if the tool is one of those delicate creations with a blade running around 2½" or so in length, then you've got a tough chore ahead of you when it comes time to field dress, skin, and possibly quarter the animal.

This may be a poor way to introduce the topic of this chapter, but I think it describes rather well my attitude towards the matter of selecting a knife for deer: just as a good big man will almost always beat a good little man, so will a good, full-sized knife generally prove preferable to a smaller version.

Notice, please, that I did not say "big knife" in the last paragraph. I said "full-sized knife", and there is a vast difference. I do not think for a moment that a hunter needs one of those over-blown Bowie-style knives with an eight-inch blade. On the other hand, if a man packs around a sheath knife with a blade of less than 3", I think he's making a mistake. In the first place, if a blade of less than 3" will handle the job at hand, a folding knife should be selected. In the second, there is nothing of a practical nature that can be accomplished with a blade of say, 2¾" that cannot be better handled with a blade of around 4".

If weight is that important, pack a good folding model with a lockblade of at least 2½" and have at it. Me? I generally carry both a sheath knife and a pocket model. Nothing like being prepared.

The question of a fixed bladed knife versus a folding version is one that comes up pretty often when folks discuss hunting knives, but in all truth, I feel I have answered that one. If you honestly feel that things can be handled with a knife possessing a blade no longer than 3", then a folding knife *should* be the order of the day. If you feel that something larger is desirable, then you should select a good sheath model. It's that simple.

When choosing a knife for your venison preparation, there are a number of factors in addition to the length of the blade that must be resolved, including custom or factory, steel and/or handle material, blade shape, and a couple of other considerations. Let's examine these points, one by one.

CUSTOM OR FACTORY?

Several years ago, I would have voted strongly in favor of the custom knife. Now, I'm not so sure. In recent years the factories have dramatically upgraded both their designs and the materials employed. Mind you, I'm speaking here of the upper strata of mass-produced cutlery-knives that, for the most part, retail for well over $25.00, and in some cases, over $50.00. When it comes to sheath knives, some of the finest factory models I've used include the Buck Kalinga, the Shrade-Loveless, any of the Gerber Presentation line, the Case Cheyenne, G 96's "3030", and the Western Westmark line. These mass-produced knives will stand comparison with many handmade models.

Looking at folding models, first make certain that the knife you are considering possesses a blade lock. This will prevent the blade's closing on your fingers when in use. I have heard many arguments pro and con concerning a blade lock, but I have never heard anything against them that I would consider valid. Next, the component parts of the folder should fit well; if you can see obvious gaps between the handle liners and spring, or between the handle slabs and liners, reject the knife immediately. In the handmade field, be prepared to pay a minimum of $65.00, or so, for a good, well-made folder with a blade lock. Good factory models are available for approximately one-third to one-half this amount. Some of my favorite factory folders include the Buck Ranger, many Gerber models, Western's new lock-blade, the Puma Backpacker, Case's Shark Tooth, and the No. 88 Camillus.

Now, let's take a brief look at some of the custom offerings.

In this area you will find many relatively famous names, many of which cater primarily to the collector market. These knives will feature superb craftsmanship and the best of materials, and they are almost certain to increase in value, but in almost every instance, such knives will cost in excess of $150.00, often much more. Included in this group would be knives bearing the names of Buster Warenski, Corbet Sigman, W. M. Moran, Jr., Ron Lake, Jess Horn, T. M. Dowell, D. E. Henry, and Lloyd Hale. These will do an excellent job in the field, but few of us actually use them – they're too valuable!

More apropos are handmade knives selling from $50.00 to $100.00, and there are a large number of makers specializing in such models. Included in such a listing would be such names as Morseth, George Herron, the Nolen Brothers, Harvey McBurnette, Jim Barbee, Jimmy Lile, Steve Davenport, Randall, and T. J. Yancey.

Some people apparently believe that "homemade" is the same as "handmade." Not so. A good handcrafted knife should be very, very slick – as slick as the better factory knives and often possessing superior workmanship. In no case should a crude knife be accepted on the grounds that it is a handmade model.

Once upon a time custom knives could be justified for all serious hunters because they would hold an edge at least twice as long as the better factory models. Now, however, the big factories have knives that will be at least 75 to 80 percent as effective in terms of edgeholding and tensile strength as the rank and file handmade knife. I still believe there is a definite place for the custom models, but that place is in the hands of those who want only the best, those who are not satisfied with the commonplace. There are those who appreciate and desire custom gun stocks, slick rifle and shotgun actions, and excellent quality guns. The same applies to knives. Do not purchase a handmade knife with the idea that it will perform twice as well as your good Puma or Gerber, to cite but two examples of better factory cutlery. They won't. Do purchase a handmade knife if you're willing to pay a premium for pride of ownership and a slight edge in actual performance.

BLADE SHAPE

A lot of drivel has been written on this topic. There are, after all, only a few things that can be done with the shape of a knife blade and still retain a high degree of practicality. You can raise the point above the back line of the blade and have an upswept point, or you can lower it and have a dropped point. Either has its virtues. An upswept point is admittedly superior for skinning, but for almost any other function, the dropped point is to be preferred. If I could have only one hunting knife, it would possess a dropped point blade approximately 4" to 5" in length.

In a folding version, it is possible to have one blade of each style, particularly if you order a handmade job. In single bladed folders, I especially like the dropped point blade such as that furnished on the new Western lock-blade folder. Last time I checked, this model retailed at only $30.00 complete with belt sheath, proving that you don't have to spend a fortune for a good lock-blade folder with excellent blade design.

BLADE STEELS

For many years, most knife blades were made of relatively simple steels which had been forged to bring out the finest qualities of the metal. Now, forging is largely a lost art, although it seems to be regaining some of its ground. Within the last quarter of a century complex stain resistant steels have

Here is a veritable bevy of good factory folders suitable for the deer hunter. From left to right they are made or imported by Browning, Puma, Precise, Gerber, Gerber, Buck, and Buck. All have blade locks.

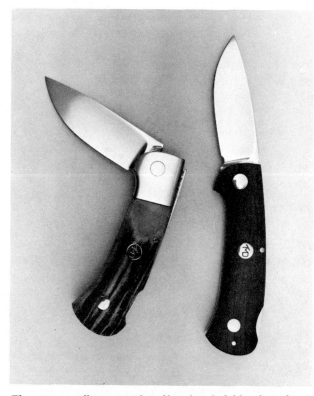

These two excellent examples of handmade folders bear the mark of T. M. Dowell. Both have blade locks and the designs are excellent for field-dressing deer.

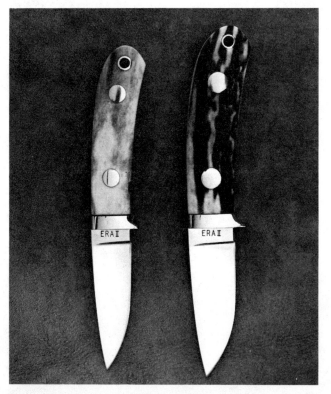

Both of these lock blade folders by Russ Andrews feature handle slabs made of sambar stag. This material is beautiful and functional, but it is becoming very difficult to obtain.

215

This large Buck folder would seem to be an excellent hunting model, but the lack of a blade lock would excuse it from consideration as far as the author is concerned.

This Gerber Magnum Hunter is one of the very finest factory folders available today, thinks Hughes. Its dropped point blade is made of 440-C, one of today's better stain resistant steels.

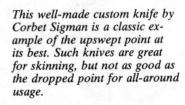

This well-made custom knife by Corbet Sigman is a classic example of the upswept point at its best. Such knives are great for skinning, but not as good as the dropped point for all-around usage.

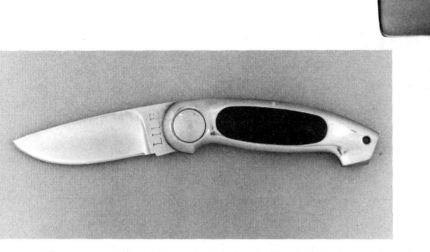

This custom folder is the work of Arkansan Jimmy Lile. A novel but functional design, this model features a blade lock incorporated into the pivot pin.

The author's favorite hand ax, or hatchet, is this one made by Buck. Such tools are useful, but few hunters actually carry them on the belt. It is not a bad idea to keep one in camp or in the hunting vehicle.

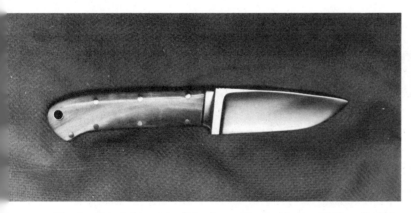

This handmade hunter is of the dropped point design. The handle is the style called a "full-tang," consisting of a slab on each side of the blade extension. This knife was made by Lloyd Hale.

The Gerber Magnum Hunter and the Gerber steel make up the combo favored most by Hal Swiggett, who put this book together. Hal caped a near record elk using this steel as a chisel separating the hide from the base of the antlers, along with this knife. Showing the steel to have more than just the capability of maintaining blade sharpness.

come into wide use, and while some of the early stainless blades were pretty grim, those made in recent years from such steels as 440-C and 154-CM are actually very good.

It should be noted that for the most part it is impractical for the factories to try to mass produce blades from such steels as the two mentioned in the preceeding sentence. There are exceptions, such as Gerber's wide use of 440-C. Most simply advertise that they use steel "of the 400 series" or "440 steel." There is a 440-A, a 440-B, and a 440-C. The latter is the type used by the custom boys and by a few factories. The two former steels are satisfactory, but not outstanding by any means. It suffices to say, granting equal skill and manufacturing techniques, a much better blade will result from the use of 440-C than from either 440-A or 440-B.

Such materials as A-2, W-2, D-2, F-8, O-1, and many others have been used with great satisfaction for knife blades. In addition, there are special materials, such as Morseth's laminated blade where a very hard portion of steel which forms the cutting edge is sandwiched between two softer pieces of steel.

Most of the modern steels will result in a good cutting edge if properly heat-treated, and, if you are purchasing a factory knife, you'll have nothing to say about this matter. If you're ordering a custom model, I suggest that you specify either 440-C, 154-CM, O-1, or a properly forged blade should you order from a smith.

HANDLE MATERIALS

Several years ago, most good quality hunting knives came with sambar stag handles. Alas, such stag is becoming increasingly difficult to obtain. Domestic stag has a soft core and is not nearly as desirable for handles. One of the better materials for a "using" knife is one of the various Micartas. These are available in wood grain, linen, and paper base in a variety of colors including red, blue, green, natural, and ivory. My favorite is the so-called ivory

218

Micarta, which is so close to the genuine article in feel and appearance that the average knife buyer can't tell the difference. This man-made material is virtually indestructible, and I strongly recommend it for knives that are to be used in the field.

Hardwoods are not used as much as they were a few years ago, but good walnut and maple both make excellent knife handles.

Ivory, pearl, and ebony cannot be recommended for knives intended for use in the field, as they are too prone to cracking and chipping.

Delrin, another man-made substance, is now being widely used on several factory models, and this is a fine material.

On sheath knives, handles may be of either the full-tang variety or the narrow-tang. On the former, the blade is of the same size and configuration as the handle slabs, which are generally affixed to the blade by means of pins and epoxy. The blade material is clearly evident between the slabs of the handle, and this probably does result in a slightly stronger knife. The latter features a narrowed section of the blade fastened into a hole which has been previously drilled in the handle. The majority of factory knives are made in this pattern, and there is nothing wrong with the resulting product.

The bolsters of folding knives and the guards and butt caps of sheath knives are often made of brass. This is a good enough material, but I much prefer nickle silver, or, even better, stainless steel. Most custom makers will gladly furnish such items, usually at a slightly higher price, but finding the exact factory knife you desire with these features may be a problem. If everything else about a given knife pleases you, I wouldn't dismiss it because it has a brass guard, cap, or bolster.

AXES, HATCHETS, AND SAWS

Every well-equipped deer camp will almost assuredly have an ax available. Such a tool is handy if you have several deer to dress out, but certainly it is not a necessity. If you're in the market for one for your deer camp, I suggest a single-bit model with a relatively light head. Actually, deer are rather fragile animals, and a person doesn't really need an ax. A hand ax, or hatchet as they are usually called, will do the job just as well, and a person can carry a hatchet on the belt, although I never do. There are so many good hatchets on today's market that recommending one is fruitless. I'll simply say that I

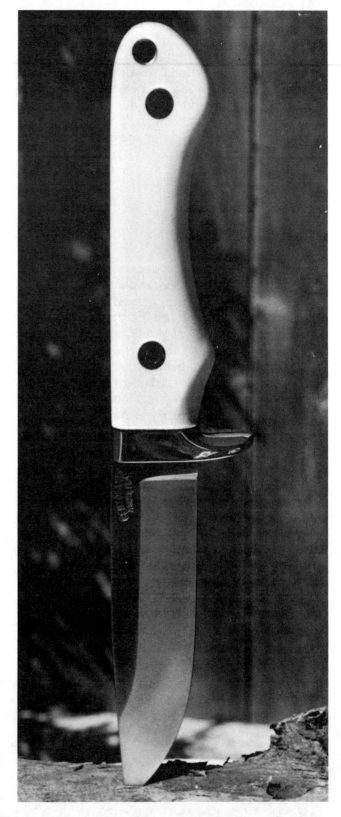

This sheath model made by Frank Centofante features handle slabs of ivory Micarta, which is the author's favorite handle material for "using knives".

219

use a Buck hand ax when I use one, and let it go at that.

Saws are extremely useful for halving deer. While an ax or hatchet is optional, if you're going to dress out many deer, I consider a saw a must. I've used a standard crosscut hand saw with a 26" blade more than anything else. Such saws may be purchased virtually anywhere; they are flat and pack easily into a truck, etc. They are inexpensive, and a decent saw will permit you to halve a deer lengthways muy pronto.

SHARPENING YOUR KNIFE

Every good knife will, sooner or later, need to be sharpened. An entire chapter could be written on this subject, but, for our purposes, it suffices to say that if a hunting trip is to last for more than one day, a sharpening instrument should be carried by the nimrod.

Among the best sharpening tools I have used may be included Russell's Arkansas Oilstones, the Gerber steel, and the Case Moon Stick. Any of these will do the job quickly and well, if you know how to sharpen a blade.

The secret of sharpening a knife is to maintain a constant angle between the blade and the stone, steel, etc. I like an angle of approximately 20 degrees. If you will make one pass on each side of the blade and maintain constant pressure and the same angle at all times, your blade will be shaving sharp when you finish. If you change your angle or permit the blade to waver during the passes, it will remain dull. Once the procedure is learned, it is possible to sharpen almost any properly ground blade within a matter of a couple of minutes. Some blades are not ground properly when they leave the factory, and they are a genuine headache!

In every community, if you ask around, there is always someone who knows how to sharpen a knife. If you simply cannot seem to learn the knack, go to that person and offer to pay him a nominal sum to teach you how. For a buck or two, it will be a genuine bargain! The greatest knife in the world is no better than its cutting edge.

SUMMING UP

Every person who takes deer hunting seriously should own at least one good knife. If you follow the suggestions given in this chapter, it will be relatively simple for you to select a good, useful knife. Provided the quality is there, the correct knife for you is the one whose appearance you find appealing and which feels "right" in your hand. Don't worry about what Cousin Jack or Uncle Frank thinks about your selection – it's your money, and it will be your knife. Select one that pleases you.

This Buck "Caper" has a blade of approximately 3⅛".
Such knives are very useful, but if a shorter blade is desired, a folder is to be recommended.

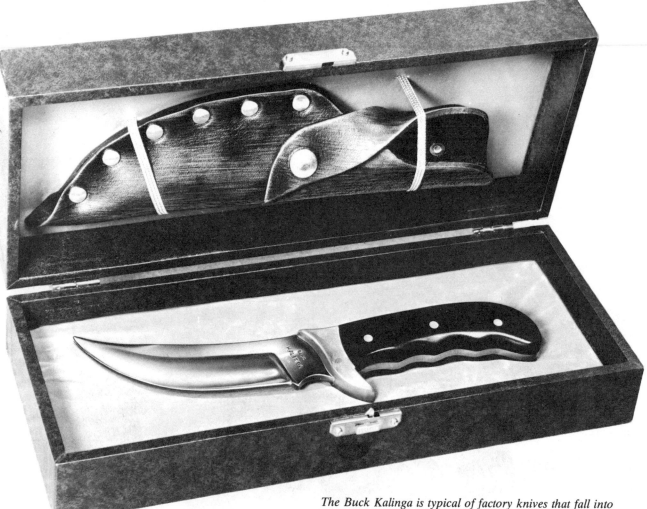

The Buck Kalinga is typical of factory knives that fall into the "over $50" category. Such knives are well-made and perform very well in the field.

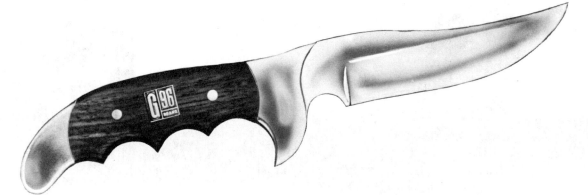

A good example of first-rate factory sheath knives is this Model 3030 offered by G96. An import, this model won't strain the pocketbook, and it will do a fine job in the field.

221

Chapter 19

CARE OF MEAT

Years ago I had the privilege of killing a rather good whitetail buck with a prototype .30-06 rifle that never made it to the open market. As a matter of fact, I think only three ever got out of the plant.

Though we were not deer hunting at the time (it was midseason) one of the guides and I had gone to one of the furthermost points of the ranch to help with a chore. On the way back, this bigger than usual buck was spotted, and killed. Sorry about that, but I'm never out without a rifle or handgun in anybody's hunting country. After a few pictures my knife went to work. The job was about half finished when it dawned on me the guide, the professional hunter, was leaning over my shoulder watching every little movement. When asked why he was so interested in what was going on, his response nearly floored me. "I've never seen anybody else gut a deer," he said, "I'm just trying to see how it's done."

Back in the pickup I couldn't help but ask the obvious question, "How did you get into guiding deer hunters if you've never seen a deer gutted?" Followed by another before he had time to answer, "What do you do when one of your hunters kills a deer?"

His story was simple. He had never killed a deer. He had initially come to the ranch several times bow hunting, loved the place, loved hunting, and talked his way into a guiding job with only that background. He was able to get away with it only because the ranch had an abnormally large deer population.

Then came the kicker. I thought his answer to my second question was terrific. If more folks would think in his terms the field dressing of big game would hold less horrors for neophytes. "I walked up to that first dead deer, looked down at him and said 'deer, you're nothin' but a great big rabbit' and went to work." How's that for common sense?

And he was right!

A deer has all those same parts as rabbits — and they are in the same place. Size is the only difference.

With a deer on the ground let's talk about what should be done and in what order. Here, we're back to that little tidbit known as "If you want three answers, ask three hunters." Since I'm the caretaker of these pages we'll stick to my methods. First off — once the deer is dead the flow of blood has stopped. There is absolutely nothing to be gained by cutting a throat, sticking, or any other act aimed at causing blood to drain. When the heart stops pumping that's it.

In Chapter 17, towards the end, I mentioned what has come to be the most important accessory a hunter can carry, except that it isn't an accessory nowadays — it is a mandatory item. The first thing to do after killing a deer is to use that little pencil. Fill out the tag and attach it to your dead deer. Make it legally yours. Only after that official act of bureaucratic appeasement, is the deer yours to do with as you see fit. Killing had nothing to do with your right to possession. It's that all-powerful little piece of paper that's of utmost importance.

Do not cut the throat of a deer to bleed him. If already dead it serves no purpose because the heart has stopped pumping. In this case the hunter is killing a buck that wouldn't give up. Hopefully he didn't intend to have it mounted. Such a cut would ruin the cape for mounting. Note the antler in the foreground. It came off when the hunter grabbed it to finish the buck. This happens occasionally during late season hunts.

Roll the deer over on his side to pull out the viscera.

This buck was dragged more than half a mile but didn't get dirty inside because only enough opening was made to get out his "innards." It doesn't take much of an opening to perform this task.

Linda Swiggett and her daughter Kathy pose with a good many venison dinners as represented by the white fallow doe shot by Linda. She can cut up a deer with the finesse of a professional meat cutter. Kathy, her sister and brother have almost been raised on wild meat.

225

Black lines indicate the basic cuts. This happens to be an Axis deer but all species are the same. Ham — backstrap — shoulder — neck. Separate all of these, bone out what's left for hamburger or sausage, and a lot of good eating is headed for the freezer.

Now, and only now, can you legally gut your deer.

There has been a lot of mish-mash printed on removing those rather large glands from the back legs. And it is exactly that — mish-mash. More meat has been contaminated by handling those glands and cutting them off than was ever contaminated by leaving them where God put them in the first place. With both the knife and hands messed up what chance does the rest of the deer have?

I usually remove the genitals first. Cut away the penis and testicles back to where the tube enters the body. If help is available have the back legs held and pulled forward to raise the rectum. If not, slip a rock or piece of wood under the hindquarters. Cut around the rectum as if cutting the core out of an apple. Use the surrounding bone as a guide. This needs to be cut loose as far into the body cavity as can be reached with the knife. A lot of mention is usually made of tying off the rectal tube. I guess that's all right, but when the deer is gutted properly I've never seen any need. Some folks tend to complicate things simply because they can't stand an easy way out.

Mentioning "as deep into the body cavity as possible" provides the opportunity to talk a moment about blades. Long bladed knives are not necessary. Not only are they unnecessary, but they are undesirable, too. Three to five inch blades are more than adequate. Either a sheath knife or folder. It makes no difference. I once gutted a deer with a tiny pocket knife, the blade was very delicate and only $1\frac{1}{8}$ inches in length. Shortly after, just to go my act one better, another guide gutted a deer with a miniature sheath knife made for a tie-tac. It wore a blade $\frac{3}{4}$ of an inch long. Folding hunting knives with $2\frac{3}{4}$ to 4 inch blades are ideal for gutting anything up to elk.

The primary cuts are shown by heavy black lines. This whitetail doe, by the way, would head up any list of prime venison. Cut off the legs, separate the hams, shoulders, backstraps and neck, cut to the serving proportions of your choice, trim the remains closely for hamburger or sausage and the job is finished.

That's the biggest I've tackled with a pocket knife. It should be a heavily built knife designed for field use. Also, the blade should be slightly drop-pointed for best all around use.

Once the rectum has been severed, cut the abdominal cavity open by inserting the tip of the knife blade through the skin in front of the pelvis. Just the tip and make this initial opening large enough to accept the first two fingers of the off hand. Insert these fingers and use them to guide the upturned blade as it does its job. Insert only enough blade tip in the animal to go through that belly skin. With a sharp knife, and that's all that should ever be carried, it takes only a moment. Don't forget, the keen edge of the blade is up, away from the intestines. Done in this manner it isn't necessary to try and get the head of the deer higher than the rump. Care and a sharp knife are all that's needed.

Cut only to the breastbone. There is no need to go into the rib section ever at this point. Under the edge of the rib line you will find the diaphragm that separates the animals lungs and heart from the intestines. This must be cut loose from the carcass all around. If the deer is gut shot it is messy and if lung shot, it is bloody. That's just the way it is.

With the diaphragm free (hopefully your sleeves were rolled up to above the elbows before this was started – and your wrist watch removed) reach as far into the throat as possible and sever the windpipe. Be cautious here, and in cutting that diaphragm loose, as warm blood destroys any feeling in cold hands. It is easy to give yourself a bad cut and not know it until the windpipe is pulled out, the blood wiped off, and you find you are the one providing it.

227

That's the end of the cutting except for occasional spots where the intestines hang stubbornly to the carcass. Start by pulling out the windpipe. With it comes the heart and lungs. The liver is on the intestines side of the diaphragm. Some remove it before the diaphragm is cut loose. Others, like me, wait and get it afterwards. After the heart and lungs are out, keep pulling. With the carcass rolled over a bit on its side this all comes out easily. The intestines, stomach and bladder all are rolled out quickly. This is possible because the rectum had already been cut out.

Your deer is gutted. Field dressed, if you prefer.

If you took your time and worked very carefully maybe three or four minutes have elapsed. I have done it often in less than a minute as has every other guide I know. I think something like 28 seconds is the record on one popular hunting ranch.

Drain the blood out by turning the carcass over and letting it lay belly down a few minutes.

If the deer is to be dragged any distance this form of field-dressing offers the least possible exposed flesh for picking up dirt. If it is to be left any length of time it's best to hang the deer and prop open the belly cavity for circulation of air. In spite of what you might have heard or read, use a little water in cleaning the inside, if possible. A clean deer will always taste better. If lacking water, wipe the cavity with paper towels and, if no towels, dry grass is better than nothing.

If you are a heart and liver fan retrieve them from the viscera. Both are good. I never eat either except that, on occasion, the liver is used in camp.

Now comes a problem I can only add from what I've heard. Apparently some parts of the country are blessed with thieves who delight in stealing deer from successful hunters. That doesn't happen in Texas. Maybe because we're not too gentle. A deer thief here would literally be taking his life in his hands. 'nuf said. Anyway, identify the carcass as yours in some manner should you have to leave it. Do this by concealing something in an out of the way spot, not easily detected.

In camp, the carcass can be opened up to the chin if the trophy isn't to be mounted. Or delivered to a locker plant for storage, skinning or whatever. Skinning is the best way to cool out a carcass but don't do this unless you have something to wrap it in. Dirt must be kept off and, if the weather is warm, flies are even more of a problem. Should temperatures get no higher than 40 degrees or so during the day your kill will keep great. Much warmer, and it needs to be kept in a cooler. It is much better to cut your trip short or make a lengthy trip to the nearest town than to lose the meat by trying to leave it hang in warm weather. The difference between aged and rotten can be borderline at times.

Never, if the deer has to be dragged, hauled on horseback or transported in a pickup or Jeep, cut it open from rectum to chin for field dressing. Never split the pelvis on a deer that will be handled as above. Leave as little meat exposed as possible, until it can be properly taken care of.

In splitting the pelvis sometimes it is possible, especially on younger deer, to stand with your feet on the deer's back legs then reach down, grab the tail, and snap it upward as hard as you can. This is impossible on an old deer. There is a hairline seam between the two sides. Start the knife blade in this seam and push down hard. If it requires pounding use a small piece of wood from a nearby tree. Do not use a rock on the back of your knife blade. This is one way to ruin a good knife in a hurry.

Obviously you can't eat the deer until it is cut up. Here again there needs to be nothing complicated about it. Go back to all those rabbits and squirrels you've cut up and you will know exactly what to do with this bigger animal. Work on a solid table with a sharp knife. To facilitate handling I like to cut the carcass in half at the ribs. A saw is necessary for this. My next move is to remove the forelegs at the shoulders. There are no bones to cut here. These shoulders make good roasts and the lower part of the leg is trimmed for hamburger or sausage. Use the saw again and cut off the neck. This might make a roast but it's better for stew meat, hamburger or sausage.

The ribs can be cut into portions for barbecue or trimmed out for hamburger or sausage. It's your choice on any of this. My point is only to show how easy it is.

Remove the hams from the back. There is a big knuckle here to be separated. It might take a bit of searching but once it is found you won't have any trouble. A rump roast can be cut or whatever other roasts you might want. My preference is for steaks so the hams are always sliced for that purpose.

Peel out the backstraps. These are the long pieces of delicious meat laying alongside the backbone from the hams to the shoulders. Which reminds me of a story—I know the man who perpetrated the act. My friend came across a hunter who had just killed a deer. The man was obviously dumbfounded as to what to do next. Unidentified friend offered to help.

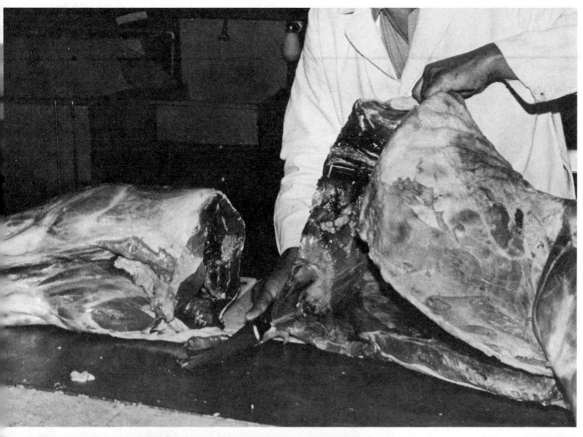

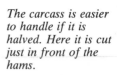

The carcass is easier to handle if it is halved. Here it is cut just in front of the hams.

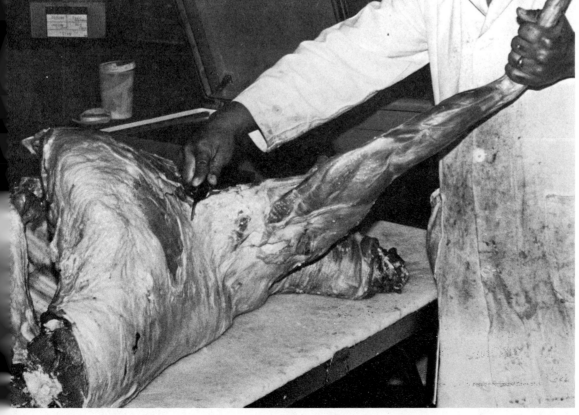

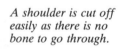

A shoulder is cut off easily as there is no bone to go through.

*A saw
is necessary
to cut off
the neck.*

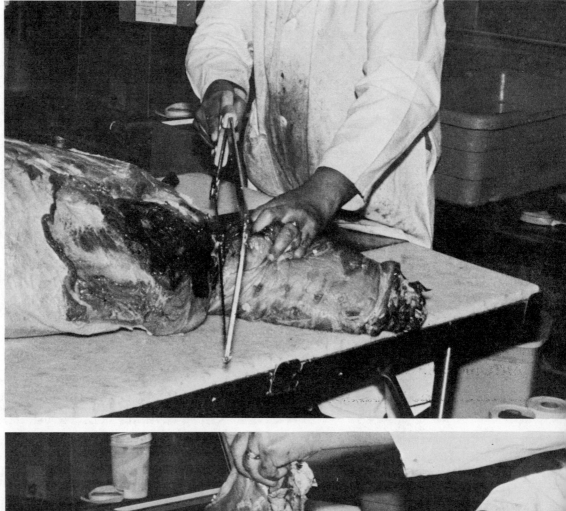

*Cut away
waste from the
back then saw
through
the ribs.*

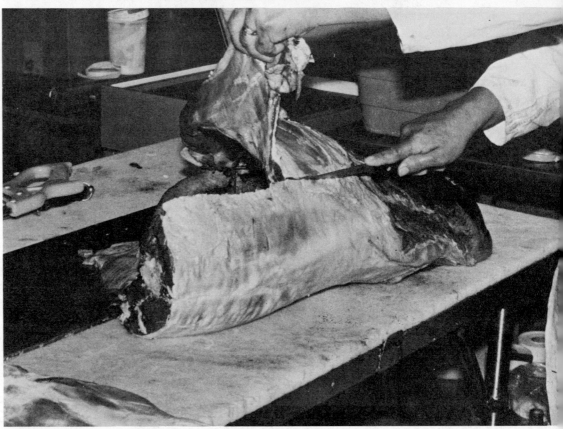

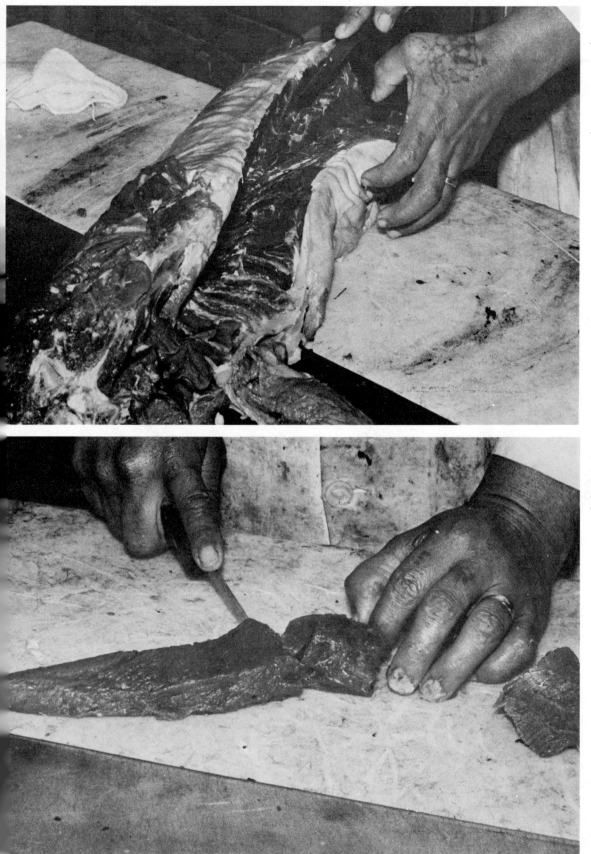

The best part of a
deer. A backstrap is
peeled away from the
backbone. That
tough outer skin can
quickly be removed
by handling the
backstrap as you
would a fish to be
fileted.

Backstrap being cut
into filets. Some like
to leave it in larger
chunks for roasts.
However served, it is
delicious.

231

*Split
the hams with
a saw.*

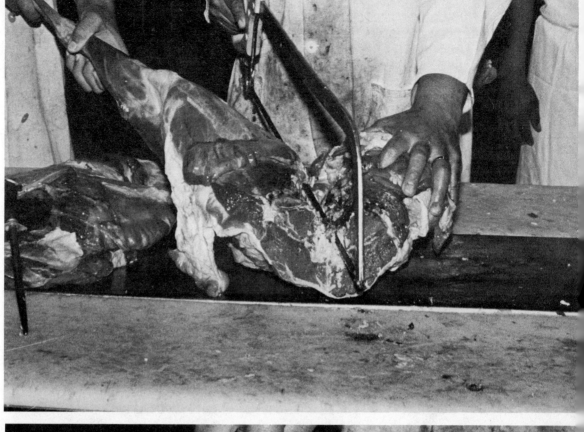

*It's steaks here but
excellent roasts are
also possible. The
author has had many
hams barbecued
whole, with suet and
spices inserted before
cooking. A great way
to handle a fine piece
of meat.*

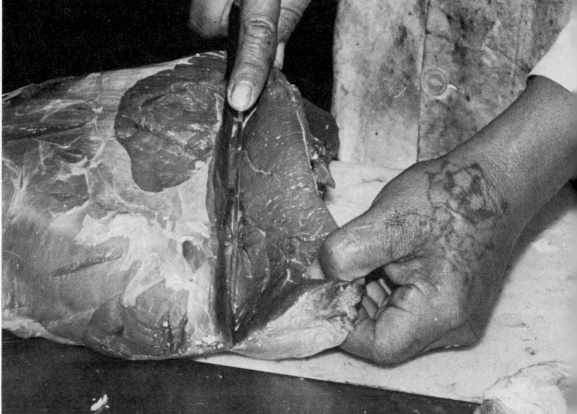

232

He gutted the deer, then dragged it to a road so the hunter could get his car and pick it up.

At this point the hunter tried to pay him for his trouble. Unidentified friend refused money saying, "I'm glad I happened along to help – and by the way – I'd better finish my job. These pieces of meat along the back need to come out as they are the first to spoil. I'll just take them along with me". And he did! These backstraps can be left in roast-sized segments or sliced for frying or broiling. Flattened with a cleaver they make excellent filets. However they are prepared, this will be the most delicious part of your deer. Trim the bones of all meat and toss it in the sausage and hamburger pile.

Here again, cutting up a deer is only a matter of minutes. One person, doing the cutting and wrapping alone, can do it all in an hour. One of my daughters-in-law can do it faster than most professional meat cutters.

Venison sausage is prime fare in my part of the country. It is made both as sausage to be cooked and as a dry summer sausage for just cutting off a hunk and chewing. That's my favorite. Venison hamburger is also delicious. Some prefer the trimmings as pan sausage rather than rings.

But that part belongs to Sylvia Bashline in the next chapter.

Here's one more tale I feel compelled relate. Concerning big knives and field dressing deer. Most guides gut game as soon as it's on the ground. This one was no exception. As he opened his knife his hunter stopped him with, "No, let me do that." And he drew from a belt sheath a real biggie with about a 7 or 8 inch blade. Placing himself over the belly up deer he raised both hands above his head with the knife firmly grasped by the pair. One swift movement plunged the blade into the deer just below the breastbone, all the way to the hilt. With pure brute strength he dragged that long blade full length down to the pelvis. Withdrawing his bloody, gunky, knife covered with stomach contents, intestinal contents and pure undiluted urine he reached for some grass to wipe it off as he said, "You can finish it now – I just wanted to try out my new knife." Kill your deer with either a chest or neck shot, gut it immediately, keep it clean, cool it out quickly, and it will provide excellent meat. Gut shoot it (or pull a stunt like above), don't work very hard in cleaning it up, let it get hot, and you will be a top-ranked candidate for the "I like to hunt but don't like venison" crowd. Even Sylvia won't be able to help you.

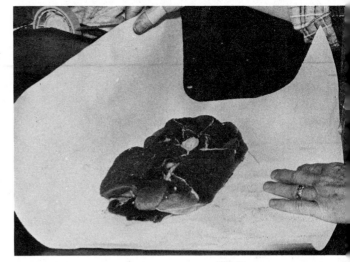

Wrap the cuts and the job is almost finished.

Bone out everything that's left. Trim every tidbit of meat for hamburger or sausage. Sausage is such a Texas tradition that many an entire deer has gone that route. Not a bad way to go, either, with a few rings for cooking, a few as "Summer Sausage" for eating as it's cut from the ring and a few pounds of pan sausage for breakfast.

233

Chapter 20

VENISON IS ROYAL FARE
by Sylvia Bashline

Europeans have always respected their hunters and the meat they provide. This is probably because, at one time, only royalty was allowed to hunt. Today, hunters in Europe have to undergo a series of tests to be allowed to practice their sport. Even then the game downed often belongs to, and is claimed by the landowner and not the sportsman.

Things are different in the United State. We harvest a record number of deer every year *and* we're allowed to keep all the meat. But this privilege brings a responsibility to use the venison wisely without waste. Venison does not need to be soaked to "kill" the gamey taste. With the exception of the improperly gutted deer, or one that has been dining on something strong, most venison does not have an unpleasant taste. If you kill a deer that has a layer of fat, it should be removed when the meat is cut up. Deer fat becomes rancid quickly and can affect the flavor of the meat. If a deer is over 5 years old the meat may need to be tenderized with marinades and long cooking recipes but for the most part, venison should be treated with as much respect as you would offer a filet mignon from your favorite meat market. Venison is truly royal fare and we can enjoy it for the price of a hunting license and a box of shells.

Following are some favorite recipes from my kitchen, all guaranteed to please the most discriminating palate. Some of my recipes use alcoholic beverages but the cooking process will evaporate all the alcohol, leaving only the good natural flavors.

BARBECUE SHOULDER ROAST

In a deep pan, melt 2 tbsp. of margarine and brown a shoulder venison roast on all sides.

Sauce:
1 cup catsup	1/8 tsp. cinnamon
1 tsp. salt	3 slices lemon
2 tbsp. steak sauce	1 onion, sliced thin
1/4 cup vinegar	1/8 tsp. allspice
1 tbsp. butter	

Simmer sauce for ten minutes, then pour it over the roast, cover and bake in a 350 degree oven for about 2 hours, or until the meat is tender. Slice thin and serve with sauce spooned over the meat.

VENISON IN A BAG

5 pound venison roast
Salt & pepper
6 slices of bacon
1 onion, sliced
2 bay leaves
2 beef bouillon cubes
1 small bottle of beer

Salt and pepper the roast and place in a cooking bag. Lay the bacon on top of the roast. Add onion, bay leaves and bouillon cubes to the bag and then add the beer. Close the bag according to directions and roast in 350 degree oven approximately 2 hours. Thicken pan juices with flour for gravy.

Note: If you don't have a cooking bag, heavy duty aluminum foil could be used. However, you must use care not to pierce the foil and let out the juices.

VENISON POT ROAST

4 pound shoulder roast
Flour, salt & pepper
2 tbsp. butter
¼ tsp. basil
¼ tsp. parsley, chopped
1 onion, chopped
1 carrot, chopped
1 celery stalk, diced
1 cup beef bouillon
1 cup dry red wine
4 potatoes, cut in quarters
4 carrots, cut in quarters

Dust roast with seasoned flour and brown in a heavy Dutch oven using the butter. When brown on all sides, sprinkle the roast with basil and parsley and add the next five ingredients to the pan. Cover and simmer for 1½ hours turning the roast several times. Add rest of carrots and the potatoes to the roast and simmer another 45 minutes. Will serve 4 to 6.

SMOKED VENISON

4 pound rolled, boneless, venison roast
1 cup white sugar
1 medium onion, sliced
3 bay leaves
½ tsp. marjoram
1 tsp. chili powder
1 tsp. coarsely ground black pepper
2 tbsp. soy sauce
Enough water to cover roast

Mix all of the ingredients together in a deep roasting pan or bowl. Add the venison roast to the marinade. Place in the refrigerator for 48 hours. After removing the roast from the liquid, drain on paper toweling and then air-dry on a cookie sheet for two hours.

Smoke the roast in an electric smoker (such as Little Chief or Outers) for 25 hours – 5 pans of smoke. If the weather is cold, you may have to finish cooking the meat in the oven – 300 degree oven for 2 hours. A little of the finished product goes a long **way,** so slice thinly.

SMOKED VENISON – The finished product, compact and full of proteins.

SMOKED VENISON – These venison roasts are marinating before they go in the smoker.
This is an excellent way to use the tough cuts.

HUNGARIAN VENISON ROAST

5 pound venison roast	1¼ tsp. oregano
2 cloves of garlic	1 tsp. parsley
Several strips of salt pork	½ cup beef bouillon
Flour, salt & pepper	½ cup dry vermouth
3 tbsp. butter	1 tbsp. Hungarian paprika
2 onions, chopped	1 cup sour cream

HUNGARIAN VENISON ROAST – With salt pork strips throughout the meat.

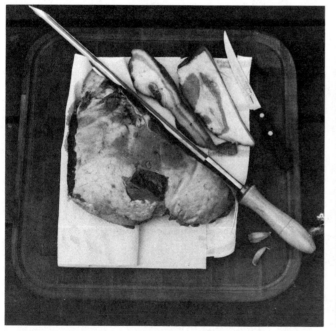

The roast, larding needle and salt pork.

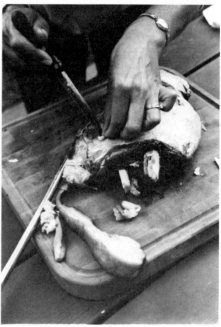

*HUNGARIAN
VENISON
ROAST –*

Push slivers of garlic into roast.

Using a larding needle (available from a restaurant supply store) or a sharp, thin knife push the strips of salt pork into the roast. Sliver the garlic cloves and push into slots cut in meat. Rub the roast with salt & pepper and roll in flour. Sear quickly on all sides in the butter in a Dutch oven. Add onions, oregano, parsley, bouillon and wine to the pot, cover and simmer for 2 hours. Add paprika, check for doneness and add more broth if necessary. When done, remove to a hot platter. Add sour cream to the broth and heat until almost boiling.

Serve the roast sliced with cooked rice on a platter. Pour sauce over meat and rice. Serves 6.

237

FOILED VENISON ROAST

6 pound roast
1 can condensed cream of mushroom soup
1 envelope dry onion soup mix

Lay roast on a large piece of heavy duty aluminum foil. Pour the soups over the roast. Using the drugstore wrap, seal the roast and place in a roasting pan in a 350 degree oven. Roast for approximately 2½ hours.

RARE FRIED STEAK

4 venison steaks, cut ½ to ¾ inch thick
2 tbsp. butter
2 tbsp. cooking oil
2 tbsp. parsley
Salt & pepper

If your deer is a young one, try this quick and delicious way to cook steak. Have your frying pan hot and the butter and oil sizzling. Sear the steak for about 3 minutes on each side. Serve immediately, sprinkling with salt, pepper and parsley. It will be rare and juicy. Serves 4.

CHINESE PEPPER STEAK

2 pounds venison steak
1⅓ cups of beef bouillon
Cooking oil
1 medium onion, coarsely chopped
1 green pepper, coarsely chopped
1 stalk celery, coarsely chopped
2 tbsp. water
3 tbsp. cornstarch
2 tbsp. soy sauce
2 tsp. sugar
Pinch ginger
1 16-oz. can La Choy chinese vegetables (drained)

Partially thaw venison steak, cut into thin strips (⅛ inch slices) and brown in oil. Add bouillon and simmer for 20 minutes. Add onion, green pepper and celery and simmer for 10 minutes. Mix water, cornstarch, soy sauce, sugar and ginger and add to the pan. Cook until slightly thick and add vegetables. Serve with rice. Makes 6 servings.

VENISON STROGANOFF

1 pound venison steak, cut in long thin strips
3 tbsp. flour
Salt & pepper
Margarine
1 garlic clove, minced
1 onion, chopped
1 cup tomato juice
1½ cup water
1 tsp. sugar
1 can mushrooms
1 tsp. steak sauce
5 drops Tabasco sauce
½ cup sour cream

Douse meat in flour. Add salt and pepper. Brown lightly in margarine with onion. Add tomato juice, water, sugar and sauces. Simmer until tender – 1 to 1½ hours. Ten minutes before serving add mushrooms and sour cream. Serves 4. Goes well with spaghetti noodles.

MARINATED VENISON STEAK

4 venison steaks, ¾ inch thick
1 clove garlic
1 cup dry red wine
1 cup water
6 black peppercorns
1 bay leaf
1 tsp. pickling spice
1 onion, sliced
1 tsp. sugar.
Butter

Rub steaks with the garlic and place in a bowl with the wine, water, pepper, bay leaf, spice, onion and sugar. Let marinate for six hours. Dry steaks on paper toweling. Fry quickly in hot frying pan with the butter. Serve on hot plates and sprinkle with salt.

SWISS STEAK

4 venison steaks, cut 1 inch thick
2 onions, sliced
1 small can tomatoes
1 bay leaf
Salt & pepper, & flour
1 can mushrooms

Dredge steaks in seasoned (salt & pepper) flour. Pound with a mallet to force flour into meat. Brown steaks in fat on each side. Add tomatoes, onions, bay leaf, cover and simmer for 1½ hours. Add mushrooms, heat and serve. Will serve four.

BROILED VENISON CHOPS

8 chops, at least 1 inch thick
Meat tenderizer
Butter
Salt & Pepper

One half hour before broiling time, moisten the chops and sprinkle with meat tenderizer. Pierce in several places with a fork. Butter both sides of meat just before broiling. Place on aluminum foil on a broiler pan. Broil 4 inches from the heat, 5 minutes on each side and serve immediately. Salt and pepper to taste at the table. Serves 4.

VENISON CHOPS WITH SOUR CREAM

8 venison chops
1 onion, chopped
2 tbsp. butter
1 cup burgundy
1 small tomato, chopped & seeded
1 cup sour cream
Salt & pepper
1 tsp. basil

Saute chops and onions in butter until lightly brown. Add wine, tomato, basil and cover. Simmer until tender. Transfer chops to a heated platter. Add sour cream to the pan juices and heat. Pour sauce over chops. Serve with buttered noodles. Will feed four.

SWISS STEAK – The makings.

SWISS STEAK – Simmering.

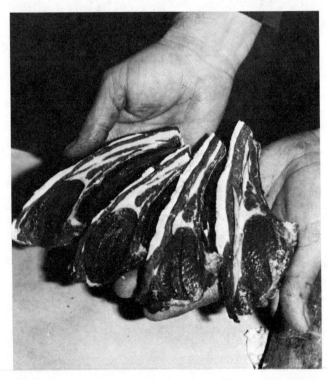

ROUNTREE STEW

1 pound venison stew meat, cubed
2 tbsp. butter
1 large can tomatoes
1 tsp. steak sauce
Salt & pepper
1 onion, chopped
1 stalk celery, chopped
4 carrots, sliced
4 potatoes, quartered.

Brown stew meat in butter. Add tomatoes, cover and simmer for 1¼ hours. Add rest of ingredients and cook until done – about 45 minutes. Thicken the juices with instant flour. Salt & pepper to taste.

WHITETAIL CHOPS – Too good for ordinary people.

*FRIED VENISON STEAK –
RARE.*

HUNTER'S STEW

1½ pound venison stew meat, cubed
1 large onion, chopped
1 cup celery, diced
Butter
½ cup uncooked rice
1 can cream of chicken soup
1 can cream of mushroom soup
1 can mushrooms
4 tsp. soy sauce
Salt & pepper
1 package peas & carrots (frozen)
1 cup water

Brown meat, onion and celery in butter. Add water, cover and simmer on top of stove for 1 hour. Add rest of ingredients, mix well, cover and place in 350 degree oven until rice is cooked and meat is tender – another 45 minutes to 1 hour. Will serve 4 to 6.

241

VENISON LASAGNE

2 pounds ground venison
1 jar (32 oz.) Ragu spaghetti sauce
1 lb. ricotta cheese (or 1 lb. cottage cheese)
½ lbs. mozzarella cheese
2 eggs, beaten
1 tsp. parsley flakes
Salt & pepper
1 lbs. lasagne noodles (cooked 5 minutes)
1 cup grated parmesan cheese

Brown venison in large skillet, add spaghetti sauce and heat to just a boil. Cut 12 thin slices of mozzarella for topping and shred the remaining. Mix it with ricotta cheese, eggs, parsley, salt and pepper. Ladle 1 cup of meat sauce into bottom of each baking dish (2 dishes – 12" x 8"). Layer 3 noodles, then about 1 cup of cheese mixture and 1 cup of meat sauce in each pan. Repeat twice. Sprinkle parmesan on the top with mozzarella slices. Bake at 350 degrees for 30 to 40 minutes – until bubbly.

VENISON ▶
MOUSSAKA

VENISON MOUSSAKA

1 16-ounce can cut green beans, drained
1½ pounds venisonburger
1 8-ounce can tomato sauce
½ tsp. garlic salt
⅛ tsp. cinnamon
2 eggs, slightly beaten
1½ cups cream-style cottage cheese
⅓ cup grated parmesan cheese
2 tbsp. ripe olive juice
4 ripe olives, sliced

Place green beans in a buttered casserole. Brown meat in a skillet and drain off excessive fat. Add tomato sauce, garlic salt and cinnamon, spread over the beans. Combine eggs, cottage cheese and olive juice and spread over the meat mixture. Sprinkle with parmesan cheese. Bake in a 350 degree oven for 30 minutes. Garnish with the olive slices. Makes 6 servings.

VENISON STUFFED CABBAGE LEAVES

2 pounds ground venison
¼ cup chopped onion
4 tbsp. butter
2 cups cooked rice
½ tsp. dill weed
½ tsp. celery salt
Salt & pepper
12 cabbage leaves
1 8-ounce can tomato cauce
½ tsp. basil

Brown meat and onion in butter. Mix in rice, dill weed, celery salt, salt & pepper (to taste). Place cabbage leaves in boiling water for 1 minute. Drain and dry on paper toweling. Place meat mixture in the center of each leaf, roll and secure with toothpicks. Place filled leaves in a greased casserole. Mix tomato sauce and basil and pour over leaves. Bake in 325 degree oven for about 45 minutes. Serves 6.

VENISON SAUSAGE

5 pounds venison
2 pounds fat salt pork
5 tbsp. sage
1 tsp. fennel
3 tsp. salt
2 tsp. cayenne pepper
1 onion, minced
1 garlic clove, minced

Grind meat fine and mix with other ingredients. Make into patties and fry.

VENISON LIVER

Slices of fresh venison liver
4 tbsp. butter
Salt & pepper
Splash of dry vermouth

Liver is traditional in hunting camp but often it is fried in bacon grease and overcooked. For a new taste, try slicing the liver paper-thin. Heat the frying pan until the butter is hot. Saute the liver for a couple minutes on each side. Add vermouth and simmer for an additional 2 minutes. Serve immediately. The liver should be a bit pink in the center. Salt and pepper to taste.

VENISON CASSEROLE

½ package egg noodles
1 pound ground venisonburger
1 tbsp. green pepper, chopped
1 onion, chopped
1 clove garlic, minced
4 tbsp. cooking oil
1 can tomato soup
1 can corn
1 can mushrooms
1 can tomato sauce (small)
Salt & pepper
Pinch of Italian seasonings

Cook noodles in salted water until tender. Saute meat, green pepper, onion, garlic in the cooking oil. Add other ingredients. Mix in noodles and pour into a greased casserole dish. Bake for about 30 minutes in 325 degree oven.

PICKLED HEART

1 venison heart
8 peppercorns
1 tsp. salt
2 bay leaves
2 onions, sliced
Vinegar
Salt & pepper

Place heart in a deep saucepan and cover with water. Add 1 sliced onion, peppercorns and salt. Cover and simmer until it is tender. Cool the heart on paper toweling. Slice thinly, removing all cords and fat. Place slices in a bowl with the other sliced onion, salt and pepper. Cover with vinegar water (1 part vinegar/6 parts water). Pickle for 24 hours in refrigerator. Can be used in sandwiches or for low calorie snacking.

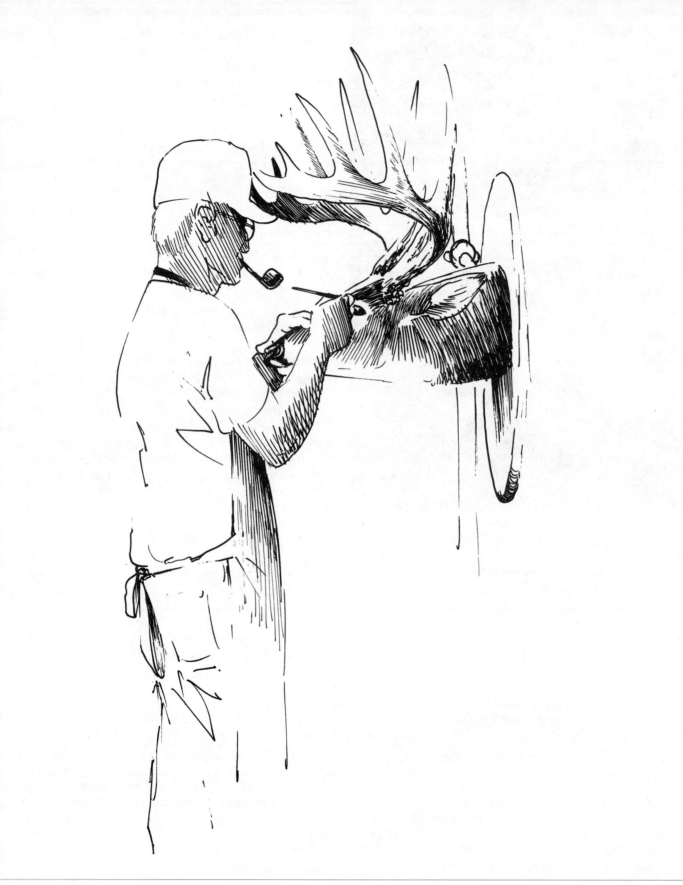

Chapter 21

TAXIDERMY

Seldom have I killed a game animal and not skinned and caped it for mounting, even if I didn't want it for myself.

One of the biggest problems confronting taxidermists is hides that have been allowed to go bad so they can't be tanned without hair slippage. As a result, there is no trophy for the hunter. More often than not, that same hunter will blame the taxidermist for the slipping hair. Because of this most shops try to have a few spare capes on hand.

One of San Antonio's oldest taxidermy shops is run by a close friend of some three-plus decades. My kills are always handled carefully and given to him for "spares," unless I want the trophy myself. I save all antlers and horns from my kills, it's just the cape I give away.

I have still another idiosyncrasy. Lots of them, according to my wife, but this one concerning hides: I skin all my animals out whole and let the taxidermist cut off what he wants for the mount. The remainder is tanned into buckskin. By doing it this way he has plenty to work with and I get a good supply of buckskin for gloves, vests, jackets, etc. All too often a hunter wants a shoulder mount but cuts the cape so short he leaves barely enough for a neck mount. Usually, the taxidermist gets blamed for this too. My method solves that problem.

But let's start at the beginning and see what happens.

The caping of a deer takes only a little time. Even a first-timer should need little more than an hour. Tool requirements are simple. A sharp — spelled SHARP — knife, a steel to keep it that way and a good stone to get it that way in the first place. A screwdriver can come in mighty handy. Make it a long one. You will find out why as this project develops.

For a shoulder mount the buck should have been field dressed through an incision from the anal opening to the rib cage. Never cut into the ribs. Roll up your sleeves and dive in all the way to your shoulders if necessary but do not cut into the ribs if a good cape is desired.

Cut around the body starting at the forward end of this incision by going up one side, across the back and down the other side to where it all started. Remove the front legs at the knee or whatever you want to call that first joint below the shoulder. Make a cut down the inside of a front leg running it straight across to the center of the chest. Now do the same thing to the other front leg. If there is any hide beyond this, back towards the body cavity, go ahead and split it to that encircling cut. Peel out the legs leaving no meat on the hide. And that's it for this side of the deer.

Turn him over and split the hide from the shoulders up the back of the neck to about three inches short of a line between the antlers. Go to the base of an antler and cut diagonally to where the preceeding cut stopped. The same from the other antler. When this section of hide is peeled from the skull it will form a perfect triangle.

Go back to that around the chest cut and carefully remove the hide. Pull as much of it loose as possible

The dotted black line indicates where the cape should be cut behind the shoulders and where the cut up the back of the neck is made.
Raymond Rhodes was the guide on this Y. O. Ranch hunt. Not readily visible in the photo, but there is a heavy, palmated-tip, tine running off the left antler base back of the right antler almost to the right ear. Needless to say, the trophy was mounted.

cutting only where absolutely necessary. Take no more meat than you have to because, sooner or later, it all has to come off, one way or another. In using the knife try to avoid cutting the hide. Each puncture has to be sewn up by the taxidermist. Be sure, when stripping meat from the hide, to never go through to the roots of the hair. The hair will come out, upon tanning, when roots are exposed.

After the shoulders and neck are skinned, some like to stop. If conditions are such that the head can be left intact, by all means do it. What is necessary here is that it be possible to either freeze the head or at least keep it very cold – and dry – until it can reach the taxidermist for finishing.

Be alerted to that "dry" notation; using ice doesn't always work. Sometimes watersoaking ruins the hide. If ice can be kept in plastic bags so no water is in contact with the hide, you'll have no problem. Moist, it can sour and spoil rather rapidly.

Backing up a bit – if you can get by in this manner it is not necessary to cut up the back at all. Just pull the hide as far up the neck as possible then cut off the head. The taxidermist will split it where he wants.

To finish the caping chore, skin out to the skull then move carefully along the back of the jaw and up to the antlers. Now comes time to use that screwdriver. And a hammer or rock. Chip the hide

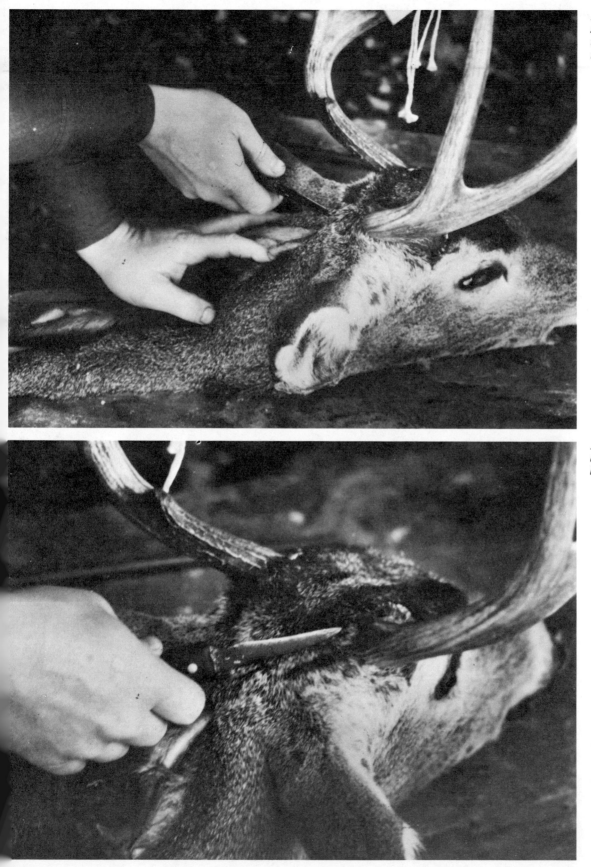

*David Nowotny
shows where the cut
up the back of the
neck stops.*

*And here – how it
angles over to the
base of the antler.*

247

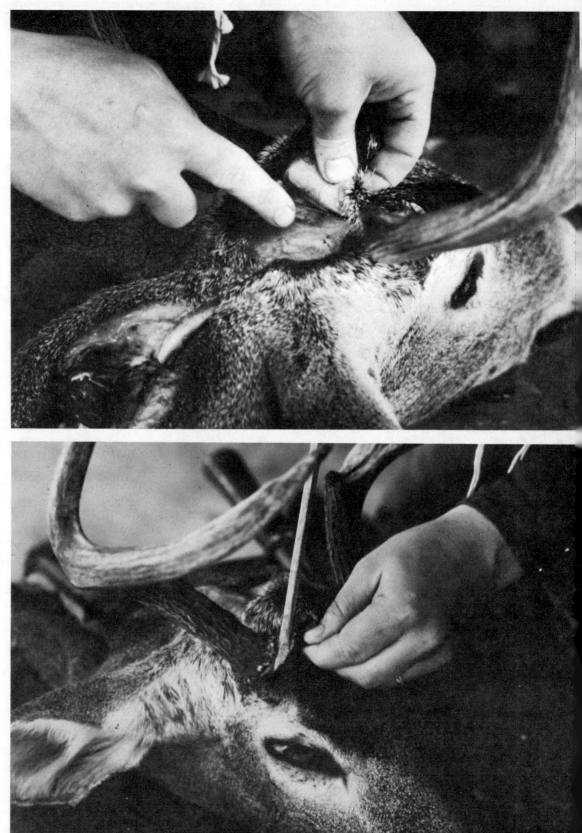

With the triangular cut made to each antler base the hide is lifted from the skull.

The screwdriver is used to chip the hide away from antler bases. A knife can be used but is dangerous in that the hide can be cut beyond repair.

248

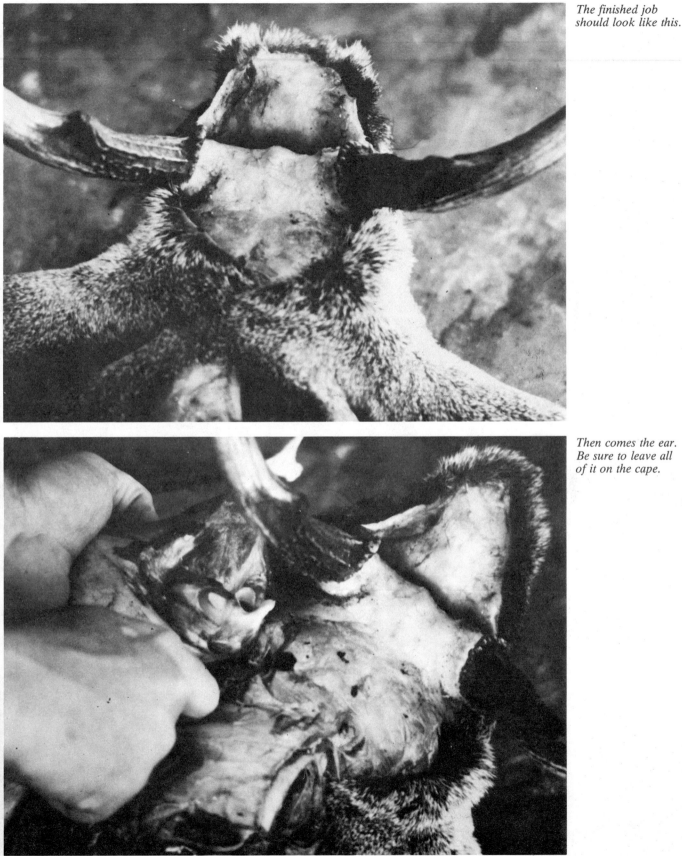

The finished job should look like this.

Then comes the ear. Be sure to leave all of it on the cape.

249

Eyes demand even more care than ears. All of the lid must be on the cape. Work very slowly here.

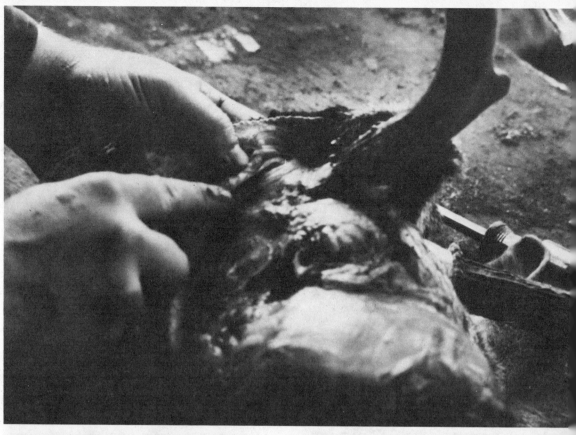

The finished eye will look like this.

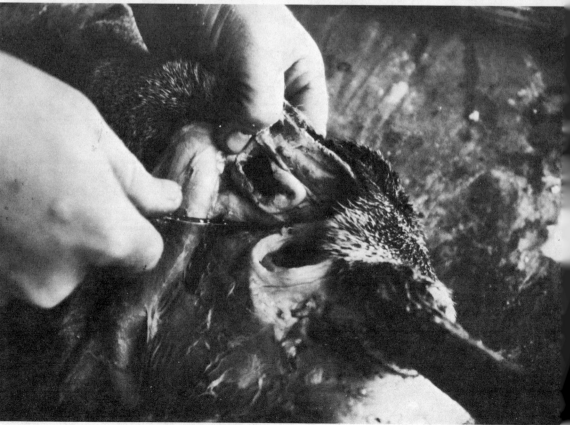

250

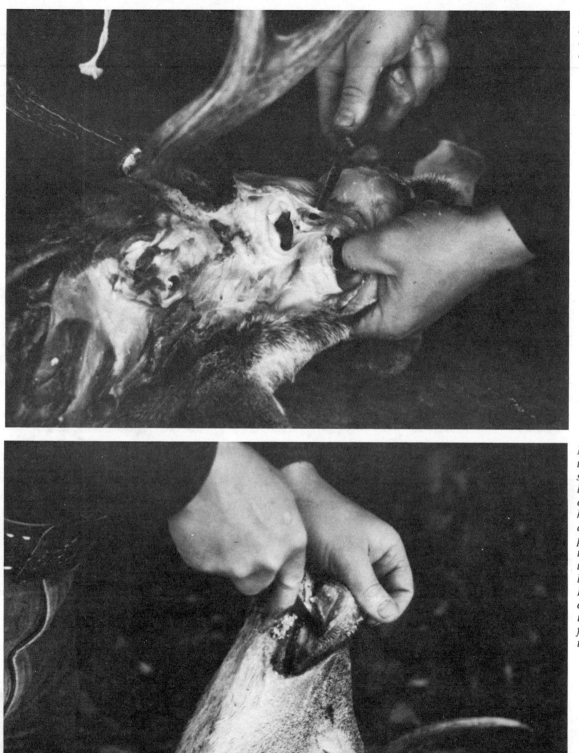

The tear duct is below the eye. Be sure all of it is on the cape.

Nowotny likes to cut the lips from the outside as shown here, by reaching in to the edge of the teeth with his knife. Whether done this way or by pulling the cape over the skull it is important that all of the lip be left on the cape. It is cut from the edge of the teeth. All that skin is needed for tucking-under on the finished mount.

251

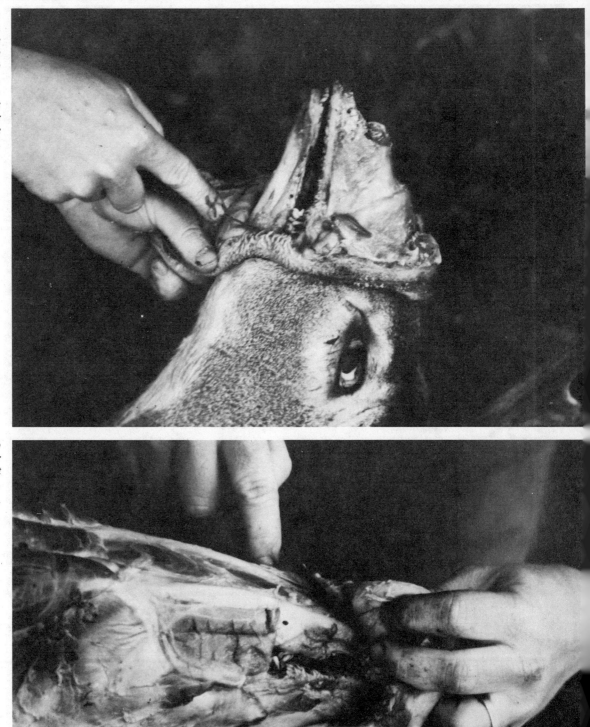

Nowotny still works from the outside in skinning the nose and front of the lower jaw. Taught by his grandfather Lin, an old-time taxidermist, the method is obviously good or they wouldn't be using it.

Now he's back to pulling the cape over the skull and is almost finished.

252

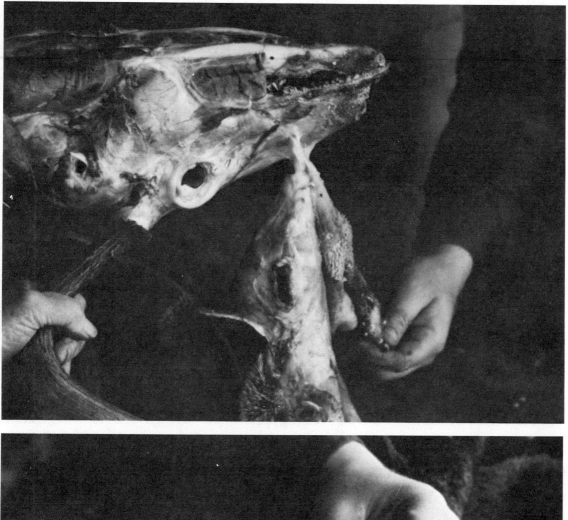

Only this one cut to be made and the caping is finished.

Skinning the bottom of the ear, getting ready to turn it inside out.

253

David uses his steel to push the ear inside out. A long screwdriver serves the same purpose.

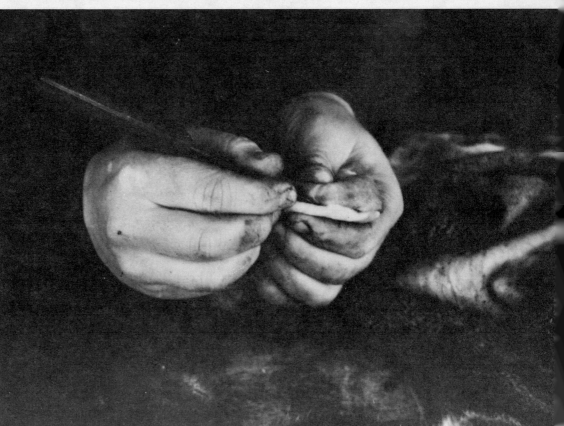

Almost finished. The ear must be turned inside out all the way to the tip.

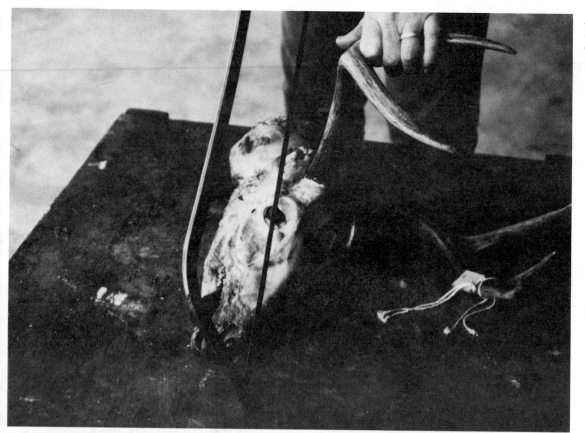

A single cut through the eye removes the antlers.

One cut from the back of the skull through the eyes gets the antlers off easily. Except for salting, the caping job is finished. If it can be frozen, do so. If salting use table salt. It will take about two pounds for the cape. Another four pounds if saving the rest of the hide for buckskin (a great idea).

away from the base of each antler with the point of the screwdriver, working from the burr down. And around. It's easy and much safer than trying to cut it free with a knife. As the hide is freed from both antlers peel it on over the skull. Watch closely for the ears. It often works best to put a finger as far into the ear as possible then work against it from the other side.

Once to the base, cut the ear off. Make sure all the ear is left on the cape. There should be nothing left but the hole into the skull when the cut is made.

Now it's time for the eyes. Even more care is needed here than with the ears. The entire eye must be left intact. All of the lid and tear duct has to be on the cape. Work cautiously. Slowly. Don't make any cut until you are sure it's the right one. The tear duct is below the inside corner of the eye. It must be cut off against the skull which actually means into it. There should be no skin at all left around the eye socket or tear duct. If there is, you've goofed!

That same care used around the ears and eyes is now necessary for the lips. There are two schools of thought here. One cuts the lips free from the outside working carefully along the edge of the teeth. The other, the one I've always used, peels the cape down over the skull and very carefully cuts the lips away from the jaw at the edge of the teeth. It's six of one and half a dozen of the other. The important thing is that painstaking care is required as all of the lip and skin has to be on the cape for sufficient material to be available for tucking-under on the finished mount.

With the lips freed there is nothing left but to finish peeling the cape off the skull and to cut through the cartilage where the nose begins.

Voila! That's all there is to it!

Well, almost.

If the cape can be frozen, you are finished. If it can be kept very cold and will be at the taxidermist's in a few days, you are finished. If the hide is to be salted, the ears have to be turned inside out. Use the longhandled screw driver by bracing it against the thigh. Pull the ear down over the point to separate the hide from the cartilage. After this is started it can usually be completed with the fingers. Pull down hard, cutting carefully only where the hide can't be separated with the fingers. The ear must be turned inside-out clear to the tip.

Lay the cape out flat and scrape away any meat or fat that remains. If there is any tissue residue the salt can't do its job. As soon as it is clean, rub salt thoroughly into the pelt, then roll it up, pelt side in. Tie it into a bundle and keep it in deep shade in the coolest spot you can find. If several days are to elapse before getting to your taxidermist it can be advantageous to open up the cape at night and let it cool. Providing you are where it does get cooler at night. Re–salt and roll it back up in the morning. Hides can be kept fresh quite a while this way.

To remove antlers make a single cut with a saw from the back of the skull on a line through the center of the eyes. This will come out more or less halfway between the base of the antlers and the nose.

If, by chance, you want a life-size mount the only extra work is to field dress the animal through a small incision between the ribs and the genitals. And, naturally, do not cut off those front legs as mentioned in caping for a shoulder mount. Start at the edge of a back hoof and cut up the inside of a leg to the first joint, then let the cut veer to the back side of the leg and up to just behind the scrotum. Likewise on the other side. Very carefully split the hide along the penis, staying in a straight line down the center of the abdominal cavity, and peel out this organ. Next cut the testicles loose and peel them out. Continue this cut on to the anal opening. Then on out to the tip of the tail.

Work carefully around the hoof and cut the leg off at the joint you will find inside the top of the hoof (hooves remain attached to hide). Do the front legs the same way, except that here the cut stays down the inside of the leg to that center line.

Once the hide is peeled from the carcass (be very careful with the tail as it is easy to tear off), up to where you would have cut around the chest for a shoulder mount, the process is the same as related earlier.

In cutting up the back of the neck for a life-mount, start just beyond the shoulders at the base of the neck. It doesn't go all the way back as for shoulder mounting.

There is nothing hard about caping. Yet many trophies are ruined. Sometimes it's lack of care, sometimes lack of knowledge.

I'll never forget two mule deer I left at a locker plant to be skinned, caped, and the meat processed and frozen. A week later I picked up the frozen meat, neatly bundled frozen capes, and antlers. Two days later, at my taxidermists (one of the capes was a spare for him and the other to be shoulder mounted for the hunter) it was discovered the skinner had split the hides from tail to chin.

Ruined! Both of them!

Grabbing the phone I called that locker plant a couple of states away and in no uncertain terms I informed the owner that by the end of that week he would have two proper mule deer capes on the way to my taxidermist. I didn't ask this – I ordered it! He got the message. The following Monday morning my taxidermist called and said two nicely skinned capes had just arrived.

How or where that locker plant owner got them, I don't know, but I have the feeling that never, again, did one of his men rip a trophy buck from one end to the other.

Chapter 22

EXOTIC (FOREIGN) DEER

No book on deer hunting in North America could be complete without considering those foreign species that are imported and hunted in some areas. In some instances individual animals have escaped and built up huntable herds in the wild, but most are under private ownership and are hunted on a year 'round basis. There are few restraining laws concerning these animals on private land. And there shouldn't be. After all, these landowners paid hard-earned money for their stock. They feed it, even some of the smaller ranches, until harvestable. Others, the bigger ranches, watch over them, same as their native herds, wait out their growth, same as conservation-minded landowners do with their whitetails and mule deer, and harvest the surplus, which wouldn't have been there if they hadn't invested both money and time.

Exotics, same as the native varieties, will be harvested whether hunted or not. Nature takes a terrible toll when over-population brings on under-nourishment, then sickness, and finally death by disease and starvation, a far more cruel death and a total waste. Hunting is not just killing – it is harvesting a crop, be it whitetail deer, mule deer, exotic deer, or whatever the species of animal or bird. But let's get on to the animals themselves which include Axis deer, the Chital of India; Sika deer, the Japanese, Formosan and Dybowski of Manchuria; and the Fallow deer from countries bordering the Mediterranean. These are the ones of primary concern. The occasional Red deer (from Europe) and even fewer Sambar (from southern Asia) are to be found, but only on scattered ranches.

By far the most handsome is the beautiful Chital, or Axis, deer from India. Wearing lifelong spots as with fawn whitetails the rufous (reddish-brown) colored coat tops out with a dark, almost black, stripe from the mane down the back to the tip of the tail. The belly, rump, throat, and the insides of the legs, tail and ears are white. There seems to be no set breeding season for these animals. Though most bucks drop their antlers from late summer to fall there are always a number of hardened antler bucks in any herd thus making them the only deer that can be hunted year around. By the same token bucks in velvet can be seen at all times of the year. Likewise for fawns. It is confusing to those of us familiar with whitetails and mule deer, but interesting to the hunter or wildlife observer because of the possibility of finding a buck with hardened antlers, one in velvet, and one just starting antler growth in the same herd.

Some say the Axis runs to 200 pounds but I'm of the opinion 140–150, field dressed, would be a lot closer. A good many real trophies with magnificent antlers might not hit over 125–130 pounds on a set of scales – minus what is normally left in the field.

Axis antlers are impressive – there is no other way to put it. Whitetail hunters have been known to go drooling, lip-quivering mad over a little 24-incher that an Axis hunter wouldn't look back at. To approach trophy proportions antlers need to close in on 30 inches along the main beam. Exceptions would be either extremely heavy beams or very long tines. In these instances 27 or 28 inches would be readily acceptable. The peak of growth

Number One – Extra Typical – Primitive Arms. That's the standing of this Sika killed by the author, right, on the Y. O. Ranch. Bobby Snow was the guide. Primitive Arms means muzzle loaders. Swiggett used a .58 caliber Buffalo Hunter.

seems to occur at six, seven and maybe even up to eight years of age. Before that, they aren't big enough, and after, the antlers start going downhill. There are usually 3 points on each beam. At least this is typical; anything more will, as a rule, not be evenly matched on both sides, therefore not so desirable as a trophy.

The author has a life-sized Axis mount that was taken on the Y.O. Ranch with a .50 caliber muzzle loading (Thompson/Center Hawken) rifle. It measures only 28½ inches along the beam and has the typical 3 points. Each of the tines are extremely long and both sides match almost to perfection. They are so long and so perfectly matched that in the Burkett Trophy Game Records of the World book it is ranked Number Two – Primitive Arms.

Axis deer like cover and are never found far from something to hide in – that is until the sun starts down. Their primary feeding time seems to be those few hours just before and after dark and another two or three hours before and after daylight. Both browsers and grass eaters, they appear to eat more grass than do whitetails.

The most important thing to remember, in hunting Axis deer, is to avoid buck fever. Those antlers look mighty big to the first-timer and sometimes to more experienced hands, too. Another point – if one is spotted and not disturbed, the odds would be in your favor to go back to that area later in the day and find him. This just in case one is seen that is good, but maybe borderline. Hunt a few hours longer, then go back and seek him out if nothing

Number Two – Primitive Arms is where this Axis stands in the BTGRW book. Killed on the Y. O. Ranch by Hal Swiggett using a T/C .50 caliber Hawken – scope sighted. Harvey Goff, his guide, poses with the trophy.

better is found. This will work only where the animals aren't hunted hard and are not disturbed.

One final comment on Axis deer: when you get your trophy, regardless of how big he is, carefully field dress him and keep the meat as clean as possible. It is by far the best table fare of any deer that ever walked the woods, in my opinion. Except for elk. It's not any better than elk, to my taste buds, but also isn't any worse and I've always given elk meat my vote as the best of big game. I've been told Big Horn sheep meat is even better, but I'm not a sheep hunter so guess I'll never find out.

Sika deer are about the size of a small whitetail. Their darker color and shaggier coat sometimes reveals a hint of spots. Never like those on an Axis, but spots nevertheless. The different varieties of Sika vary in color from almost black in the smaller

Japanese animals to a dark to medium brown on the biggest, the Dybowski. This latter one is more revealing of his spots, maybe because of the lighter color.

Sika antlers are quite elk-like in appearance though much smaller, of course. The Dybowski's antlers can be as large as those of a red deer or even a small elk. (Very small elk, I'd better add.)

Sika are brush lovers, seldom found away from heavy cover. I like to hunt draws and the thickest cover in the area, as that's where the better bucks will be found. Shots are seldom long in hunting these fascinating deer. Both browsers and grass eaters, they seem more like native whitetail in their eating habits by preferring tender browse over grass. Unlike any of the other deer, Sikas have

261

A trophy Axis – big of antler and big of body.

This Axis buck is still in velvet.

A good spotted Fallow buck.   *Photo by Albert Dean*

Axis herds such as this can be found on the Y. O. Ranch in the Hill Country of Texas.

A Fallow buck of trophy quality.

A fine Fallow buck in velvet. This photo by Albert Dean shows the palmated antlers in detail.

A typical Sika buck. The spots are more visible here than usual for the species.

been known to cross with both Red deer and Sambar.

Working with one of the larger exotic game ranches, to be more specific, the largest in the world, I had occasion some years back to trade Sikas for a small herd of Zebus. These are little cattle from Tibet that can best be described as miniature Brahmas. Mentioning two or three other exotics I thought the rancher might be interested in, none hit a receptive note – then I mentioned Sikas. This rancher, an old-timer, looked me right in the eye and said, "Young feller (this was a long time ago), I wouldn't be able to keep Sika on my ranch. Them danged things can go through any fence water can get through."

Without a doubt – he knew his Sika.

Because of this trait they can be found in most any pasture of any ranch that ever stocked them, as well as on most of the surrounding ranches, even in the original pasture where they were stocked to begin with. A biologist on the Y.O. Ranch, the world's largest exotic game hunting ranch, told me he had actually seen them swimming in rain-swollen draws waiting for fence gaps to be washed out.

Fallow are most thought of in their white coloration. "Park deer" I guess best states their case, except that in the wild they don't even remotely resemble the gentleness of nature that would endear them to the hearts of park goers. In other words, they get wild quick! There are three distinct colors of Fallow deer. The white, as mentioned, a chocolate that closely resembles the whitetail, and a spotted edition. This last one is of a lighter brown, almost yellow at times, having a background with white spots.

Antlers are palmated at the top with projections along the back a la moose. They drop them, like Sika, in January and February, which means they can be hunted usually from September or early October until that time; sometimes as early as August, depending on the area.

As to their wild nature, the Y.O. has a thriving herd, as they do also of Sika and Axis, well represented by all color variations. A huge white buck long claimed one of their larger pastures as home. Of tremendous size, he was sought out by many a guide and hunter. All came back with the shakes. None ever did get him. A few got a shot, but those who were so lucky never touched a hair as he disappeared over a ridge or into heavy cover not to be seen again that day. He finally disappeared. Probably died of old age.

Unlike native deer all of these are rather vocal. Axis deer are known to emit a shrill whistle when disturbed or alarmed. During the rut they don't always have to be alarmed or disturbed to whistle and usually the rutting whistle is more drawn out than the bark-like whistle of normal alarm. Though I've never heard it, others have reported both Axis does and bucks have been known to scream when in pain.

Sika bucks, during the rut, have an unusual whistle which often changes into a high pitch towards the end of a note, much on the order of an elk bugle. At other times they utter a very realistic bark.

Fallow bucks sound off with a sort of drawn out grunt when rutting, and while they produce similar sounds throughout the year, you'll detect much less enthusiasm.

A fine trophy Sika taken by this woman hunter on the Y. O. Ranch.

Red deer can weigh close to 200 pounds or about twice that of Fallow or Japanese Sika, comparable to the Axis according to some, but I've never seen a Chital that heavy. Maybe on the hoof but not field dressed. Antlers are elk-like, sometimes as heavy and long and often with more points.

Sambar are big deer. "Deer of the World," by G. Kenneth Whitehead, lists them as about 600 pounds with exceptional animals going as heavy as 700 pounds. Only a very few are available for hunting in the United States and this only on rare occasions. Red deer are more plentiful but nowhere near on a par with Axis, Sika and Fallow. To be truthful one would really have to seek out a hunt for a Red deer.

Sika almost have a personality – and I know that's dangerous to say because of the Bambi syndrome –

but I'll stick to it. They are a blockier deer than any of the others and have a pure white rump patch that is totally distinctive as they hop off into the brush. And hop they do – stiff legged – like mule deer. Not always, sure, but often enough that they are always fun to watch.

The Y. O. Ranch has a rather sizable herd of elk. As you know, a bull elk can weigh 600 to 750 pounds without half trying. Sometimes even more. A great big Japanese Sika buck might, soaking wet, tip the scales all the way over to 100 or a few more pounds. Yet they get very buddy-buddy. It's quite a sight to see a Sika buck and a big bull elk feeding along together.

As I type this I can look up on the office wall at a Sika buck, shoulder mounted. He is dark gray-brown with longer than whitetail hair on his neck

265

White Fallow mount.

and February can hop on a plane and in a matter of hours be on a Texas ranch for a few days of deer hunting. Hunters wanting an early hunt before whitetail and mule deer seasons open can get after them in August and September. Year around hunters, those who dream of their sport during off seasons, can put on a short-sleeved shirt and go Axis hunting in the middle of the summer. Late winter and late summer hunters can have their choice of all three.

Exotic game ranches are not always that, unfortunately. Some are little more than cow lots with fences visible in every direction. Not exactly conducive to a real "hunt." These are put and take outfits just after the quick dollar. Select your hunt with care. Ask questions. There are real hunting ranches – but not very many. The Y. O. Ranch, for instance, hasn't bought an Axis, Sika or Fallow deer in years. Instead they live trap and sell to others as a method of keeping their herd under control. A hunt there is really seeking the animal as he survives on his own. In the Schreiner family since 1880, the Y. O. is very jealous of its reputation and guards it with an iron hand. Nothing even remotely out of the way takes place on that vast acreage covering more than 100 square miles. Hunting is for real and whether or not a trophy is bagged is totally dependent on the hunter's ability with his rifle. For more information on this great ranch located approximately 100 miles northwest of San Antonio, write to Y. O. Ranch, Box 200, Mountain Home, Texas 78058.

Dolan Creek Ranch, north of Del Rio some 70 or so miles, is another of that type. Not so large as the Y. O. but plenty big, it's been in John Finegan's family since back before the turn of the century. It is an entirely different type of country than the Y. O., much more open. John has built up a good herd of exotics and takes the hunting of them seriously. Neither does he go in for any of the so-called "like shooting fish in a barrel" hunts. He can be reached at 310 E. 17th Street, Del Rio, Texas 78840.

Both of these ranches also hunt native whitetail in season. The Y. O. on a "No Game – No Pay" basis, same as they hunt exotics. Dolan Creek, I think on a flat fee, but his success ratio is very high since he takes no more hunters than he feels he can satisfy. The Y. O. also operates on a very high hunter success ratio because of the same reason. Neither ranch allows hunters out on their own. A guide is with them at all times.

and back. His antlers are a bit heavier than some, but not any longer than any really good trophy Sika. The tines, four to a side as seen from the front, might be longer than most. But this isn't what sets him off. Unknown to me until after he was on the ground, was a pair of extra tines that protrude straight back, from just above the base of each antler, one on each beam, making him an extra typical Sika of rather unusual proportions. So much so that he ranks as Number One – Extra Typical – Primitive Arms in the Burkett Trophy Game Records of the World. Yes, he too was killed with a muzzle loader, more than a decade ago on the Y. O. Ranch, with a .58 caliber Buffalo Hunter.

Exotic deer serve a very useful purpose. They are available throughout Central Texas, primarily in what is known as the Hill Country, and in a few of the eastern seaboard states as well as along the west coast and even in the north-central region. British Columbia has a huntable herd in the wild. Most of those in the States are on private land and are hunted for a fee.

By so being, year round hunting is possible in the case of Axis. A hunter with cabin fever in January

Darker than usual this Fallow is almost black. This one was killed by 13 year old Steven Sun on the Y.O. Ranch.

Both ranches are very conservation-minded. Deer are a crop. They will not take more than their herd will stand. They can do this because both are full working ranches with hunting paying only a partial share of the upkeep. Little outfits have to over-kill to stay alive. The two I mentioned count their herds after hunting season and again prior to the next one. It is after that second count that they set the number of animals to be taken. With the advent of helicopters game counting can be extremely accurate nowadays.

There is only one way to grow a trophy deer, be it whitetail, mule deer or exotic, and that is through aging. He has to be allowed growing time. Because of this all hunts are guided. No hunter is allowed to take less than a trophy specimen. When trophies are not available, hunts for that species are stopped. That's the reason you will find the addresses of only two ranches included. There are probably other good ones, but unless I know first hand, I will never recommend a ranch, outfitter or guide.

If you haven't hunted exotic deer you have been passing up a great opportunity. Their presence lengthens hunting time in the field and the trophy adds immeasurably to any den. And besides that, especially in the case of Axis, they sure do taste good.

I hope this book has given you a greater knowledge of deer in North America. What he is. Where he is. How to hunt him. Perhaps, even stimulated the flow of adrenalin in your system enough so that you will want to take on an off-season hunt or a journey into new-for-you section of this continent.

> "May the road rise to meet you,
> the wind be always at your back,
> the sun shine warm upon your face,
> the rain fall soft upon your fields,
> and, until we meet again, may God
> hold you in the palm of His hand."

267

Chapter 23
APPENDIX

DIRECTORY OF STATE GAME DEPARTMENTS

<u>State Agency to contact concerning hunting:</u>

Alabama .... Department of Conservation and Natural Resources, 64 North Union Street, Montgomery, AL 36104

Alaska .... Department of Environmental Conservation, Pouch 0, Juneau, AK 99811

Arizona .... Game and Fish Department, 2222 W. Greenway Road, Phoenix, AZ 85023

Arkansas .... Game and Fish Commission, Game and Fish Commission Bldg., Little Rock, AR 72201

California .... The Resources Agency, 1416 Ninth St., Sacramento, CA 95814

Colorado .... Department of Environmental Protection, State Office Bldg., 1313 Sherman – Rm 718, Denver, CO 80220

Connecticut .... Department of Environmental Protection, State Office Bldg., 165 Capitol Ave., Hartford, CT 06115

Delaware .... Department of Natural Resources & Environmental Control, The Edward Tatnall Bldg., Legislative Ave. & Wm. Penn St., Dover, DE 19901

Florida .... Department of Natural Resources, Crown Bldg., 202 Blount St., Tallahassee, FL 32304

Georgia .... Department of Natural Resources, 270 Washington St. S. W., Atlanta, GA 30334

Hawaii .... Department of Land & Natural Resources, Box 621, Honolulu, HI 96809

Idaho .... Fish & Game Department, 600 South Walnut, Box 25, Boise, ID 83707

Illinois .... Department of Conservation, 605 State Office Bldg., Springfield, IL 62706

Indiana .... Department of Natural Resources, 608 State Office Bldg., Indianapolis, IN 46204

Iowa .... State Conservation Commission, State Office Bldg., 300 4th St., Des Moines, IA 50319

Kansas .... Forestry Fish & Game Commission, Box 1028, Pratt, KS 67124

Kentucky	Department of Fish & Wildlife Resources, Capitol Plaza Tower, Frankfort, KY 40601
Lousiana	Wildlife & Fisheries Commission, 400 Royal St., New Orleans, LA 70130
Maine	Department of Conservation, State Office Bldg., Augusta, ME 04333
Maryland	Department of Natural Resources, Tawes State Office Bldg., Annapolis, MD 21401
Massachusetts	Department of Fisheries, Wildlife and Recreational Vehicles, 100 Cambridge St., Boston, MA 02202
Michigan	Department of Natural Resources, Box 30028, Lansing, MI 48909
Minnesota	Department of Natural Resources, 300 Centennial Bldg., St. Paul, MN 55155
Mississippi	Game & Fish Commission, Robert E. Lee Office Bldg., 239 N. Lamar St., P.O. Box 451, Jackson, MS 39205
Missouri	Department of Natural Resources, 1014 Madison St., P.O. Box 176, Jefferson City, MO 65101
Montana	Department of Game & Fish, 1420 East Sixth, Helena, MT 59601
Nebraska	Department of Environmental Control, State House Station, Box 94844, Lincoln, NE 68509
Nevada	Department of Fish & Game, Box 10678, Reno NV 89510
New Hampshire	Fish & Game Department, 34 Bridge St., Concord, NH 03301
New Jersey	Division of Fish & Game, Department of Environmental Protection, P.O. Box 1809, Trenton, NJ 08625
New Mexico	Department of Game & Fish, State Capitol, Santa Fe, NM 87503
New York	Department of Environmental Conservation, 50 Wolf Rd., Albany, NY 12233
North Carolina	Wildlife Resources Commission, Albemarle Bldg., 325 N. Salisbury St., Raleigh, NC 27611
North Dakota	State Game & Fish Department, 2121 Lovett Ave., Bismarck, ND 58505
Ohio	Department of Natural Resources, Fountain Square, Columbus, OH 43224
Oklahoma	Department of Wildlife Conservation, 1801 N. Lincoln, P.O. Box 53465, Oklahoma, OK 73105
Oregon	Department of Fish & Wildlife, P.O. Box 3503, Portland, OR 97208
Pennsylvania	Game Commission, P.O. Box 1567, Harrisburg, PA 17120
Rhode Island	Department of Natural Resources, 83 Park St., Providence, RI 02903
South Carolina	Wildlife & Marine Resources Department, Bldg. D – Dutch Plaza, Box 167, Columbia, SC 29202
South Dakota	Department of Game, Fish & Parks, Sigurd Anderson Bldg., Pierre, SD 57501

Tennessee	Wildlife Resources Agency, P.O. Box 40747, Ellington Agricultural Center, Nashville, TN 37204
Texas	Parks & Wildlife Department, 4200 Smith School Rd., Austin, TX 78744
Utah	Division of Wildlife, Department of Natural Resources, 1596 W.N. Temple, Salt Lake City, UT 84116
Vermont	Fish & Game Department, Agency of Environmental Conservation, Montpelier, VT 05602
Virginia	Commission of Game & Inland Fisheries, 4010 W. Broad St., Box 11104, Richmond, VA 23230
Washington	Department of Game, 600 N. Capitol Way, Olympia, WA 98504
West Virginia	Department of Natural Resources, 1800 Washington St., East, Charleston, WV 25309
Wisconsin	Department of Natural Resources, Box 450, Madison, WI 53701
Wyoming	Game & Fish Department, Cheyenne, WY 82002

In Canada:

Alberta	Department of Recreation, Parks & Wildlife, 10363–108 St., Edmonton, Alberta T5J 1L8
British Columbia	Fish and Wildlife Branch, Department of Recreation and Conservation, Parliament Bldg., Victoria, British Columbia V8V 1X4
Manitoba	Manitoba Government Travel, 6100, 200 Vaughn St., Winnipeg, Manitoba R3C 1T5
New Brunswick	Tourist Information Services, P.O. Box 1030, Fredericton, New Brunswick E3B 5C3
Newfoundland and Labrador	Tourist Development Office, Confederation Bldg., St. John's, Newfoundland AOK 3E0
Northwest Territories	Travel Arctic, Yellowknife, Northwest Territories X1A 2L9
Nova Scotia	Department of Tourism, P.O. Box 456, Halifax, Nova Scotia B3J 2R5
Ontario	Ontario Travel, Ministry of Industry and Tourism, 900 Bay St., Toronto, Ontario M7A 2E1
Prince Edward Island	Fish & Wildlife Division, P.O. Box 2000, Charlottetown, Prince Edward Island C1A 7N8
Quebec	Tourist Branch, Department of Tourism, Fish and Game, 150 St. Cyrille Blvd. East, Quebec City, Quebec G1R 2B2
Saskatchewan	Saskatchewan Travel, 1825 Lorne St., Regina, Saskatchewan S4P 3N1
Yukon Territory	Director of Game, Yukon Game Department, Box 2703, Whitehorse, Yukon Territory Y1A 2C6
And in Mexico	Director General de Fauna Silvestre, S.A.G., Aquiles Serdan No. 28–7 Piso, Mexico 3, D.F., Mexico

DIRECTORY OF MANUFACTURERS

If it concerns guns, ammunition, scopes, binoculars, bows and arrows, knives, hunting clothing, boots or sleeping bags you can find out from:

Bob Allen Sportswear, 214 S.W. Jackson St., Des Moines, IA 50302
American Archery Co., Box 100 Industrial Park, Oconto Falls, WI 54154
American Field Corp., Pink Hill, NC 28572 (hunting clothing)
American Footwear, 1 Oak Hill Rd., Fitchburg, MA 01420 (insulated boots)
Atlanta Cutlery, Box 839, Conyers, GA 30207
Baker Mfg. Co., 428 N. St. Augustine Rd., Valdosta, GA 31601 (tree stands)
Bear Archery, Rural Route 1, Grayling, MI 49738
Ben Pearson Archery, P.O. Box 270, Tulsa, OK 74101
Bianchi Leather Products, 100 Calle Cortez, Temecula, CA 92390
Bonanza Sports, 412 Western Ave., Faribault, MN 55021 (reloading tools)
Bootmakers of Sturgeon Bay, 245 E. Vine St., Sturgeon Bay, WI 54235
Bowen Knife Co., P.O. Drawer, 590, Blackshear, GA 31516
Brauer Bros., 817 N. 17th St., St. Louis, MO 63106 (holsters, cases, slings)
Browning, Route 1, Morgan, UT 84050 (firearms)
Buck Knives, 1717 N. Magnolia, El Cajon, CA 92022
Buehler Scope Mounts, 17 Orinda Way, Orinda, CA 94563
Burris Co., 331 E. 8th St., Box 747, Greeley, CO 80631 (scopes)
Bushnell Optical Co., 2828 E. Foothill Blvd., Pasadena, CA 91107
Butler Creek Corp., P.O. Box GG, Jackson, WY 83001 (black powder accessories)
Camillus Cutlery, Main St., Camillus, NY 13031
W. R. Case & Sons Cutlery, 20 Russell Blvd., Bradford, PA 16701
CCI-Speer, P.O. Box 856, Lewiston, ID 83501 (reloading components)
Challanger Corp., 118 Pearl St., Mt. Vernon, NY 10550 (gun cases)
Charter Arms, 430 Sniffens Lane, Stratford, CT 06497 (handguns)
Chippewa Shoe Co., 925 First Ave., Chippewa Falls, WI 54729 (boots)
C-H Tool & Die, 106 N. Harding, Owen, WI 54460 (reloading tools)
Coleman, 250 N. St. Francis, Wichita, KS 67201 (sleeping bags, etc.)
Colt, 150 Huyshope Ave., Hartford, CT 06102 (handguns and rifles)
Comfy, P.O. Box 1007, Sioux Falls, SD 57101 (down clothing, bags)
Conetrol Scope Mounts, Hwy 123 South, Seguin, TX 78155
Connecticut Valley Arms, Saybrook Road, Haddam, CT 06438 (black powder guns)
Converse Rubber Co., 55 Fordham Rd., Wilmington, MA 01887 (footwear)
Doskocil, P.O. Box 1246, Arlington, TX 76010 (gun cases)
Du Biel Arms, 1724 Baker Rd., Sherman, TX 75090 (fine rifles)
Duofold, P. O. Drawer A, Mohawk, NY 13407 (insulated underwear)
Federal Cartridge Corp., 2700 Foshay Tower, Minneapolis, MN 55402
Firearms Center, 308 Leisure Lane, Victoria, TX 77901 (fine rifles)

Forster Products, 82 E. Lanark Ave., Lanark, IL 61046 (reloading tools)

Game Winner, 1900 Peachtree Cain Tower, 229 Peachtree St. N. E., Atlanta, GA 30303

Gerber Legendary Blades, 14200 S. W. 72nd Ave., Portland, OR 97223

Gutmann, 900 S. Columbus Ave., Mt. Vernon, NY 10550 (hunting knives)

Harrington & Richardson, Industrial Row, Gardner MA 01440 (firearms)

Himalayan Industries, 301 Mulberry St., Pine Bluff, AR 71611 (down sleeping bags and garments)

Hornady, P.O. Box 1848, Grand Island, NB 68801 (bullets and Frontier ammunition)

Hodgdon Powder Co., 7710 W. 50 Hiway, Shawnee Mission, KS 66202

Interarms, 10 Prince St., Alexandria, VA 22313 (firearms)

Jennings Compound Bow, 28756 N. Castaic Canyon Rd., Valencia CA 91355

Kershaw Cutlery, 100 Foothills Rd., Lake Oswego, OR 97034

Kleinguenther, P.O. Box 1261, Seguin, TX 78155 (fine German rifles)

George Lawrence Co., 306 S. W. First Ave., Portland, OR 97204 (gun cases, slings, etc.)

Leupold & Stevens, P.O. Box 688, Beaverton, OR 97005 (scopes, mounts, bullets)

Lyman Products, Route 147, Middlefield, CT 06455 (sights, loading tools and bullet moulds.)

Marlin Firearms, 100 Kenna Dr., N. Haven, CT 06473

Michaels of Oregon, 7323 N. E. Glisan St., Portland, OR 97213 (firearms accessories)

O. F. Mossberg & Sons, 7 Grasso Ave., North Haven, CT 06473 (firearms)

Mowery Gun Works, P.O. Box 28, Iowa Park, TX 76367 (black powder rifles)

MTM Molded Products, 5680 Webster St., Dayton, OH 45414 (ammo boxes)

National Rifle Association, 1600 Rhode Island Ave. N. W., Washington, D. C. 20036

Norma Precision, Auburn Rd., Lansing, NY 14882 (ammunition)

Numrich Arms, Williams Ln., W. Hurley, NY 12491

Olsen Knife Co., 7–11 Joy St., Howard City, MI 49329

John Olson Co., 294 West Oakland Ave., Oakland, NJ 07436   (sports books)

Omark Industries, P.O. Box 865, Lewiston, ID 83501 (ammunition, primers, bullets)

Original Mink Oil, 10652 N. E. Holman, Portland, OR 97220

Pachmayr Gun Works, 1220 S. Grand Ave., Los Angeles, CA 90015 (scope mounts, recoil pads)

Ranging, Inc., 90 Lincoln Rd. N., E. Rochester, NY 14445 (handheld optical range finders)

RCBS, P.O. Box 856, Lewiston, ID 83501 (reloading equipment)

Redding Hunter, 114 Starr Rd., Cortland, NY 13045 (reloading equipment)

Redfield, 5800 E. Jewell Ave., Denver, CO 80224 (rifle scopes)

Red Head Brand Corp., 4949 Joseph Hardin Dr., Dallas, TX 75236 (hunting clothin, sleeping bags, gun cases, etc.)

Remington Arms, 939 Barnum Ave., Bridgeport, CT 06602

Rigid Archery, 445 Central Ave., Jersey City, NJ 07307

Rigid Knives, 9919 Prospect Ave., Santee, CA 92071

Royal Red Ball, 8530 Page Ave., St. Louis, MO 63114 (boots, clothing)

A. G. Russell, 1705 Highway 71 N., Springdale, AR 72764 (knives)

Saeco Reloading, 526 Maple St., Carpinteria, CA 93013

Safariland, 1941 S. Walker Ave., Monrovia, CA 91016 (belts, holsters, slings)

San Angelo., P.O. Box 984, San Angelo, TX 76902 (racks for guns, bows, etc.)

Saunders Archery, P.O. Box 476, Industrial Site, Columbus, NE 68601

Savage Arms, Springdale Rd., Westfield, MA 01085

Buddy Schoellkopf Products, 4949 Joseph Hardin Dr., Dallas, TX 75236 (sleeping bags, hunting clothing, gun caases)

Schrade Cutlery, 1776 Broadway, New York, NY 10019

Service Armament Co., 689 Bergen Blvd., Ridgefield, CT 07657 (black powder guns, accessories)

Servus Rubber Co., 1136 Second St., Rock Island, IL 61201 (waterproof hunting footwear)

Sierra Products for Shooters, 10532 S. Painter Ave., Santa Fe Springs, CA 90670 (jacketed bullets)

Smith & Wesson, 2100 Roosevelt Ave., Springfield, MA 01101 (handguns, knives, leather, ammunition)

Sterling Arms, 4436 Prospect St., Gasport, NY 14067 (autoloading pistols)

Sturm, Ruger, Co., Lacey Pl., Southport, CT 06490 (firearms)

10-X Mfg., 6185 Arapahoe Rd., Boulder, CO 80302 (insulated jackets and vests)

Texan Reloaders, P.O. Box 5355, Dallas, TX 75222

Thompson-Center Arms, Farmington Rd., Rochester, NH 03867 (single shot pistol, black powder firearms)

Totally Dependable Products, 513 High St., Pottstown, PA 19464 (lubricants)

Trail Guns Armory, 2115 Lexington, Houston, TX 77006 (muzzle loading rifles)

Utica Duxbak, 815 Noyes St., Utica, NY 13502

WD-40, 1061 Cudahy St., Dan Diego, CA 92110 (lubricant)

Weatherby, 2781 Firestone Blvd., South Gate, CA 90280 (fine rifles)

W. R. Weaver, 7125 Industrial Ave., El Paso, TX 79915 (scopes, mounts)

Dan Wesson Arms, 293 Main St., Monson, MA 01057 (handguns)

Western Cutlery, 5311 Western Ave., Boulder, CO 80306

Wigwam Mills, 3402 Crocker Ave., Sheboygan, WI 53801 (socks, headwear)

Williams Guns Sight, 7389 Lapeer Rd., Davison, MI 48423 (hunting and shooting accessories)

Winchester-Western, 275 Winchester Ave., New Haven, CT 06504

Wolverine Boots, 9341 Courtland Dr. N. E., Rockford, MI 49351

Woods Bag & Canvas, 90 River St., Ogdensburg, NY 13669 (sleeping bags, comforters, clothing)

Woolrich, Inc., Woolrich, PA 17779 (outdoor clothing)

York Archery, 1450 W. Lexington, Independence, MO 64051

Carl Zeiss, Carl-Zeiss-Straße, Oberkochen, Germany 7082

For information on scoring procedures contact:

Firearms . . . . Boone and Crockett Club, 424 North Washington Street, Alexandria, VA 22314

Burkett Trophy Game Records of the World, Route 2, Box 195-A, Fredericksburg, TX 78624

Archery . . . . Pope and Young Club, Box J, Basset, NE 68714

Burkett Trophy Game Records of the World, Route 2, Box 195-A, Fredericksburg, TX 78624